Jung and Kierkegaard

Jung and Kierkegaard identifies authenticity, suffering and self-deception as the three key themes that connect the work of Carl Jung and Søren Kierkegaard. There is, in the thinking of these pioneering psychologists of the human condition, a fundamental belief in the healing potential of a religious outlook. This engaging and erudite text explores the significance of the similarities of thinking between Kierkegaard and Jung, bridging the gap between the former's particular brand of existential Christian psychology and the latter's own unique philosophy.

Given the similarity of their work and experiences that were common to both of their personal biographies, particularly the relationship that each had with his father, one might expect Jung to have found in Kierkegaard a kindred spirit. Yet this was not the case, and Jung viewed Kierkegaard with great scorn. That there exists such a strong comparison and extensive overlap in the life and thought of these towering figures of psychology and philosophy leads us to question why it is that Jung so strongly rejected Kierkegaard. Such hostility is particularly fascinating given the striking similarity that Jung's own analytical psychology bears to the Christian psychology upheld by Kierkegaard.

Cook's thought-provoking book fills a very real gap in Jungian scholarship and is the first attempt to undertake a direct comparison between Jung and Kierkegaard's models of development. It is therefore essential reading for academics and postgraduate students with an interest in Jungian and Kierkegaard scholarship, as well as psychology, philosophy and religion more generally.

Amy Cook graduated with a degree in History from the University of Aberdeen in 2005. She then went on to study a Master's Degree in Philosophy and Psychoanalysis at Essex University before completing another masters in Jungian and Post-Jungian Studies. After a brief spell teaching overseas, Amy returned to the UK and began a PhD at Bangor University. She currently lives in North Wales, where she works with young carers to encourage and support them to reach their full potential.

Research in Analytical Psychology and Jungian Studies

Series Advisor:
Andrew Samuels,
Professor of Analytical Psychology, Essex University, UK.

The *Research in Analytical Psychology and Jungian Studies* series features research-focused volumes involving qualitative and quantitative research, historical/archival research, theoretical developments, heuristic research, grounded theory, narrative approaches, collaborative research, practitioner-led research, and self-study. The series also includes focused works by clinical practitioners, and provides new research informed explorations of the work of C. G. Jung that will appeal to researchers, academics, and scholars alike.

Books in this series

Eros and Economy
Jung, Deleuze, Sexual Difference
Barbara Jenkins

Towards a Jungian Theory of the Ego
Karen Evers-Fahey

A Japanese Jungian Perspective on Mental Health and Culture
Wandering Madness
Iwao Akita
Translated by Waka Shibata and Kittredge Stephenson

Jung and Kierkegaard
Researching a Kindred Spirit in the Shadows
Amy Cook

Jung and Kierkegaard

Researching a Kindred Spirit
in the Shadows

Amy Cook

LONDON AND NEW YORK

First published 2018
by Routledge
2 Park Square, Milton Park, Abingdon, Oxon OX14 4RN

and by Routledge
711 Third Avenue, New York, NY 10017

Routledge is an imprint of the Taylor & Francis Group, an informa business

© 2018 Amy Cook

The right of Amy Cook to be identified as author of this work has been asserted by her in accordance with sections 77 and 78 of the Copyright, Designs and Patents Act 1988.

All rights reserved. No part of this book may be reprinted or reproduced or utilised in any form or by any electronic, mechanical, or other means, now known or hereafter invented, including photocopying and recording, or in any information storage or retrieval system, without permission in writing from the publishers.

Trademark notice: Product or corporate names may be trademarks or registered trademarks, and are used only for identification and explanation without intent to infringe.

British Library Cataloguing-in-Publication Data
A catalogue record for this book is available from the British Library

Library of Congress Cataloging-in-Publication Data
A catalog record for this book has been requested

ISBN: 978-1-138-68027-2 (hbk)
ISBN: 978-1-315-56373-2 (ebk)

Typeset in Sabon
by Apex CoVantage, LLC

For Arthur

Contents

Acknowledgements ix

PART I

Introduction 3

1 A holy kind of healing 7

2 Some striking similarities: personal and philosophical 12

3 Introducing Kierkegaard 21

4 Presenting Jung 34

5 The wounds of the father: a shared inheritance 43

PART 2

6 An unconventional Christianity 59

7 Jung and religion 63

8 The therapeutic value of faith 76

9 Grounding ethics in spirit: the medium of our self-realisation 85

10 Suffering and the pain of personal growth: perrissem, nisi perissem 94

11 Authenticity: the creation of one's genuine self 107

viii Contents

PART 3

12 'That Religious Neurotic': Kierkegaard on the couch   129

13 Keeping mum: a powerful silence   135

14 Søren's spiritual castration: a father's influence   143

15 To marry or to martyr   154

16 The final years of Søren Kierkegaard: a story of archetypal compensation   167

PART 4

17 The nature of a Kierkegaardian neurosis: Jung's reception of Kierkegaard   177

18 Kierkegaard and Nietzsche: polar opposites in the mind of Jung   192

19 Summary of discussion   206

20 Conclusion   219

    Epilogue: Jung and Kierkegaard: a legacy considered   228

    Bibliography   233
    Index   242

Acknowledgements

First and foremost, I would like to offer my heartfelt thanks to Philosopher, Jungian Scholar and Cincinnati Bengals Superfan, Dr Lucy Huskinson. Dr Huskinson's patience, guidance and generosity whilst supervising the PhD thesis that this book grew from has been phenomenal. I suspect such an endeavour was indeed the definition of a thankless task. I am extremely grateful for our many useful discussions and her invaluable insights, suggestions and friendship over the years. The better ideas in this book almost certainly owe their existence to her.

To David Parker (University of Northampton) and Professor Eryl Davies (Bangor University) – the designated examiners of my Doctoral thesis, I should like to extend a warm thanks for their constructive comments and encouragement to publish.

I am also extremely indebted to Thomas Fischer for cheerfully digging into the Jung archives on my behalf. Thank you Thomas.

And finally to Richard, my thanks and apologies in equal measure are due. I am not the easiest person to live with and I really do not know how you put up with me. However, you are a perfect nuisance to me. So fair's fair.

In this book I have made particular reference to the *Collected Works* of C.G. Jung and Soren Kierkegaard's *Journals and Papers* (edited by H.V. Hong & E.H. Hong), reproduced by the kind permission of Princeton University Press and Indiana University Press. Extracts from Jung's autobiography *Memories, Dreams and Reflections* have been reprinted by permission of Harper Collins Publishers Ltd. (© 1963 (Jung)).

Part I

Introduction

Søren Kierkegaard is widely acknowledged today as one of the most insightful philosophical and religious thinkers of Western history. Until very recently psychologists have been more interested in him as a subject of analysis, rather than as a psychologist in his own right. Jon Stewart (2011) notes that many scholars, perhaps inspired by Georg Brandes's 1877 famous study of Kierkegaard (Søren Kierkegaard, a literary character),[1] have treated him not as a psychologist or even a source of inspiration for psychological insight but rather as a case study[2]. Fortunately, the tide has now turned and Kierkegaard's particular brand of Christian psychology has been documented in dedicated monographs; however, these monographs certainly do possess a particular leaning towards Freudian psychology (see Nordentoft 1978; Ferguson 1995; Cole 1971). It is notable then that whilst Kierkegaard has been exhaustingly investigated from a Freudian perspective, with the exception of a few very brief comparisons by Jungian scholars, it remains that an extensive Jungian-orientated study has yet to be completed.

Carl Jung, like Kierkegaard, is another complex and controversial figure in the world of psychology: there are those who worship him with a fierce loyalty, whilst others are more interested in discrediting and pathologising the mystically inclined old man of analytical psychology. At the heart of this book is the psychological theories of these two revolutionary thinkers and the relation that their own individual psyches and life experiences have upon the formulation of such theories. When confronted with a psychology that is primarily conceived through self-analysis and which claims to bring to light and lay bare the human condition, it is absolutely necessary to study that individual as deeply as possible and to pose questions that others might find questionable. And yet it is all too easy to lapse into the pathologising of deficiencies. I do not intend, nor am I qualified, to diagnose either Kierkegaard or Jung. Instead I have striven to balance their extraordinary brilliance with the demons that they faced, without reducing their achievements to mere pathology. It is my hope that through the course of this book it will become readily apparent to the reader that Kierkegaard's rightful place is amongst psychologists, not as an object of psychological investigation but as an incredibly gifted and insightful psychologist. Indeed, a psychologist whose insights bear comparison with Jung's own.

This inquiry will seek to provide an in-depth commentary of the many striking similarities between Jung and Kierkegaard, both in terms of their work and their personalities. In Jung's psychology we see the continuation of Kierkegaard's project of selfhood as a divine call to become a self before God. There are aspects of these thinkers' insights that so easily converge with one another and this points towards a significant conceptual parity and complementarity in their thought. We might summarise the most important points of commonalities as: the creation of meaningful existence through inward deepening; the overcoming of self-deception through self-creation/recovery; and self-determination through the creative exercise of freedom in conjunction with a reference (guiding) point outside of one's own. Such complementarity between these two significant figures illustrates the possibility for philosophy and psychology to complement each other in their respective visions of authentic selfhood.

In addition to exploring the inherent and exciting similarities between these thinkers, what makes this a particularly fruitful discussion to be had is the fact that whilst there are works that associate the thought of Jung and Kierkegaard, very few have attempted to directly compare the convergence of their models of development. Though such a comparison seems really very compelling and perhaps obvious to scholars of Jungian and Kierkegaardian thought, it is one that has largely escaped attention. The extensive overlap in their thinking reveal both an intellectual and spiritual correspondence that serves to illuminate just how surprising and odd it is that Jung was not able to find in Kierkegaard a kindred spirit. In written correspondence with Kunzli, Jung refers to Kierkegaard as 'that Grizzler' whose 'problems and his grizzling' served to allow him to settle 'everything in the study' so he 'need not do it in life. Out there things are apt to get unpleasant' (16th March, 1943). Writing to Rudolf Pannwitz, he confides, 'That you find Kierkegaard "frightful" has warmed the cockles of my heart' (March 27, 1937). Such comments are unfair, unwarranted and undoubtedly illuminate and reflect Jung's own psychological vulnerabilities more so than they address the failings of Kierkegaard's 'insupportable' philosophy. It is clear that the affinity in the thought of Kierkegaard and Jung is much greater than Jung himself, at least consciously, realised. It is to Jung's Library that we shall later turn in order to establish the extent of Jung's knowledge of Kierkegaard. Tackling the question as to why Jung rejects Kierkegaard is a primary concern, the reason behind which we shall try to discover in the following pages.

Not only is there no single Jungian-orientated monograph devoted to Kierkegaard's psychology or its possible bearing on Jung's own psychology, there are no Jungian studies of Kierkegaard, the man. This alone strikes me as surprising, but when we combine this Kierkegaardian absence with the very emotive and negative comments Jung makes of Kierkegaard in regards to both his philosophy and character, then such absence seems remarkable. This is not to say that these negative comments or the similarity between the respective psychological projects of Jung and Kierkegaard has gone unnoticed. Prominent Jungian analyst Ann Casement (1998) very briefly explores the 'striking affinity' between these two deeply spiritual men, both of whom 'were antipathetic to conventional Christianity'. However, she merely alludes to, rather than analyses, what she insightfully perceives to be a shared psychological inheritance between Kierkegaard and Jung. John Dourley (1990) in his 'Jung, Tillich, and Aspects of Western Christianity' notes Jung's rejection of Kierkegaard and interprets its origins to Kierkegaard's distancing of the realities between man and God[3].[4] This interpretation, as we will later discover, readily enforces Jung's own distorted view of Kierkegaard, and as a consequence, Dourley unquestionably reinforces the idea that what Kierkegaard lacks and needs is the corrective of the immanent presence of God.

The most substantial exploration of Jung's relation to Kierkegaard's psychology is to be found in Anthony Rudd's essay 'C.G. Jung: A missed connection' which forms part of *Kierkegaard's Influence on the Social Sciences* (Stewart, 2011). Notably Rudd draws together Kierkegaard and Jung's view of the self and argues that the achievement of selfhood for both men requires that the various aspects of the self are consciously taken up as parts of who one is. The failure to integrate and balance the various aspects of the personality leads, according to Kierkegaard, to despair in its various forms. Whereas, for Jung, these aspects of unintegrated self can potentially become pushed into the unconscious where they assume crude and undeveloped forms (becoming what Jung calls 'the shadow'). Rudd draws attention to Jung's apparent unawareness that Kierkegaard was involved in the same cultural and religious problem situation as himself; namely, the banalisation of Christian concepts that arises in modern misappropriations of 'Christian' society and 'Christian' culture. However, he downplays Jung's hostile response to Kierkegaard by pointing towards Kierkegaard's relative anonymity outside of Scandinavia during Jung's student days. Furthermore, Rudd reflects that whilst the work of Kierkegaard had begun gathering a momentum amongst the intelligentsia following World War I, Jung's main ideas were already formed, and, though 'he considerably elaborated on them, he showed little interest in considering new perspectives from philosophy or theology'. Rudd makes no mention of Arnold Kunzli, a frequent correspondent of Jung and whose dissertation thesis on Kierkegaard Jung possessed two copies of in his library. This PhD thesis is crucial in revealing what Jung could have known of Kierkegaard's personality and religious philosophy. Moreover, whilst Jung may well have been uninterested in new perspectives as Rudd claims, he does make use of philosophy that reinforces his own views and this would not preclude Kierkegaard. This book seeks to rectify these issues and proposes to attempt to bridge the gap in Jungian

6 Introduction

scholarship regarding the figure of Kierkegaard, particularly in regards to addressing Jung's outright and venomous rejection of him. It will thereby be the most thorough study to date to explore the extensive overlap and affinity between their models of psychological development and illness. It will also be the first, albeit tentative, attempt at a Jungian analysis of the melancholy Dane.

Part One of this book outlines some striking similarities between the works of Jung and Kierkegaard, whilst drawing together Jung's conception of the unconscious and Kierkegaard's notion of spirit. The ideas here are presented abstractly and generally are given a more intensive treatment in Part Two. These chapters therefore seek to trace and concretise the essential similarities in their respective works through a thorough exploration of three key themes of overlap: authenticity, suffering and self-deception. Everything in this exposition is carefully interconnected, and consequently this means that in a certain sense new aspects of the same parallels between the life and works of Jung and Kierkegaard are continually being developed. Having worked towards establishing a strong comparison between Jung and Kierkegaard, Part Three is devoted solely to a Jungian analysis of Kierkegaard, setting the scene for Part Four, 'In the Shadow of Jung'. This concluding segment will revisit these scathing comments of Jung with a view of ascertaining why – given the otherwise strong affinities between his work and Kierkegaard's – he made these very odd and curious remarks.

Notes

1
2 Stewart, J. (Editor) Kierkegaards Influence on the Social Sciences (Ashgate, 2011).
3 Dourley, John. 'Jung, Tillich, and Aspects of Western Christianity,' *Thought: Fordham University Quarterly*, Vol 52, Issue 1, March 1977.
4

Chapter 1

A holy kind of healing

For many, Jung's appeal lies in the optimistic tone of his thought for there is no sense in his writing that psychological characteristics are inborn and without the potential of development or change. There is a distinct absence of the ridding of symptoms that we find in Freud's therapeutic model and a rather abundant concern that the analyst help his or her patients to engage with their symptoms in an attitude of acceptance. The essence of Jungian therapy lies not in asking what is missing or repressed but in focusing upon that which is available within the therapeutic alliance and the potential this gives the individual. In fact, it appears that Jung wanted to dispel the Freudian perception that analysis simply alleviates and removes troublesome symptoms. He writes, '[T]here is a widespread prejudice that analysis is something like a "cure" to which one submits for a time and is then discharged healed. That is a layman's error left over from the early days of psychoanalysis' (1916/1957: par.142). For Jung, the analytic task is altogether more comprehensive and focused on the 'whole man', not just his missing or repressed parts. For,

> The object of therapy is not the neurosis, but the man who has the neurosis. . . . Nor does it [neurosis] come from an obscure corner of the unconscious, as many psychotherapists still believe: it comes from the totality of a man's life and from all the experiences that have accumulated over the years and decades.
>
> (1934: par.337)

It seems apparent to me that such an insight, contrary to Freud's psychoanalysis, stems from a realisation that one's personality and symptoms are intimately interwoven and entwined. He expresses this much more directly when he states outright that 'psychotherapy knows first and foremost – or rather should know – that itsproper concern is not the fiction of neurosis, but the distorted totality of the human being' (1945: par.199). Since it is likely that symptoms are deeply embedded within the patient's personality, this distorted totality requires the healing of the psyche through a process

8 A holy kind of healing

that Jung terms 'individuation', which concerns the evolution of the whole personality towards the attainment of greater wholeness. This process of evolution is brought about through the integration of unconscious complexes, which demands that the individual increasingly accept the self that he or she is:

> Individuation means becoming a single, homogeneous being, and, in so far as 'in-dividuality' embraces our innermost, last, and incomparable uniqueness, it also implies becoming one's own self. We could therefore translate individuation as 'come to selfhood' or 'self-realisation'.
>
> (1929a: par.266)

Rosemary Gordon (1979), an influential member of the 'London School' of analytical psychology, draws out the very useful distinction between cure and healing: 'to cure' means to 'take care of', 'to take charge of'; it also denotes 'successful medical treatment'. Whilst, on the other hand, 'to heal', which means basically 'to make whole', is a very ancient word in the English language, and is closely related to the word 'holy'. Interestingly, Gordon goes on to explain that both 'healing' and 'the holy' derive from the same roots, *haelen*, or *helag*, in Old Friesians, or *haelen* in Old Teutonic, or *haeloz* and *halig* in Old English. Such a process is a spontaneous and natural occurrence within the psyche, even if the vast majority of us are unaware of it, it exists as something potentially present in all human beings.

In 1958 Jung wrote, 'my raison d'être consists in coming to terms with that indefinable being we call "God"' (1951–1961). To do this, he wrote,

> the knowledge I was concerned with, or was seeking, still could not be found in the science of those days. I myself had to undergo the original experience, and, moreover, try to plant the results of my experience in the soil of [modern] reality.
>
> (1963)

In many respects we might view the recently published *Red Book* as a product of this very endeavor, in the sense that it is a visual and written record of a six-year encounter with 'God', culminating in his own self-revelation and enlightenment. Jung considered *The Red Book* his most important work; 'everything later was merely the outer classification, the scientific elaboration, and the integration into life,' wrote Jung, 'but the numinous beginning, which contained everything, was then' (Jung 2009). His position as we shall see in detail, though simply stated now, is that all neurotic problems are generally speaking religious problems. Consequently the basic process of development and maturation that Jung terms individuation becomes a religious process.

The Terry Lectures (1938/1940) represent Jung's most powerful and forceful insight into religion as a psychological experience. It is here that he

A holy kind of healing 9

highlights the similarity between the development of 'a religious attitude' that facilitates self-acceptance with that which we try to capture when we say of someone that they have made their peace with God. He claims,

> If you sum up what people tell you about their experiences, you can formulate it this way: They came to themselves, they could accept themselves, and thus were reconciled to adverse circumstances and events. This is almost like what used to be expressed by saying: He has made his peace with God, he has sacrificed his own will, he has submitted himself to the will of God.
>
> (1938/1940: par.138)

Given that psychological healing is expressed, albeit indirectly, in terms of the religious, we might then view the analytical process of individuation as equivalent to one's personal search for a relationship with God. At the very least we can certainly conclude that healing consists in finding what can best be described as a religious attitude. Especially if we remind ourselves that individuation shares with religion its goal of union, wholeness and completeness.[1] Given that individuation has 'for its goal the development of the individual personality' (Jung 1921), it can be construed as the natural birth process of the personality. It is both the goal and natural outcome of life, fundamentally a process of becoming in which we become more truly ourselves. Essentially by separating one's conscious self from the unconscious images that lead us to blind illusions and ultimately self-deception, we are able to facilitate a metamorphosis of the personality that encourages self-acceptance. Whilst individuation should occur naturally, it must be understood that it can all too readily be thwarted by any number of factors – by heredity, the adverse influences of one's parents' education and environment. Clinical analysis therefore catalyses a natural development process. If a patient is able to commit himself to a dialectical relationship with his unconscious then not only is there resolution of conflict between ego and unconscious but also the energy-laden symbols that foster individuation are given space to emerge. Perhaps we might say that the principle task of analytical psychology is to remove those elements that obscure the process of individuation and thus free the personality to pursue its particular path. Jung's psychology is fundamentally philosophical in the classical sense, a dialectic whose dynamics bring to consciousness not only a more complete understanding of the problem involved, but also the emergence of a new insight. Jung quotes a letter from a former patient that evocatively describes the emergence of such insight and the healing capabilities that it possesses:

> Out of evil, much good has come to me. By keeping quiet, repressing nothing, remaining attentive, and by accepting reality – taking things as they are, and not as I wanted them to be – by doing all this, unusual knowledge has come to me, and unusual powers as well, such as I could

never have imagined before. I always thought that when we accepted things that they overpowered us in some way or other. This turns out not to be true at all, and it is only by accepting them that one can assume an attitude towards them. So now I intend to play the game of life, being receptive to whatever comes to me, good and bad, sun and shadow forever alternating, and, in this way, also accepting my own nature with its positive and negative sides. Thus everything becomes more alive to me. What a fool I was! How I tried to force everything to go according to the way I thought it ought to!

(Jung 1929c: par.70).

To reiterate, Jung's analytical psychology does not seek cure for 'the fiction of neurosis' or other psychological symptoms as its *raison d'être*, but rather strives to bring about a change of attitude in oneself and consequently a new attitude to life in general. The subject undertaking this journey of healing, as is illustrated above, takes a very active role in coming to terms with his or her nature, which is an incredibly empowering and integral part of the healing process. In place of the extinguishing of symptoms and the eradication of suffering there is instead the notion of rebirth, the sense that an individual is to undergo a renewal or perhaps even a transformation of personality through this process of individuation. Jung seems almost to seek the resurrection of man into new life through the regenerative power of the psyche. We might very well conclude that the process of individuation is far from being a method of medical treatment and is instead a spiritual quest – a secular path to salvation. Indeed, Jung concedes as much when he writes, 'the very aim of religious education, from the exhortation to put off the old Adam right back to the rebirth rituals of primitive races, is to transform the human being into the new, future man, and to allow the old to die away' (1930/1931: 766).

Jung's understanding of 'healing' is I believe in total accord to the ancient derivation of the word. In many ways we might say that Jung's conception of healing falls within the more general psychological understanding of healing as a process of evolution of the whole person towards an ever greater and more complex wholeness. However, where Jung differs significantly from the norm is where I believe the strongest link between Kierkegaard and Jung is to be found; namely that the journey towards the self is a religious one. In the works of Kierkegaard and Jung, immediate experience is the defining quality of religion; it is a very direct, personal encounter that emanates from within, and by the same token, one's religious experience of the encounter – which Jung refers to in direct allusion to Rudolf Otto (1917) as a *numinous* encounter, is individual and personal. That is to say, authentic religious experience is not something that is taught or passed down by a religious authority. Individuation then is understood as our relation with the God within:

The seat of faith, however, is not consciousness but spontaneous religious experience, which brings the individual's faith into immediate relation with God. Here we must ask: Have I any religious experience and immediate relation to God, and hence that certainty which will keep me, as an individual, from dissolving in the crowd?

(1957: 563).

Inherent in the works of Jung and Kierkegaard is the ethereal sense that when wholeness is attained God is found. The experience of the psyche's wholeness is, for Jung, an experience of God. Similarly, Kierkegaard's understanding of the personality focuses on its potential for becoming whole, understood as a union/synthesis with God. As I shall expound upon later, Jung and Kierkegaard share an understanding of self as that which transcends ego-consciousness. We might best describe the self for Jung and Kierkegaard as one's totality of potential and purposefulness. Individuation means becoming that which 'God' intended and not that which the ego desires. Whilst the ego must possess the strength to take life by the coat tails, Jung's 'Self-like "God"'[2] is full of ambiguity – it does not refer to an entity as such but rather something altogether much more mysterious. Jung's psychology requires that the ego be strong enough to take on life but also humble enough to allow the individual to discover the deeper dimensions of life. What is required is the submission to one's calling as a person, an act of humility that allows the deeper mysteries of the personality to be engaged with – those that exist beyond the ego's everyday awareness. In other words, to submit and engage with the religious experience that constitutes the Jungian Self.

Notes

1 The goal of individuation for Jung is the Self, and the Self is equivalent in its archetypal image to God. 'The self', wrote Jung, 'is our life's goal, for it is the completest expression of that fateful combination we call individuality' (1928:par.404). The subjective experience of the self and that of God are so similar as to be unable of being distinguished from one another. It is through the psyche that we experience all phenomena, including the divine, thus Jung used the term 'God-Image' to describe that aspect of the psyche that receives the experience of God. Therefore, Jung's understanding of the imitation of Christ perhaps offers the perfect unification of human and divine self, whereby one does seek to be as true to his or her own unique incarnation of the spirit as Christ was to his.

2 It is important to note that Jung's Self is capitalized so as to distinguish its transcendent qualities from the ordinary sense of self that he identifies as ego. This usage sets the understanding of self as ego and the transcendent Self (that contains and transcends ego) apart, this allows us to clearly denote where Jung is referring to that sense of self 'that expresses the unity of the personality as a whole . . . a transcendental concept, for it presupposes the existence of unconscious factors on empirical grounds and thus characterises an entity that can be described only in part, but for the other part, remains at present unknowable and illimitable' (1921:par.789).

Chapter 2

Some striking similarities
Personal and philosophical

As I shall expound, Jung's therapeutic perspective and Kierkegaard's theological perspective share a common goal: the development/maturation of personality to its highest potentiality. Subjectivity is not only the core of human existence for both these thinkers; it is the foundation of one's religious life. Kierkegaard and Jung sought what can be described as the 'true' self within the grounds of the Godly[1]; consequently the urge towards greater self-knowledge takes on a religious significance. The most important insight we might take from such a reading of Jung alongside Kierkegaard is that through choosing one's true self over the self that one hides behind, an individual discovers that which was latent or unconscious within, and it is this hidden potential that is the driving force of all life. Indeed, this idea that salvation is sought through this particular kind of healing that brings about the birth of a new orientation towards life is the most important link between Kierkegaard and Jung.

The Undiscovered Self (1957) is one of Jung's last works and one that largely focuses upon religion. It is in this work of Jung that we find this curious passage that could quite as easily have appeared in any of Kierkegaard's works: 'Theindividual who is not anchored in God can offer no resistance on his own resources to the physical and moral blandishments of the world'. What Jung describes as being anchored in God, Kierkegaard with a greater sense of poetry describes as 'rest[ing] transparently'.[2] At the heart of Jung's psychological treatment and Kierkegaard's existential synthesis is the shared belief that man has the capacity through the discovery of his unconscious life to heal himself. Whilst such overtones of optimism inherent in Jung's psychology will not come as a surprise to Jungians, what will no doubt come as a surprise is the affinity that Jung shares with Kierkegaard – the philosopher regarded by many as the most melancholic of Danes.[3] Much is made of the prominence of despair in Kierkegaard's work, whilst little time is devoted to the hope that flows like warm currents throughout the stream of Kierkegaard's thinking. In the following chapters, I will pursue the idea that the aim of Kierkegaard's religious education is at one and the same time the very goal of Jung's analytical psychology. I will also contend that Kierkegaard, so ardently obsessed with finding the truth that will transform one's being, was similarly concerned with one's personal rebirth and salvation. And like Jung, this coming into the possession of one's personality and winning through to one's own true and authentic Self relied upon a particular process of self-healing. A self-healing that demands of the individual that he or she suffer and struggle after a life that is completely and wholly one's own, where God is sought in the innermost sanctuary of the Self. Essentially, one is to encounter oneself through encountering God.

Whilst Jung maintained that he himself was only a psychologist of religion and, as such, not a philosopher of religion,[4] we shall see that he has much in common with Kierkegaard, a self-proclaimed philosopher of religion. In the works of Kierkegaard and Jung we find very little to differentiate psychological and theological approaches to self-understanding. Instead, what we do discover are two thinkers out of kilter with their times, each seeking to understand the process of passage from the conventional experience of the world to an experience of it from the position of the new self, and more importantly, whose solution to the sickness of modern man (his lost soul and superficial Christendom) is almost identical. Whilst Jung did not preach Christianity to be the answer to modern man's ills, he certainly believed religious experience to be fundamental to one's self-development. That Jung viewed the aims of religion and analysis of the human mind as the functional equivalent of one another is, I contend, hard to argue against. Especially if one is to consider here his numerous writings concerning the malady of modern or mass man. As he puts it 'modern man has lost all the metaphysical certainties of his medieval brother' (1928/1931). Which I understand to mean that mankind has drifted away from his transcendental moorings, which perhaps could be said to distinguish conventional Christianity. And again:

> The psychological interest of the present time is an indication that modern man expects something from the psyche which the outer world has not given him: doubtless something which our religion ought to contain, but no longer does contain, at least for modern man.
>
> (1938/1940: par.163)

The recovery of the living religious experience was for Jung the most pressing spiritual need of the Western world. In the same vain Kierkegaard asserted that an individual, in relating to himself, relates to God. Kierkegaard's synthesis is a creative force that allows the self to choose and develop itself. Kierkegaard writes directly about relating to God as self in *Sickness Unto Death* (1849):

> A human being is spirit. But what is spirit? Spirit is the self. But what is the self? The self is a relation that relates itself to itself or is the relation's relating itself to itself in the relation: the self is not the relation but is the relation's relating itself to itself. A human being is a synthesis of the

> infinite and the finite, of the temporal and the eternal, of freedom and necessity, in short, a synthesis. A synthesis is a relation between two. Considered in this way, a human being is still not a self. In the relation between two, the relation is the third as a negative unity, and the two relate to the relation and in the relation to the relation. . . . If, however, the relation relates itself to itself, this relation is the positive third, and this is the self. . . . The human self is . . . a relation that relates itself to itself and in relating itself to itself relates itself to another.

Synthesis is a relation posited by the spirit in freedom that allows the self to give birth to itself.[5] The essential element in the fulfilling of our eternal destiny is for Kierkegaard to be found in despair. 'It is perfectly true' states Kierkegaard 'that only terror to the point of despair develops a man to his utmost – though of course many succumb during the cure; but it is also useful for a man to be handled as roughly as all that' (JP: 1850). Despair is the necessary foundation upon which to develop the right kind of passions – in other words, to cultivate faith.[6] His belief that Christian faith could not grow in superficial soil is reflected in Jung's emphasis on genuine religious experience. In his *Literary Review* (1846) Kierkegaard speaks of his age as the age of reflection: lacking in enthusiasm, a pretentious and superficial culture, spineless and apathetic. It is an age that seeks to create security as a replacement for naturalness of self-understanding of which change has deprived it: such an age 'lets everything remain but subtly drains the meaning out of it' (Kierkegaard 1846b). In other words, Kierkegaard speaks of the age-old conflict of freedom versus security. Spiritlessness is reified consciousness, 'the stagnation of spirit'; such a state is regarded by Kierkegaard to be the lowest form of despair denoting a lack of inwardness and is analysed as a psychological and cultural phenomenon (Kierkegaard 1844b). This is indeed comparable to Jung's reports of the loss of symbolic sense that results in a severage from the deepest resources of the capacity of religious healing.[7] This he says takes its toll on the individual who consequently experiences a sense of meaningless, emptiness and depression. In his 1912 essay 'New Paths in Psychology', Jung spoke explicitly of cultural forces at the root of clinical problems; urbanisation and the division of labour are held to account for having created an ominous psychological crisis, giving rise to modern man in place of his traditional Christian counterpart. Spiritlessness becomes a social complex for both these thinkers. And so Kierkegaard and Jung can be viewed as having put their culture on the couch and found it devoid of genuine religious subjective, personal, or 'inward' experience.

For Kierkegaard, one's salvation is sought through the decisiveness of spirit. Spirit is the restless inner longing for God that must strive against the inner and outer worlds of spiritlessness; the possibility of spirit is anxiety inducing because the spirit 'constantly disturbs the relation between soul and body' (1844b). Kierkegaard's spirit is comparable to Jung's unconscious in that out of the conflict of opposites rises the third thing:

> The human being is a synthesis of the psychical and the sensuous. But a synthesis is unthinkable if the two are not united in a third. This third is the spirit. . . . The spirit is present, but as immediate, as dreaming. Inasmuch as it is now present, it is in a sense a hostile power, because it constantly disturbs the relation between soul and body. . . . On the other hand, it is a friendly power, which precisely wants to constitute the relation
>
> (1844b).

For both Kierkegaard and Jung, without the tension of opposites there can be no forward movement. Jung writes, 'if a union is to take place between opposites like spirit and matter, conscious and unconscious, bright and dark, and so on, it will happen in a third thing, which represents not a compromise but something new' (1955: par.765). Jung's salvation (individuation) comes via the restoration of one's personality – it consists of recognising and assimilating the unconscious and bringing about a new center of consciousness. Whereas the achievement of transparency before God constitutes both health and one's salvation for Kierkegaard. The truth of Christianity is, for Kierkegaard, a truth belonging to each individual's existence. His entire literary corpus is an earnest attempt to communicate with the reader the very truth about his life. Kierkegaard's Christianity is not a dogmatic set of beliefs, the emphasis is always upon living one's life inwardly in relationship to God. His mission is to awaken his reader to make him or her aware of their existence. The aesthete, for Kierkegaard, really represented the majority of those who considered themselves Christian. These Christians, whom Kierkegaard believed to live in aesthetic categories, do not engage themselves truly in life, nor do they have a sense of inwardness, as they fail fully to accept responsibility for themselves or heartedly commit themselves to anything. The aesthetic life is despair, but one can recognise his spiritual character through becoming conscious of this despair. Kierkegaard sought to seduce his reader to Christianity and to lure him into Christianity.

Kierkegaard accords this power born of *vismedicatrix nature* to the individual that psychoanalysts for the most part would seem to deny. Both Kierkegaard and Jung assert that the individual is in a privileged position to undertake the investigation of himself or herself, unaided by factors outside themselves. Despair, one of Kierkegaard's most prominent themes, open or disguised, conscious or unconscious, is the constant characteristic of life;

> there is not one single living human being who does not despair a little, who does not secretly harbor an unrest, an inner strife, a disharmony,

an anxiety about an unknown something or a something he does not even dare to try to know

(1849).

Yet despair is not buried in dark recesses of the unconscious but seems to be something that we have much more control over. It becomes almost a choice; that is, there seems to be a conscious decision to choose one's despair. As he describes it, 'there is no bliss except in despair; hurry up and despair, you will find no happiness until you do' (1843a). Kierkegaard's despair, much like Jung's understanding of neurosis, is a source of natural, life-giving, underdeveloped positive potentialities. He writes,

if I were to wish for anything, I should not wish for wealth and power, but for the passionate sense of the potential, for the eye which, ever young and ardent, sees the possible. Pleasure disappoints, possibility never. And what wine is so sparkling, what so fragrant, what so intoxicating, as possibility!

(1843a)

Kierkegaard, whilst a keen observer of the lives of people around him, was a keener observer of himself. The primary sources for his insight come from his introspection. His unhappiness and personal suffering become the material on which he draws upon to educate others, those who are still capable of happiness, about how to live well. Yet Kierkegaard also had a critical, analytic distance from this sickness. Indeed, this is exactly how he portrays himself in *Sickness Unto Death*; 'this book is written as if by a physician. I, the editor, am not the physician; I am one of the sick' (1849). Kierkegaard is patient and physician, the object and the subject of his psychological investigation. His interest in psychology is profoundly personal, *Sickness Unto Death* and *The Concept Of Anxiety* being especially anecdotal, but in his attempt to share it and to build a Christian mode of development around it, is testament to his ideas not being private or abstract and dogmatic. According to the Nietzschean scholar Walter Kaufmann, Kierkegaard's psychology suffers most seriously from his peculiar self-centeredness. Consequently, as a psychologist he somewhat limits the applicability of his ideas in arriving at conclusions from a small range of experiences, of which he obsessed for the rest of his life. Notably, his father's sin in cursing God when he was a poor boy, long before Kierkegaard was born; his father's dissoluteness, particularly his problematic seduction of Kierkegaard's mother when she was a maid in his house; his own dissoluteness after he first found out about his father's debauchery; and the way he broke his engagement, pretending that he was a frivolous person, unworthy of his fiancé, Regine (Kaufmann 1980). And yet, the genuine effort to give universal interpretations to his experiences leads me to believe that his works are not limited in their application to himself alone. Indeed, arguably, all understanding is self-understanding to a significant extent. Kierkegaard's psychology is based upon self-analysis, and like Jung, Freud and other analysts of the psyche, he chose to understand himself first and foremost before tackling the great project of understanding all people. But is this not the basis of all Socratic wisdom? Is not to know oneself the precondition for knowing others? There is no reason to think that Kierkegaard's psychology is any more limited than any of those who have founded schools of psychology. Jung's own self-analysis is similar in method to Kierkegaard's attempts to reflect introspectively on his own experiences. In both instances there is an interesting connection between their introspective orientations and the curious relationship that each had with their father. We will discover in due course that it was very much the fathers who set their sons on their respective inward journeys – if it were not for the incurable religious melancholy of their fathers, Jung's and Kierkegaard's psychology would have been very different indeed.

There are many similarities between Kierkegaard and Jung, both biographically and in terms of their work, and the influence these aspects have upon each other. They are both dialecticians of existence, who share a strong commitment to the central position of the individual; the fundamentally religious nature of the psyche; the limits of rationality; the developments of personality and subjectivity; and finally, of salvation through psychological insight – whether this involves the aid of an interventionist God, ethical code or a particular therapeutic alliance to a certain school of thought. Both individuals possess a deep and extensive understanding of human life and its problems; a sense of the consolation of those who experience life in its deepest emotions, and who suffer greatly for a deeper understanding of life as it is available to us. What Kierkegaard and Jung really bring to life is the profound relationship between human and eternal realities; in fact we could say that their very existence was devoted to understanding the conflict between our immediately given nature and our capacity for transcendence – of finding that tenuous connection with a sense of infinite reality. Essentially, both these thinkers postulate a transcendental element that facilitates our journey towards wholeness. Common to both Kierkegaard and Jung is a profound insistence upon a uniquely personal and individual experience leading to 'religious' truth. This mode of being, characterised by a highly subjective awareness of truth within one's own existence culminates in coming to know what you are and what you are capable of becoming. There are then similar goals in both Kierkegaard's philosophy and Jung's analytical psychology. They both aim for truth as the honest reacquaintance and acceptance of oneself. Furthermore, both advocate journeys of a spiritual nature initiated by and conducted through a deep sense of despair and spiritual disquiet. Fundamentally, both Jung and Kierkegaard stress that in a world where too many are in despair of being themselves, it is necessary for the development of personality, if it is to attain its highest potentiality,

18   Some striking similarities

for the individual to willingly choose to be himself. I shall expound the similar theories of these thinkers concerning development of self, particularly their respective notions of what can be described as neurosis; whereby a painful lack of the feeling of wholeness is remedied through a spiritual self-healing that brings about the emergence and expression of the true self – or perhaps a more appropriate description would be the rediscovery of the greater 'moral' self. The progressive steps of Jungian analysis and the Kierkegaardian stages of a life-philosophy offer up a salvation that is to be understood with regards to the maturation of this very idea of the healthy self. And whilst regression and despair are the means by which a self-cure is attempted, this is not the illness itself – for the illness exists in the falseness of personality, a self-deception that marks the defeat of the self by the self. Such self-deception is characterised for both Kierkegaard and Jung as a loss of the unifying power of the personality; this is an important point of correspondence between our two thinkers that will be discussed later in Part two, Authenticity: The Creation of One's Genuine Self.

Jeffrey Sobosan (1975) in his article, 'Kierkegaard and Jung on the Self' astutely describes the point at which consciousness and unconsciousness, or the finite and infinite, come together, as one where human problems arise. Furthermore, he states that 'to Jung these are psychological problems; to Kierkegaard they are theological ones'. This is not strictly true, for that which is for Kierkegaard primarily theological is profoundly psychological, and that which is essentially psychological in Jung is also deeply theological. How could it be otherwise for a psychologist whose study of religion and religious experience, his wrestling with the self in relation to the divine clearly impacted upon the formation of his psychology? Similarly, Kierkegaard, foremost a philosopher of religion, offers us his own psychology which like Jung's is the product of the analysis of his own pathology in conjunction with his religious philosophy; as a result his works contain an immense amount of biographical detail. What I suggest in place of this stark distinction that Sobosan draws, is that there is a greater fluidity between the realms of the psychological and the theological than appears at first glance. Kierkegaard's spiritual development is profoundly psychological, just as Jung's process of self-development through individuation is fundamentally spiritual. There is this fascinating entwining and interweaving of religious and psychological development that underpins the overlap between Jung and Kierkegaard; self-development proceeds through what can be best understood as moral development of a fundamentally religious nature across the works of these men. Their exploration into the inner world of human subjectivity and the consequent melancholic isolation that accompanies such a search has a common religiously inspired undercurrent. We must not make the assumption that here we have in Jung an atheist intent upon the quest for authentic self-actualisation; rather Jung too emphasises the need for meaningful religious experience and the discovery of the hidden

God of an inner faith. We should not ignore Kierkegaard's claim that he is a religious author, nor should we ignore Jung's claim to be a scientist. However, we can and ought to take these claims absolutely seriously whilst also appreciating Kierkegaard's brilliance as a psychologist and Jung's passionate reinterpretation of orthodox Christian religion.

However, the potential problem in such an endeavor is that with both Jung and Kierkegaard it is quite possible that one will read into a text that which is looked for in the first instance. Scholars and avid readers alike are able to find the Kierkegaard/Jung that they seek owing to the seemingly contradictory nature of their works. Indeed, both figures surely possess a great appeal to those who seek to canonise their own psychologies/theologies through some sort of association. In short, there seem to be as many different ways of reading Jung and Kierkegaard as there are readers of Jung and Kierkegaard. So rich and alive are these texts that this is an extremely difficult problem to counter; perhaps the best one might do in such a situation is to be acutely aware of this nature inherent in both the works of Kierkegaard and Jung. What I shall take care to avoid is the temptation to detect likeness in unlikeness, so as to resolve diametrical differences into identity. Alongside this endeavor not to misinterpret or misread, in so far as this is possible, I hope to allow Jung and Kierkegaard to speak for themselves. There exist important differences and oppositions in their thinking, perhaps the most notable being Kierkegaard's profoundly Christian experience of the religious and the unhealthy rigorism of his conception of the authentic Christian that lacks *joie de vivre*. What demands to be addressed here is whether these differences and incompatibilities culminate providing justification for Jung's complete disregard of Kierkegaard. The question as to whether we might characterise Jung's process of individuation as religious is particularly interesting and contentious. Whilst Charles Hanna (1967) claims that by studying Jung 'we gain an insight into the ways by which men become aware of God', Edward Glover (1950) writes that 'so far from being religious in tendency, Jung's system is fundamentally irreligious. Nobody is to care whether God exists, Jung least of all'. This seems more than a divide between what could be said to be a typically Jungian versus a particularly Freudian perspective and is thus deserving of our attention. But first we shall become more acquainted with the life and thought of Søren Abaye Kierkegaard.

Notes

1 Neither Kierkegaard nor Jung spoke literally in terms of authenticity or 'false' as opposed to 'true' self; however, that there are such inauthentic ways to exist that carry pathological implications makes the use of such terms relevant and useful.

2 'The formula that describes the state of the self when despair is completely rooted out is this: in relating itself to itself and in willing to be itself, the self rests transparently in the power that established it' (1849).

3 See H. V. Martin, *Kierkegaard: The Melancholy Dane*. Martin is one of the many scholars who has invoked the figure of Kierkegaard as the melancholy Dane, predisposed to the tragic and prime representative of the gloomy, guilt-ridden aspect of Christianity. Podmore (2011) remarks that 'this oft-repeated legend for Kierkegaard – "the melancholy Dane" – represents a perception that only sees half the face, as it were, of one of modern theology and philosophy's most insightful exponents of the triumph of faith over despair.' (Unfortunately, the darker aspect of Kierkegaard's work has prevailed to the neglect of the divinely lit redemptive elements. There is no denying the presence of darkness; however, the individual must first navigate his or her way through the darkness of the abyss before the divine light may be discovered – again, we see a very clear parallel with Jung's own thinking.

4 Jung states at the very beginning of *Psychology and Religion* that 'I am an empiricist and adhere as such to the phenomenological standpoint. . . . I restrict myself to the observation of phenomena and I eschew any metaphysical or philosophical considerations' (1938/1940).

5 To put it simply, spirit is freedom – it is the third thing that is able to establish and substain the synthesis between body and soul so as the individual is posited as spirit.

6 'The only way in which an existing individual comes into relation with God, is when the dialectical contradiction brings his passion to the point of despair, and helps him to embrace God with the "catergory of despair" (faith). Then the postulate is so far from being arbitrary that it is a life-necessity. It is then not so much that God is a postulate, as that the existing individual's postulation of God is a necessity' (1846a).

7 'The world had not only been deprived of its gods but had lost its soul. Through the shifting of interest from the inner to the outer world, our knowledge of nature was increased a thousand fold in comparison to earlier ages, but knowledge and experience of the inner world were correspondingly reduced' (1912/1952:par.113).

Chapter 3

Introducing Kierkegaard[1]

Kierkegaard was born on 5th May 1813, in Copenhagen, the seventh and youngest son of a somewhat elderly father, Michael Kierkegaard, a retired well-to-do merchant. He was born into a pietistic strict Lutheran home, the mood of which was largely dominated by his father's feelings of guilt and depression (Ostenfeld 1978). Søren possessed a remarkable immunity to the rigorous rationalism all-prevalent in the late nineteenth century and sought to do away with systematic philosophical thinking altogether. From a reader's perspective this is particularly problematic, since his own viewpoint is consequently never conveyed and presented simply in the form of a system. Kierkegaard is rarely an easy read and comprehension in the first sitting would denote a formidable intellect or, rather, a misreading, but perseverance is often rewarded by a greater gradual understanding of an author whose thinking is unique, challenging and revolutionary in the sense that he earnestly attempts to redefine what it means to be a Christian. It has often been the case in the past that psychologists have been all the more interested in Kierkegaard as the subject of their analysis than a theorist in his own right, as a psychological case study, for instance. He has been diagnosed, amongst other things, as paranoid (Thompson 1974), schizoid (Frank Lake 1986; Thompson 1974; Helweg 1933; La), manic-depressive (Helweg 1933), and as a sufferer of sexual anxiety and syphilis (Fenger 1980; Garff 2005) and epilepsy (Hansen 1994). Podmore (2009) notes that so prolific were rumors and speculations as to Kierkegaard's health that they led Sartre to boldly proclaim that, in spite of the unbroachable silence at the very heart of this wound in his writings, all are agreed in diagnosing a 'sexual anomaly as its kernel'. The wound to which Podmore alludes is the elusive source of Kierkegaard's 'secret suffering', which invoking the afflictions of St. Paul, Kierkegaard provocatively names his 'thorn in the flesh':

> Now Governance really had me shackled: perhaps like a dubious character I have been kept on a very restricted regimen. I am accustomed to living in such a way that at most I believe I have only one year left and at times, not rarely, when things are tightened up, I live on a one-week,

yes, a one-day prospect. I could not leave it understood in such a way that it ended with my having my life in the esthetic. Even if the religious had not been in the background, that 'thorn in the flesh' would still have kept me from it.

(Kierkegaard 1848)

The secret of the mysterious curse, inherited from his father, has long been the subject of much scholarly conjecture and continued fascination – alongside the nature of his psychopathology. Ever enigmatic, his works elicit a very personal response from the reader. The manner in which he writes often possesses the ability to unsettle his reader and it does so precisely because Kierkegaard wants the reader to engage personally with his works. It is to this end that he uses the pseudonymous authors and characters as mirrors, reflecting aspects of one's true self; whether we recognise them as such is another matter. Kierkegaard's work, and Kierkegaard himself – the enigmatic author, exerts a great fascination – the prolific speculation with regards to his mental/physical health is testament to this. Writing of his imagined legacy Kierkegaard perceptively foresaw that 'the day will come when not only my writings, but precisely my life – the intriguing secret of all the machinery – will be studied and studied'. Regardless of Kierkegaard's psyche and the various psychological and psychiatric diagnoses that scholars may seek to adorn him with, it remains that his psychology demands to be taken seriously. His work on suffering and despair may well be the literary autobiography of a religious neurotic but it is also a genuine psychological theory that seeks to put the individual onto the path of becoming – becoming the self one is and becoming an authentic Christian.

One year before his father's death Kierkegaard met Regine Olsen, daughter of a high-ranking civil servant then 14 years old, ten years younger than Søren. He fell in love with her at first sight and in 1840, two months after being awarded his degree in theology he had announced his engagement to Regine, now a girl of just 18 years of age and he a man of 27. But as soon as he had made this commitment, the image of his fervent hopes changed into the pale image of his memories. Søren became the victim of doubts. Could he, burdened by depressive mood swings, carry the responsibility of this commitment? Was he not going to destroy her and himself? Was it not selfish to ask for salvation through love? (Weigert 1960). For one year Kierkegaard tried to play the part of the considerate conventional fiancé. He tried to convince Regine that he was unworthy of her love. He was deeply distressed by her clinging attachment. His conflict was a double bind: 'Do it and you will regret it. Do it not and you will regret it, too'. At last he broke the engagement, deeply humiliated by his defeat, Regine's misery and the accusations of public opinion. Kierkegaard is not the only great writer to have rejected marriage and a family for the lonely rigor of art. Franz Kafka proposed twice to Felice, who accepted twice – and Kafka broke both these engagements. It is genuinely quite fascinating to note that Kierkegaard, Jung and Kafka were all products of a similar family dynamic; that of a conventional, rigid, bourgeois father and a reclusive, sensitive and spiritual mother. The focal point of Kierkegaard's being unable to marry seems to lie in the conflict between being alone with his melancholy and living intimately with another person. He believed that marriage required total honesty and since he was unable to open himself up regarding his father's curse and sensuality, he was simply unable to fulfill his engagement to Regine. This very conflict is reflected in *Either/Or*, whereby Antigone is unable to reveal the secret that would disgrace her father. The year of his broken engagement coincides with his most creative period; it is during this tumultuous year that he wrote *Either/Or*, *Fear and Trembling* and *Repetition*, alongside various discourses.[2] In these works he analysed and reanalysed his feelings, his unhappiness as the lover and betrothed of Regine; his betrothal, faith and love are at the very heart of all his writings of 1843. Kierkegaard's refusal to marry marks the beginnings of his withdrawal from life; we can speculatively suggest that his estrangement from Regine sparked his creative impulses. Yet this decidedly devoted move towards religious authorship also marks the sacrifice of his sexual self-identity; Kierkegaard's choice not to marry concretizes his orientation towards the spiritual at the expense of the body and its sexual nature.

Misunderstood and largely ignored during his lifetime it was not until the twentieth century that he was rediscovered and celebrated as a philosopher of significance. Kierkegaard found himself the victim of much public humiliation; he could go nowhere in Copenhagen without being insulted:

> Even the butcher's boy almost thinks himself justified in being offensive to me at the behest of *The Corsair*. Undergraduates grin and giggle and are delighted that someone prominent should be trodden down; the dons are envious and secretly sympathize with the attack, help to spread it abroad, adding of course that it is a crying shame. The least thing I do, even if I simply pay a visit, is lyingly distorted and repeated everywhere; if *The Corsair* gets to know of it then it is printed and is read by the whole population.
>
> (JP 1846)

It is worthy of mention that this man routinely ridiculed and humiliated on the streets of Copenhagen despite claiming 'I am positive that my whole life will never be as important as my trousers' (JP 1846), possessed a certainty that he would be celebrated as a great author long after his death. His philosophy profoundly influenced many twentieth-century thinkers, informing and inspiring the likes of Jean Paul Sartre, Albert Camus, Karl Jaspers, Ludwig Binswanger, Medard Boss, Erich Fromm, Rollo May, Erik Erickson and R. D. Laing in indirect but important ways. This alone suggests that Kierkegaard's writings are of significant psychological interest. Having lived his life in relative obscurity, his fame as a philosopher grew during the 1930s when

24 Introducing Kierkegaard

the existentialist movement identified him as a precursor. Modern existentialism essentially advocates a Kierkegaardian theory of crisis, in which an individual's crisis is thought to be brought about through the dread of infinite possibilities. Simply understood, the freedom to make choices breeds anxiety. Jean Paul Sartre, in his famous essay *Existentialism and Human Emotions* (1957), defined existentialism as the view that as far as human beings are concerned 'existence precedes essence', meaning that what we are is completely up to us to determine, for we are self-creating creatures who create through our choices. Kierkegaard then is not an existentialist as such for it was his belief that the true self is God-given – he would have absolutely deplored such existentialist self-creation as the ultimate betrayal of God. It is perhaps more fitting then that there has been a move away from this image of Kierkegaard, the father of existentialism, forerunner of Sartre, Camus and Heidegger.

Of particular influence to the theologians, philosophers and psychologists that followed him were his concepts of despair, angst, authenticity and the central importance of the individual. However, Kierkegaard was not alone in describing the existentialist predicament; Schopenhauer, Nietzsche, Pascal, Sartre, Camus and Heidegger all explore and reflect on man's purposelessness, nihilism, boredom, alienation, anxiety and despair. Yet it remains that there is no doubt that Kierkegaard is a significant and influential thinker whose insights predate the likes of Nietzsche and Pascal. And although he is considered primarily a philosopher and theologian, his insights are undoubtedly of great psychological value, possessing as they do a profoundly modern and particularly Jungian nature – sounding like the most modern of precepts for mental health. As I asserted earlier, by treating Kierkegaard solely as philosopher, we are not getting all we can from him. We can be absolutely sure that Kierkegaard regarded himself as a psychologist. As well as the frequent references to such that can be found in his journal entries, there also remains the curious subtitles that he gave to his works. For instance, *Repetition: A Venture in Experimenting Psychology* (1843), *The Concept of Anxiety: A Simple Psychologically-Oriented Reflection on the Dogmatic Problem of Original Sin* (1844) and *The Sickness Unto Death: A Christian Psychological Exposition for Edification and Awakening* (1849). These three works are given subtitles by Kierkegaard to designate them as psychological pieces. However, he is a theologian first and foremost for it is as theologian intent upon ridding Christianity of its superficiality that he understood the importance and need of psychology in the re-education of his fellow 'Christians'. In a journal entry written in 1844 Kierkegaard emphasises,

> psychology is what we need, and above all, expert human knowledge of human life and its sympathy with its interests. Thus, here is the problem

that solution of which must precede any talk of rounding out a Christian view of life.

(JP 1844)

His famous expression that 'life can only be understood backwards; but it must be lived forwards' (Journals and papers [JP] 1843) would suggest that we cannot entirely understand the possibilities of our life, until we have taken the leap into them. This is particularly pertinent with regards to depth psychology and psychoanalysis, and would certainly encapsulate their raison d'être. His greatest contribution surely and the one that intimately connects him with Jung, lies in his profound understanding of the individual's religious-psychological maturation. We could say of Kierkegaard that he is the greatest theological thinker to have penetrated and plundered psychological depths since St. Augustine, whom it is interesting to note shared a similar passionate concern for his individual existential situation. It is his concern for the authentic existence that brings Kierkegaard to his particular brand of existential psychology. Indeed, what Kierkegaard attempts in earnest to do is to offer us a way of realising an authentic religious experience. However, as a young man scarred with neurotic hatred and bitterness, frail, feeble and misshapen – he was neither a physically nor mentally healthy soul. With an upbringing that could best be described as melancholic and a love, perhaps betrayed, for his fiancée, Kierkegaard strikes a lonely and tragic figure. To use his own darkly melancholic description of himself:

> Delicate, slender and weak, deprived of almost every condition requisite for holding my own with other boys, or even, for passing as a complete man in comparison with others; melancholy, sick, in soul, in many ways deeply unfortunate, one thing I had: an eminently shrewd wit, given me presumably in order that I might not be defenseless.

(JP 1848)

Cast into emotional depths by the circumstances of his own life, he conducted a great deal of self-examination, and through plummeting into these emotional depths he made significant explorations into the self. Furtak in his much applauded work *Wisdom in Love* (2005) offers an interesting description of a man who did his best to accept everything, including his own mistakes and although his own biographical story was ultimately more tragic than happy – a narrative of unhappy love and much suffering, as he saw it – he left a sketch of what the ideal passionate vantage point would be like for those who may be able to appreciate it. Furtak reflects the view Kierkegaard presents of himself in his journal papers as the tragic figure whose task it has been to offer guidance to those who, unlike himself, are still capable of attaining happiness.

Furtak's description of a man who followed an involuntary calling – that he faithfully tried to fulfil this calling and in doing so made the most of his particular affliction – is a wonderful testament to Kierkegaard. However, I view Furtak's description of Kierkegaard as such an accepting individual deeply suspect. Kierkegaard's life was indeed a tragic one; in the inward struggle of his soul's relation to God, Kierkegaard sacrificed not only his best but his everything – his marriage, health, his means and friends. If Kierkegaard sought deliverance from his melancholy in religion then, as we will discuss later, he never found it; faith never overcame melancholy in his case and this strikes me as truly tragic. Despite Kierkegaard's prolific literary output, there is in his works the sense that his creativity never quite reconciled him with his suffering. However, personal tragedies aside for a moment, Kierkegaard shared Jung's own hope of rescuing individuals from the spiritual slavery and general malaise felt across the Europe of their respective times. That there is a commonality to Jung and Kierkegaard in this respect is evident in the spectrum of individuals that take comfort in their words.

His first book *Either/Or* (1843) presents the battle between sensuous aesthetic immediacy and endless ethical reflections that Kierkegaard was experiencing within himself at the time. Even as early as 1843 the resolution to what seems to be an irreconcilable conflict is posited on a religious plane. The three texts that are most relevant to our discussion are *The Concept of Anxiety* (1844), *Postscript* (1846) and *The Sickness unto Death* (1849). These texts weave into and out of one another, linked by a primary concern of choosing the self that you are. As has been commented upon, Kierkegaard's thinking is very much of a personal nature, related as it is to the human situation. He calls the individual, to bring him back to what is unique in himself and away from the exclusive concern with what is common to his species and from the irresponsibility of the mass minded. For Kierkegaard, the essence of man is to exist as a person who is engaged in the persistent striving to realise the highest ethical potentialities, to open himself to a multiplicity of individuating acts. The essence of man can be realised and revealed in the personal, authentic existence of an individual. This demands a psychological turning in on oneself, a highly critical self-examination, from which one must not take flight. Kierkegaard, unlike many of his existentialist followers, seems just as concerned with one's being what one is, as he is with becoming what one becomes. His concern was for the subjective needs and passions of the individual and the dread of disintegration that the dialectical tension between these passions and the prohibitions imposed upon them by reality. He saw the human being in a process of self-becoming, a process that requires tremendous courage in order to become transparent to oneself against the raging torrents of self-concealment, illusion and seclusion. For those who are even the least bit acquainted with Jung, the similarity here is too incredibly apparent to go unnoticed. For Jung believed that in order to assimilate unconscious parts of the psyche and thus to become integrated it was first necessary to nurture a sensitivity and receptivity to those aspects of ourselves that we neglect, disown and devalue. Indeed, Jung's conception of the shadow (the personification of all that one represses) has a tendency towards the darker elements of life, and this is due to its consisting predominantly of the primitive, negative, socially/religiously depreciated emotions; essentially, that which clashes with one's chosen attitude. It is, wrote Aniela Jaffe, 'the sum of all personal and collective psychic elements which, because of their incompatibility with the chosen conscious attitude, are denied expression in life' and thus are completely obscured from consciousness (1963). That which Jung terms the shadow self finds a place in Kierkegaard's conception of sin; for Kierkegaard provides a window into the deeper and darker interiority of sin and faith, much akin to the way in which Jung captures the shadow self.

Faith, as described by Kierkegaard, is surrounded in ambivalence; it is something that is neither an act of knowledge nor an act of unconditioned willing (1844a). It is a confrontation with the shadow self, leading to a mobilisation of life forces that serves to further link Kierkegaard and Jung. Jung's shadow self and Kierkegaard's notion of sin both mobilise the life forces and these are remarkably similar in nature to Freud's concept of Thanatos.[3] This really is very interesting, for it would seem that these thinkers share the same thread of thought – namely that of the creative force of destruction. However, at this stage, it would be informative and helpful to briefly sketch Kierkegaard's spheres of existence before turning again to Jung and to what I shall argue is his equivalent process of personal development: his process of individuation.

According to Kierkegaard, human beings can be classified according to types that correspond to stages of consciousness. He presents us with three differing levels of existence: the aesthetic, ethical and religious that together equate to a three-stage theory of consciousness. Each existence sphere has its own characteristic concerns and interests as well as different ways of thinking about life, which generates sphere distinctions on a whole array of emotions. As a person continues to evolve, there tends to be a progression from the aesthetic to the ethical and then onwards to the religious stage. There is also a hierarchical arrangement in each sphere, so that some humans will express a particular mode of existence in an undeveloped manner, whereas others are exemplary of more evolved versions of that life. For instance, in the aesthetic sphere he devotes most of his discussion to the lifestyle and views of the 'refined aesthete' (what we might call an ironist, or romantic), in the ethical sphere he portrays the ultimate in bourgeois virtue by revealing how the ethical judge thinks one should live (1843a). Of course he chooses the exemplarily and heroic figure of Abraham, the paragon of religious faith, as the best that the religious stage of life has to offer. Kierkegaard makes clear throughout his writings that a certain mood is necessary

28 Introducing Kierkegaard

for a certain understanding. For instance no one lost in tranquil speculation could possibly understand the concept of guilt.

The first of these three stages of development is the aesthetic, which can be understood as describing the period of one's life where the pursuit of pleasure becomes the primary aim of life; 'the aesthetic in a person is that by which he spontaneously and immediately is what he is' (1843a). This pursuit of pleasure Kierkegaard refers to as the 'first immediacy'; in this initial immediacy the ego seeks to enact the conquest of pleasure, whereas in the 'later' immediacy, the ego aesthetically and poetically relives past enjoyments:

> The poetic was the plus he brought along. This plus was the poetic he enjoyed in the poetic situation of actuality; this he recaptured in the form of poetic reflection. This was the second enjoyment, and his whole life was intended for enjoyment. In the first case he enjoyed the aesthetic; in the second case he aesthetically enjoyed his personality. The point in the first case was that he egotistically enjoyed personally that which in part actuality has given to him.
>
> (1843a)

Immediacy, freedom, egoism and lightness characterise the aesthetic life, which is immediate in the sense that it is lived for the moment rather than for a future that must be prepared for and egotistic in the sense that it consists of the pursuit of enjoyment for oneself. Aesthetical man is then, spontaneous; he seeks instant gratification and acts not through qualified reflection but mostly upon instinct. The aesthete refuses to make life-determining decisions and so everything remains a possibility and nothing can be made a reality. Having no predefined agenda or long-term goals, aesthetic life is a series of experiences, of encounters, adventures, tasks, delights and surprises. Life then has no unifying purpose; we might say that aesthetic life is then spiritless and without inner substance. This stage is, according to Kierkegaard, where most of us live out our lives of whim and caprice. For example, we could point towards the many and various quests for selfhood that ebb and flow upon the currents of celebrity and fashion as a reflection of our contemporary aesthetic leanings. Our stubborn resistance to submit to any higher power than our own ego has the result that we never truly commit ourselves and therefore the synthesis between spirit and world fails.

Whilst this aesthetic individual of immediacy, the unsubstantiated self of the aesthete, continues to regard everything with detachment, he or she will drift inevitably as a stranger within the community. Consequently, he does not possess an awareness of his moral situation, or his own place within it. In its lowest form, the aesthetic life is one of vague, floating, sensual desire – a craving for something which is not yet present to consciousness as an object, but is present in consciousness as impulse. When this sleeping desire awakes, it goes in search of what it now realises that it wants, seeking here and there, without consistency of purpose and with no sense that any one object of desire is of more value than another. In its highest form it is not mere sensuality but the art of distilling maximum pleasure out of experience – a hedonism capable of considerable refinement, where one can choose and reject pleasures till it reaches the most satisfying, yet which never acknowledges a law higher than itself. Essentially at the heart of aesthetic existence is a lack of responsibility, an absence of control over one's life; life is taken simply as it comes or, as Kierkegaard describes it, 'fortune, misfortune, fate, immediate enthusiasm, despair – these are what the aesthetic life has at its disposal' (1846a). The aesthete is dependent for the satisfaction of his desires upon conditions, within and without, which are not under his control. Eventually, then, time and life itself are against him. All efforts to make reality minister to hedonism are self- defeating in the end, because essentially such an existence is always pursuing that which can only contribute to one's emptiness and lack of substance (in Jungian terms, to one's ego and its limitations). With excessive gratification comes satiety, a weary resignation and boredom's possibility. When old sources of enjoyment become stale, they then give rise to a predominating mood of boredom, and it is at this juncture that the aesthetic life can potentially come to an end. The aesthete's boredom, emptiness and his or her consequential melancholy is inescapable. We were created spiritual beings and by making life a collection of pleasurable moments with no higher purpose we neglect this fact. Judge William, the older married man, representative of the ethical sphere of existence in *Either/Or* diagnoses depression as 'hysteria of the spirit' occurring because the 'spirit does not allow itself to be mocked; it avenges itself on you and binds you in the chains of depression' (1843a). It is the refusal to become what one should be. He writes 'there comes a time in a person's life when his immediacy is, as it were, ripened and the spirit demands a higher form in which it will apprehend itself as spirit' (1843a).

Such a situation can, however, can be temporarily avoided, just so long as aesthetical man adopts what Kierkegaard calls 'the rotation method' – the creation of one's own personalised world of pleasures. This method is doomed to eventually fail the aesthete, bringing him to a state of desperate despair. The aesthete thereby laments,

> I don't feel like doing anything. I don't feel like riding – the motion is too powerful; I don't feel like walking – it is too tiring; I don't feel like lying down, for either I would have to stay down, and I don't feel like doing that, or I would have to get up again, and I don't feel like doing that, either. *Summa summarium*: I don't feel like doing anything.
>
> (1843a)

It is at this stage that the aesthete ought to acknowledge the inadequacies of such a life and choose instead to follow that which hungers for a meaningful

30 Introducing Kierkegaard

existence. It is only by such an acknowledgement that he can begin the transition to the ethical stage of life.

He who has embarked upon the ethical sphere of existence is in pursuit of self-knowledge and struggles to become a better person. In the ethical stage of life, one 'grows up' so to speak and accepts responsibilities as defined by general principles of moral conduct. It is important to bear in mind that it is only in the ethical and religious spheres that essential knowledge is to be found:

> All essential knowledge relates to existence. . . . [This] Knowledge has a relationship to the knower, who is essentially an existing individual . . . only ethico-religious knowledge has an essential relationship to the existence of the knower.
>
> (1846a)

It is the ethical life that marks the beginning of authentic selfhood:

> The aesthetic . . . is that in which a person is immediately what he is; the ethical is that whereby a person becomes what he becomes. This in no way implies that someone who lives aesthetically does not develop, but he develops with necessity, not with freedom; there occurs no metamorphosis in his case, no infinite movement whereby he arrives at the point from which he becomes what he becomes.
>
> (1846a)

At the heart of Kierkegaard's early works is the urgent lesson that existence in the aesthetic sphere cannot ever lead to one's becoming a Christian. *Either/Or* in particular seems designed to instill within the reader a dissatisfaction for the aesthetic and its inability to bring to the fore any kind of authentic religious awareness. The religious life grows from the ethical – whilst the ethical stage allows for the religious to come about, it does in fact stand in direct opposition to the religious. Safe, secure, understandable, ultimately dutiful, the ethical stage demands that one perform his duties and responsibilities. Perhaps the most important development at this stage encompasses the awareness of ethical concepts, which are required for the growth of one's conscience. In *Works of Love* (1847) Kierkegaard writes that 'the relationship between the individual and God, the God-relationship, is the conscience' (1847b). In the second part of *Either/Or* we learn through the Judge that the 'true' life is the ethical life, and the ethical life necessitates that we make the definite choice of despair over oneself. Such a choice rests upon one's personal decision to choose oneself, not in one's immediacy, but in one's eternal validity. This marks the first step towards severing the noose of unfreedom to which the individual has tied himself; the beginnings of the transformation to a Christian existence.

Those living the hedonistic life of apparent Epicurean delight are in fact living in despair, for the Judge firmly holds that 'every aesthetic view of life is in despair, and that everyone who lives aesthetically is in despair, whether he knows it or not' (1843a). In short, the despairing man in Kierkegaardian terms is living an inauthentic existence, experienced as alienation from oneself. Essentially despair in all its forms constitutes a mis-relationship to the constituting power that grounds the all-important synthesis. Such an existence in the immediate characterises both the infant and the grown person who follows the pleasure principle. Of crucial importance is to understand that such a man has not yet begun to develop as an individual. The most substantial criticism that can be made of Kierkegaard here from a psychological perspective is that he deals only with the total cure of sickness. I find it hard to conceive in his thought any sense in which there could be a temporary alleviation of the disturbances within one's soul, but we should hardly expect otherwise of a man for whom life is either everything or nothing. What we could perhaps suggest more positively is that selfhood vacillates between inauthentic and authentic modes. That it is through inauthenticity that we find authenticity; not only is inauthenticity therefore inevitable but also a necessity. Understood more generally, the authentic existence is marked by the individual who contemplates and transforms himself, for whom the process of fulfilling one's potential is at work. This is certainly interesting to consider in relation to Jung's individuation as a project of becoming that itself has no end point.[4]

Once the realisation between one's existence in one's innermost soul and one's failure to express this outwardly has been made this leads to the ethical stage's despair. This despair, if intense enough, can precipitate a leap to faith, resulting in the religious outlook on existence. This way of life is characterised by an awareness in which the individual realises the impossibility of fulfilling the ideals of the ethical existence. In *Concluding Unscientific Postscript* (1846), Kierkegaard distinguishes between two types of religious life: a 'natural' religiosity (which he calls religiousness A), in which the individual strives to relate to God and resolve the problem of guilt by relying exclusively upon his natural 'immanent' idea of God. And, Christianity (religiousness B), which accepts that God is incarnated as a human being for the purpose of establishing a relation with humans (1846). Religiousness B can only be reached through a leap to faith, for it is a transcendent religion based upon revelation rather than an immanent religion. Kierkegaard makes the bold and controversial proclamation that in order to become a Christian proper one must first become a subjective thinker – to become 'subjective' is to become contemporary with Christ. Such a claim is controversial of course, for it is contrary to the teaching of the scriptures, where salvation is guaranteed through conversion to the Christian faith. What Kierkegaard seems to do is to add an extra criterion for salvation; belief alone, for Kierkegaard, is not enough. One must also become subjective,

32 Introducing Kierkegaard

and this is an absolutely necessary requirement to arrive at truth. Kierkeg-aard's conception of salvation, therefore, differs from that of conventional Christianity. Perhaps the simplest way of expressing this would be to say that according to Kierkegaard, mere belief falls short of what it means to be a Christian proper for one must be a Christian 'exister'. To be a Christian is to have one's life transformed; it is therefore necessary that only faith is capable of moving one to action. To believe in a Christian way then is more than believing certain doctrinal truths to be true; in fact it is all about believ-ing with one's heart, or with one's full or inner being. Salvation is not just a purified lease of life beyond the grave, but a development of self (spirit) in the here and now that recognises one's need for God. For Kierkegaard, the development of passionate inwardness is absolutely necessary in order to become a Christian, for:

> Christianity is spirit, spirit is inwardness, inwardness is subjectivity, subjectivity is essentially passion, and in its maximum an infinite, per-sonal, passionate interest in one's eternal happiness.
>
> (1846a)

Of paramount importance to our progression through the spheres to the position of being an authentic Christian, is passion – 'the essentially human element' (1843b). In fact, one cannot come to understand Kierkegaard's conception of the human self without first appreciating just how important a part passions play in its phenomenological constitution. What makes the self is the passion that it possesses. We cannot by the process of reflection transport ourselves from one sphere to the other. For within the context of these spheres, their alternative modes of existence are defined by a specific passion. The aesthetic passion is essentially for pleasure, the ethical passion is for the abidance to moral law and the religious passion is a suffering through which religious faith emerges. It is only by living intensively that one can realise oneself fully. This emphasises a key point for Kierkegaard, one that he curiously shares with Jung, that our humanity is defined by our sensibility, and not by reason: 'Passion . . . is the real measure of man's power. And the age in which we live is wretched, because it is without pas-sion' (JP: 1841). It is passion that drives us to make decisions; it is passion also that generates energy to go beyond itself and become transfigured to another sphere. Passion provides the upward flight to a higher stage and ultimately to God, from whom passion emanates. One must find such a pas-sionate vantage point through faith and not through fear or even a rational yielding to the necessities of reality. In other words, we must never wager our eternal destiny and decide to believe, because we cannot risk otherwise à la Pascal. For Kierkegaard it is the truth which alone can save me, the truth that I choose, not for the hope of salvation, but because saved or lost, I must acknowledge it to be true. It is upon such a passionate vantage point that Kierkegaard builds not only his own subjective philosophy but religion also. In terms of his own personal development, Kierkegaard succeeded in trusting his own spiritual potency and through this trust he experienced a degree of freedom that Weigert (1960) believes to have united his will with his destiny.

Notes

1 Commentaries on the various aspects of Kierkegaard's works are vast. There are many very good biographies and introductory works, amongst them are *Kierkegaard: A Critical Biography* by Josiah Thompson; *Encounters With Kierkegaard: A Life As Seen by His Contemporaries*, edited and annotated by Bruce Kirmmse (this collection of eyewitness accounts is a valuable resource for understanding Kierkegaard's life and personality); Joakim Garff's *Søren Kierkegaard: A Biography* is the most thorough biography to date and an incredible introduction to Kierkegaard's work. However, for an introductory work that weaves the overlap between Kierkegaard's life and thought into its narrative, the reader could do no better than to start with Alistair Hannay's *Kierkegaard: A Biography*.
2 There exists a clear parallel between his giving up Regine and Abraham's giving up Isaac, however, Abraham received Isaac back again; is Kierkegaard to receive back Regine? It would seem only if his faith is comparable to Abraham's. In the story of Abraham there is the teleological suspension of the ethical and the double movement of infinity. God's requirement of us is that we surrender all earthly happiness, but to those that make such a sacrifice he gives back all that is taken. The knight of faith renounces in an infinite sense the love that has been the content of his life and reconciles himself to all subsequent sufferings. However, the knight executes a further movement, for he reveals that despite his suffering and loss that his love will be returned to him, in virtue of the absurd, on the grounds that all things are possible with God. It would seem plausible to suggest that Kierkegaard at this time still hoped that something would change that would make marrying his Regine a possibility; 'but if she really does wish it, how gladly I would be reconciled with her. She has suffered for my sake, suffered what must be the deepest humiliation to a young girl, even if I did everything to alleviate the humiliation, and also proposed that she be the one to break the engagement – she has suffered for my sake, and God knows how much I want to make all possible amends. For my own sake as well: the easier the conditions on which she can be married to another, the easier my personal life will be. *In a way my personal relationship to God is a reduplication of my relationship to her*' (JP 1849).
3 Freud identified two conflicting and coinciding drives within the individual, Eros and Thanatos. Eros is the drive of life, love, creativity, and sexuality, self-satisfaction and species preservation. Whilst Thanatos, from the Greek word for 'death' is the drive of aggression, sadism, destruction, violence and death.
4 For, as we shall see, individuation for Jung has no termination point per se. The negation of inner conflict is not possible for either Kierkegaard's nor Jung's psychological models. Father Victor White wrote inquiring if anyone could finally reach a high enough level of consciousness that he would escape from the inner conflict. Jung wrote back in the negative: 'not even a person with a "higher level of consciousness [can] . . . escape the raging conflict of opposites in his soul, as God wants to unite His opposites in man'.

Chapter 4

Presenting Jung[1]

Sonu Shamdasani (2003) captures the divergent views and interpretations of Jung beautifully in the following paragraph; so prolific are such views that he asks 'what has C. G. Jung not been called?'

> Occultist, Scientist, Prophet, Charlatan, Philosopher, Racist, Guru, Anti-Semite, Liberator of Women, Misogynist, Freudian Apostate, Gnostic, Post-Modernist, Polygamist, Healer, Poet, Con-Artist, Psychiatrist and Anti-Psychiatrist. . . . Mention him to someone, and you are likely to receive one of these images. For Jung is someone that people – informed or not – have opinions about.
>
> (Shamdasani 2003)

Clearly, the variety of descriptions of Jung lays testimony to his encyclopedic learning. His library, still intact in his house in Kusnacht, presents a panoramic of human learning, without parallel in modern psychology.[2] Often portrayed as the rebel heretic of psychoanalysis, his complex psychology is much more than an offshoot, a mere modification, of psychoanalysis. Jung is a philosopher in the old fashion sense of the word: his interests were vast and this, I suspect, is the very reason why Jung has influenced developments not just in psychology but also in many disciplines from filmmaking to theology. His stout belief that the way to self-realisation lay in the rediscovery of the spiritual self seems to have a particularly strong resonance throughout our own era, with its many and appealing complementary therapies and flourishing ecological lifestyles. Jung's ideas derived from his own experiences and relationships. And this is interesting because his autobiography contains very little in the way of information concerning his relationships with others. Whereas Regine Olsen occupies a central role in Kierkegaard's thought and writing, Jung barely makes mention of his wife, Emma, or indeed his many other women.[3] Jung frequently expressed his distaste for exposing his life to public view through autobiography; however, he did relent in later life and so we have *Memories, Dreams Reflections*.[4] There is the sense in this work that Jung remained a solitary figure, and I believe this has a bearing upon his analytical psychology, particularly its development towards a balance of forces within the psyche without reference to personal relationships. And yet his personal relationships, especially those of his parents, play such an instrumental role in the shaping of his psychology.

Carl Jung was born in 1875, the fourth but sadly first surviving child of Paul Achilles Jung and Emilie Preiswerk. His father, a Lutheran pastor, seemed to have suffered bouts of depression fueled by a growing loss of faith. The young Jung was profoundly aware of his father's religious doubts, feeling 'a most vehement pity' for the demise that he perceived to be the result of a hopeless entrapment by the church and its theological teaching (1963). In contrast to a passive, depressed and weak father, Jung's mother was a much more powerful figure altogether; 'she always seemed to me the stronger of the two', wrote Jung. Far from being the conventional pastor's wife, Emilie was a domineering woman whose twofold nature fascinated and frightened her son:

> There was an enormous difference between my mother's two personalities. That was why as a child I often had anxiety dreams about her. By day she was a loving mother, but at night she seemed uncanny. Then she was like one of those seers who is at the same time a strange animal, like a priestess in a bear's cave. Archaic and ruthless; ruthless as truth and nature. At such moments she was the embodiment of what I have called the 'natural mind.' I, too, have this archaic nature, and in me it is linked with the gift – not always pleasant – of seeing people and things as they are.
>
> (1963)

It is said that she spent much of her time in her own separate bedroom, enthralled by the spirits that visited her at night;

> my parents were sleeping apart. I slept in my father's room . . . one night I saw coming from her door a faintly luminous, indefinite figure whose head detached itself from the neck and floated along in front of it.
>
> (1963)

An eccentric and depressed woman, she was hospitalised in 1878 and this had a profound effect upon the three-year-old Jung; 'my illness, in 1878', Jung reflected, 'must have been connected with a temporary separation of my parents. My mother spent several months in a hospital in Basel and presumably her illness had something to do with the difficulty in the marriage.' These breakdowns and the subsequent bouts of absence and abandonment had a great influence upon Jung's attitude of women – one of 'innate unreliability', a view that he later called the 'handicap I started off with' (1963).

36 Presenting Jung

Jung occasionally heard his mother speaking to herself in a voice of authority that seemed not to be her own:

> I was sure she consisted of two personalities, one innocuous and human, the other uncanny. The other emerged only now and then, but each time it was unexpected and frightening. She would then speak as if talking to herself, but what she said was aimed at me and usually struck to the core of my being, so that I was stunned into silence.
>
> (1963)

This 'split' that Jung had observed in his mother would later appear in himself. At around the age of 12, he came to think that he too had two personalities, which he named No. 1 and No. 2. The first personality was the child of his parents and times, whilst the latter was a timeless individual, 'having no definable character at all – born, living, dead, everything in one, a total vision of life' (1963). His childhood was lonely and unhappy and he developed a vivid fantasy life in compensation. However, this split does seem more than the usual internal fantasies of a lonely child. The psychoanalyst D. W. Winnicott (1964), who was both a pediatrician and a specialist in child analysis, reviewed Jung's autobiography and concluded that Jung suffered childhood schizophrenia.[5] Conversely, Clare Douglas (2008), admirably following the spirit of Jung's own belief in the positive value of illness, views the split in his personality as a unique combination that helped him explore the unconscious and create a visionary psychology. The rational and enlightened side, his number one character carefully maps analytical psychology and presents its empirically grounded psychotherapeutic agenda. Whilst, the second part of this personality is at home with the unconscious, the mysterious and the unknowable. We might be tempted to view Jung as following to a tee Kierkegaard's famous phrase that one is to 'simultaneously relate oneself absolutely to the absolute and relatively towards relative ends' (Kierkegaard 1846a). Kierkegaard, through his persona Climacus, seems to be advocating a balance between one's relative relationships and the God relationship that exists in the realm of the absolute. This would indeed seem comparable to Jung's two personalities. Jung later renamed and generalised these split elements of his character as ego and self – achieving the right balance between the two aspects is central to his theory of individuation.

The achievement of personality for both Kierkegaard and Jung means nothing less than the optimum development of the whole individual human being. Personality is, Jung asserts,

> the supreme realization of the innate idiosyncrasy of a living being. It is an act of high courage flung in the face of life, the absolute affirmation of all that constitutes the individual, the most successful adaptation to

the universal conditions of existence coupled with the greatest possible freedom for self-determination.

(1955: par.289)

Jung's process of individuation is the innate impulse within the personality towards growth and wholeness; 'everything living dreams of individuation for everything strives towards its own wholeness' (1906–1950). It is not about those idiosyncratic traits that comprise one's uniqueness but rather the unification of all conscious and unconscious contents. For Jung, our primary task is to be the unique individual self we were born to be, and to live our individual lives as truly as Christ had lived.[6] Such a task requires great courage, as well as the absolute acceptance of all that constitutes the individual. We might then consider Jung's individuated person and Kierkegaard's authentic Christian as almost mirror images of one another. This process of individuation and transcendence by which one strives for self-realisation finds its energy in the Self – the ultimate unifying system of the personality; 'the self is the principle and archetype of orientation and meaning. Therein lies its healing function' (1963). There is then, within the unconscious, a passionate prophetic voice calling humanity back to life in all its fullness.

In Jung's theory of personality we have two important structural considerations – the ego and the persona. Ego is defined as an experienced inner sense of self-sameness and continuity. Persona exists as a 'mask' between ego and the wider world; it is the public self that we present to others. The Self emerges as a result of dynamic changes in the relation between ego and persona. Such dynamic changes serve to establish a conscious relationship between ego and self through individuation. Importantly, it is the facilitation of a new orientation towards life, which constitutes healing, and this is to be sought through the analysis of the personal unconscious leading to deepened self-knowledge. Consequently, the unconscious functions in such a manner as to establish the individual's wholeness and thus makes an important contribution to personality. As will be explored in the following chapter, the unconscious is also the seat of religious experience, for religious experience in Jung's account is itself a psychic occurrence that bears upon one's individual wholeness. Therefore, we find that religious experience is intimately connected with the structure of the psyche/personality.

Inherent in the structure of the psyche in which consciousness and unconsciousness are complementary to one another is opposition. The principle of opposition is an extremely important one for Jung who believed that all psychic energy flows from the tension of opposing forces: 'there is no energy unless there is a tension of opposites . . . life is born only of the spark of opposites' (1917/1926/1943: par.78). For the union of opposites is a creative process that develops through the individual's ability to bear the tension of conflict in one's life.[7] To deny either unconsciousness or consciousness is resultant in one-sidedness, disequilibrium and consequently a

38 Presenting Jung

loss in wholeness: 'the union of opposites though the middle path, that most fundamental item of inward experience. . . . It is at once the most individual fact and the most universal, the most legitimate fulfillment of the meaning of the individual's life' (1929a: par.327). The resolution of opposites ends conflict, bringing wholeness. This is never to be achieved through suppression or negation since this can only ever lead to one-sidedness. Should prolonged one-sidedness occur within the conscious attitude, a countering compensatory action will take place within the unconscious since significantly for Jung the unconscious functions as an independent psychic system in dynamic partnership with the consciousness. According to Jung:

> The tendencies of the conscious and the unconscious are the two factors that together make up the transcendent function. It is called 'transcendent' because it makes the transition from one attitude to another organically possible, without loss of the unconscious.
>
> (1916/1957: par.145)

The unconscious compensates the lopsidedness in the conscious attitude, meaning that the unconscious corrects the harmful mistakes in the conscious attitude through the creation of symbols, fantasies and collective images. The more the unconscious counter-position is held back, the greater its strength and the more likely it becomes that it will burst into consciousness with unpleasant results:

> The counter-position in the unconscious is not dangerous so long as it does not possess any high energy-value. But if the tension increases as a result of too great one-sidedness, the counter-tendency breaks through into consciousness, usually just . . . when it is most important to maintain the conscious direction. . . . The further we are able to remove ourselves from the unconscious through directed functioning, the more readily a powerful counter-position can build up in the unconscious, and when this breaks out it may have disagreeable consequences.
>
> (Jung 1917/1926/1943: par.139)

Jung's medical training very much informed his understanding of a compensatory self and a self-regulating psyche, for his training had taught him that human physiology is a system of checks and balances; homeostatic mechanisms ensuring that any tendency to go too far in one direction is compensated by an opposing swing in the other. Consequently, should the self move too far in any one direction it too will be compensated – for instance, when the self is violated it will populate one's dreams, attack the body and be the cause of changes in emotional states. The unconscious compensates for that which consciousness lacks; therefore although the ego might be threatened, it is possible to learn to listen to an inner voice manifested in one's dreams, phantasies and other derivatives of the unconscious. Such an understanding of the Self and psyche carries with it the implication that the personality is intrinsically healthy, tending towards wholeness.

Individuation is neither a *summum bonum* nor a *summun disideratum* but the painful experience of the union of opposites. The greater one's maturity of personality, the more able he or she is to accept both evil and good as part and parcel of a complete existence. From this union issues forth a spiritual freedom; the unified and integrated personality has no need to seek comfort in idealistic pastures. Jung observed that it is only in later life that man becomes a spiritual problem to himself. Subsequently, he believed that the psychic problems of the young are not the same as those experienced amongst middle-aged and elderly individuals. The task of youth is one of adaptation – the young must make their place in society, seek a profession, raise a family, etc. In short, one's entire energy must be focused on the external world, and not the internal; 'The significance of the morning undoubtedly lies in the development of the individual, our entrenchment in the outer world, the propagation of our kind, and the care of our children' (1930/1931: par.787). This has the effect that the neglected parts of one's unconscious/personality lapses into shadow and consequently this individual cannot, in this state, become wholly what he or she truly is. Youth is the time for ego consolidation, it is only once we have successfully accomplished this task that yet another, spiritually important, task emerges – namely, the coming to terms with our internal world. However, should the individual refuse to heed such a call and seek instead to carry

> over into the afternoon the law of the morning, or the natural aim, must pay for it with damage to his soul, just as surely as a growing youth who tries to carry over his childish egoism into adult life must pay for this mistake with social failure.
>
> (1930/1931: par.787)

The key to Jung's psychology lies in his attempt to locate archetypal dimensions of theological doctrine, religious myth and the individuation process, and then to create interplay between these otherwise diverse and seemingly unrelated phenomena. For the execution of such a task Jung returned again and again to the religious image. Our reading of Jung here brings to mind many elements from Kierkegaard's own sense of development. For instance, Jung's emphasis on the 'turning inward' of energies that had been invested in the pursuit of the outer goals of the first half of life and that is often accompanied by depressive feeling is comparable to Kierkegaard's understanding of aesthetic man, whose energy and propulsion of life's existence similarly comes from outside himself. In this aesthetic, essentially narcisstic, stage of immediacy we live fearing the day when the external might break through revealing to us the inauthentic nature of our lives built upon comfort and deceit.

40 Presenting Jung

To have the center of one's existence outside oneself is to be perpetually blown on the winds of chance, and of events. The unconscious, much like religious experience itself is an ambiguous and dangerous thing. Kierkegaard's religion, like the Jungian unconscious, works to compensate the conscious situation. Simply stated, both religion and the unconscious strive to bring about our human wholeness. In Kierkegaard we have the metamorphosis of spirit, whereas in Jung we see transformation through that which lies at the very heart of the individuation process – the transcendent function. His understanding of the psyche contains philosophical and theological implications that unite the human and divine so intimately as to make them functions of each other working to mutual completion. Jung's self symbolises the totality, the fact that this image of self coincides with that of the deity would indicate that there is no realisation of self without a relationship to this God-image. The self is the unifying center of the person and is therefore indistinguishable from the god-image, which represents the highest unifying factor. Like Kierkegaard's own conception of the self, Jung's understanding of self is an entity of potentiality. On the divine side there is the creative call of God, and on the human side there is the response to this call, in either willing to be oneself or not willing to be oneself. For both Kierkegaard and Jung a psychological balance between the aspects of the psyche is required. Jung writes 'the utterances of the heart – unlike those of the discriminating intellect – always relate to the whole'. Furthermore, Jung observes that the absence of religious meaning is a major component in most illnesses, particularly that of neurosis; 'A psycho-neurosis must be understood as the suffering of a human being who has not discovered what life means for him.' He even offers us his own interpretation of that which Kierkegaard characterises as the 'sickness unto death':

> For thousands of years rites of initiation have been teaching rebirth from the spirit; yet, strangely enough, man forgets again and again the meaning of divine procreation. Though this may be poor testimony to the strength of the spirit, the penalty for misunderstanding is neurotic decay, embitterment, atrophy and sterility. It is easy enough to drive the Spirit out of the door, but when we have done so the meal has lost its savour – the salt of the earth. Fortunately, we have proof that the spirit always renews its strength in the fact that the essential teaching of the initiations is handed on from generation to generation. Ever and again there are human beings who understand what it means that God is their father. The equal balance of the flesh and the Spirit is not lost to the world.
>
> (1929b: par.783)

The religious spirit is our capacity for and urge towards a conscious relationship to a transpersonal deity. A disorder in our relationship to this religious instinct can lead to illness, just as we can fall ill from disorder in our relation to any other instinct. Repression of one's sexuality can lead to the development of pathological symptoms, and so too with the religious instinct – which, when thwarted, will also lead to the outbreak of pathology. The task of selfhood, a task that Jung and Kierkegaard share, is to unify opposing and incongruous elements through a synthesis that results in the self becoming itself before God.

Notes

1 There are many well-researched and informative biographies on Jung. In the course of writing this thesis I have gravitated towards those of Barbara Hannah (1976) and Ronald Hayman (1999). The former bases her biographical memoir on first-hand experiences of Jung and her acquaintances with other figures in Jung's circle. It therefore possesses a more intimate understanding of Jung that comes with Hannah's direct experience with Jung and his psychology. Hayman's *A Life of Jung* is a well-researched and enlightening portrait of Jung; however, it is clear that Hayman has his own very clear view of Jung as a monomaniacal narcissist and sometimes this view is forced more than is perhaps needed. For works pertaining to Jung's psychology and its relation to religion, Naomi Goldenberg (1979) in her *Changing of the Gods, Feminism and the End of Traditional Religions* offers an excellent critique of Jungian psychology. Whilst Charles Hanna's (1967) *The Face of the Deep: The Religious Ideas of C.G. Jung* is a wealth of information on Jung's ideas about God and the unconscious. Furthermore, Ulanov's *Religion and the Unconscious* with its discussion of the function of religion in the human psyche is another very valuable secondary source.
2 Shamdasani's recently published *C. G. Jung: A Biography in Books* (W.W. Norton, 2012) is a informative biographical study of Jung and an essential companion to reading and understanding not only Jung's *Red Book* but of appreciating the breadth of Jung's reading and its impact upon his own thought.
3 See M. Anthony, *Jung's Circle of Women: The Valkyries* (Nicolas-Hays, 1999).
4 The Evolution of *Memories, Dreams and Reflections* has an interesting and yet problematic history. In 1953, when Jung was questioned on whether he intended to write an autobiography, he cautiously responded: 'I have always mistrusted an autobiography because one can never tell the truth. In so far as one is truthful, or believes one is truthful, it is an illusion, or of bad taste' (Shamdasani 2005). Whilst *Memories, Dreams, Reflections* is widely read and considered Jung's autobiography, it is, as Shamdasani's research clearly shows, a 'remarkable biography . . . mistakenly read as an autobiography' (Shamdasani). The primary problem being that despite the first-person narrative Jung's personal secretary, Aniela Jaffé, compiled and heavily edited this 'autobiography' and therefore its authorship is not entirely Jung's own. Concurrent with *Memories* Jung also authorised his friend, the English psychiatrist E. A. Bennet, to write a biography. Shamdasani suggests that 'it is possible that . . . because Jung thought that there was no single individual with sufficient grasp of his psychology to write his biography, that he deliberately narrated some of the same material to Bennet as to Jaffé, so neither would be the only account.' Nevertheless, *Memories* is a useful complement alongside Jung's *Collected Works* but it must be noted that it does not offer a full representation of the evolution of Jung's life and works (Shamdasani, S. *Jung Stripped Bare by His Biographers, Even* [London: Karnac Books, 2005]).

42 Presenting Jung

5 It is interesting to note that it was Fordham, and not Winnicott, who first diagnosed the autobiographical Jung as a childhood schizophrenic: Jung apparently did not demur. Contrary to both Winnicott and Fordham, contemporary Jungian child analysts believe Jung to have displayed symptoms of psychotic structure rather than schizophrenia. See Meredith-Owen, W. (2011), Winnicott on Jung: 'Destruction, Creativity and the Unrepressed Unconscious'. *Journal of Analytical Psychology*, 56.

6 'The *imitatio Christi* has this disadvantage: in the long run we worship as a divine example a man who embodied the deepest meaning of life, and then, out of sheer imitation, we forget to realise our own highest meaning. . . . The imitation of Christ might well be understood in a deeper sense, namely as the duty to realise one's best conviction, which is always also a complete expression of the individual imperament, with the same courage and the same self-sacrifice as jesus did' (Jung 1929b).

7 For an analysis of the role of opposites in Jung's project of psychological development (and its relationship to that of Nietzsche) see: Huskinson (2004) *Nietzsche and Jung: The Whole Self in the Union of Opposites.*

Chapter 5

The wounds of the father

A shared inheritance

It is only natural that what Jung and Kierkegaard have to say about religion is conditioned by their own psychological dispositions. Referring to the personal element in his work Jung wrote, 'every psychology, my own included – has the character of a subjective confession . . . even when I deal with empirical data I am necessarily speaking about myself' (1929b: par.774). Kierkegaard, on the other hand, is a little more candid on such subjective confessions, warning us away with the following words of dismissal:

> After my death, no one shall find in my papers (that is my consolation) a single explanation of what, properly speaking, has filled up my life. No one shall find the writing in my inmost soul which explains everything, and which often makes huge and important events for me out of what the world would call bagatelles, and what I myself regard as insignificant, when I take away the hidden note which explains it.
>
> (JP: 1843)

However, both these men struggled to understand themselves; to understand what it means to be and become a person and as such their work cannot be detached from their personal struggle for self-acceptance. Theirs was a search for an individual freedom, for the ability to find one's self and be oneself regardless of dogma and tradition. Yet, tragically, Kierkegaard's owns life made it impossible for him to reach such a solution for he suffered the continuous misfortune of being suspended between heaven and earth. His attack upon Christendom, founded primarily upon the pursuit of self-knowledge, lays stress upon the profound solitude and interiority of the true Christian: a far cry from the complacent piety of Christendom. Consequently Kierkegaard is champion to a kind of radical individualism that seems very much akin to Jung's own. Jungian analyst Ann Casement (1998), suggests that Jung and Kierkegaard share a very similar psychological inheritance stemming from their father's relationship to religion. Whilst the material facts of Kierkegaard's life are very different from those of Jung, what is far more relevant, writes Casement, is this psychological inheritance.

44 The wounds of the father

Casement has certainly hit on something very important here; I only wish that she had drawn on her experience as an analyst to delve deeper into this. This shared inheritance of the unresolved religious dilemmas of the father is a really remarkable coincidence. Here we have two individuals whose work is molded by a tragic father figure. Antony Storr (1996) certainly believes Jung's analytical psychology originates from his need to replace the religion that he lost as a child and with good reason. Jung himself confesses as much:

> I feel very strongly that I am under the influence of things or questions, which were left incomplete and unanswered by my parents and grand-parents and more distant ancestors. It often seems as if there were an impersonal karma within a family, which is passed on from parents to children. It has always seemed to me that I had to answer questions which fate had posed to my forefathers, and which had not yet been answered, or as if I had to complete, or perhaps continue, things which previous ages had left unfinished.
>
> (1963)

Jung further confessed that 'Al of my writings may be considered tasks imposed from within.' These tasks imposed from within can also be understood as tasks that essentially evolve around the father. For this wound is one that he sought to heal not only on his own behalf but also on behalf of his father. Murray Stein (1985) takes this argument further and believes that Jung saw his spiritual vocation as the path to healing the source of his father's suffering. Stein characterises Jung's emotional involvement with Christianity as an active struggle for its psychotherapeutic transformation which evolved through his childhood experience of Christianity's representatives. He catalogues wonderfully the evolution of Jung's thinking from the fear, dread and distrust of his childhood years to the compulsion to offer Christianity his psychotherapeutic help guided by an unconscious *spiritus rector* which was linked to the memory and image of his father. Referring to the unravelling of his father's faith, Jung wrote 'it was the tragedy of my youth to see my father cracking up before my eyes on the problem of his faith and dying an early death' (1963). Paul Jung, a pastor in the Swiss Reformed Church, much like Mikeal Kierkegaard, was overwhelmed by religious doubts. In *Memories, Dreams, Reflections*, Jung writes that even in his youth he already felt the experience of God to be endemic to his consciousness and to humanity's, when not blocked by bad theology. Recalling dialogues with his minister father:

> I saw that my critical questions made him sad, but I nevertheless hoped for a constructive talk, since it appeared almost inconceivable to me that he should not have had experience of God, the most evident of all experiences. I knew enough about epistemology to realise that knowledge of

this sort could not be proved, but it was equally clear to me that it stood in no more need of proof than the beauty of a sunset or the terrors of the night.

(1963)

Whilst Jung's mother dominated the early years of his childhood, his adolescence and young adulthood is certainly overshadowed by his depressed and ill-tempered father. Jung grew increasingly disappointed with his father's doubt-ridden Protestantism and it seems highly probable that this precipitated his own loss of faith in orthodox Christianity at an early age. Laurens Van Der Post (1975) tells us that Jung had questions of an unusual, urgent and original import to ask. But whenever he turned to his father, he was cruelly disappointed and dismissed with the exhortation that first he had to believe and trust; only then could he know and understand. This seemed the wrong way round to Jung. Surely one had to experience first and then one could know and learn to understand? His father's brand of belief without understanding dogmatism not only bored Jung but also caused great hurt to his spirit at a very early age. While father and son could enjoy philosophical conversations, the moment the topic turned to theology, the quarrels began. Jung would ask his father to give him a belief in God, and his father would shrug his shoulders and turn away:

At that time, too, there arose in me profound doubts about everything my father said. When I heard him preaching about grace . . . what he said sounded stale and hollow, like a tale told by someone who knows it only by hearsay and cannot quite believe it himself. . . . Later, when I was eighteen years old, I had many discussions with my father . . . but they invariably came to an unsatisfying end. . . . 'Oh nonsense,' he was in the habit of saying, 'you always want to think. One ought not to think, but believe.' I would think, 'No, one must experience and know,' but I would say, 'Give me this belief,' whereupon he would shrug and turn resignedly away.

(1963)

Jung suspected that his father's refusal to accept the pre-eminence of experience to be the result of unacknowledged and profound doubts about his own faith. It must have become quickly clear to Jung that his father followed his religion based solely on faith without ever having had a religious experience touch him emotionally.[1] We might then propose that it is here in these frustrating and disappointing quarrels with Paul Jung that the importance of a directly experienced divinity first took seed. In later years, Jung's father experienced a religious collapse, it is clear that Jung believed the source of this to lay in his dogmatic faith: 'my poor father did not dare to think, because he was consumed by inward doubts. He was taking refuge from

46 The wounds of the father

himself and therefore insisted on blind faith' (1963). The blame of which he places at the feet of the Christian church and its theology.[2] However, the Church and its theology was not the only factor that Jung thought to have precipitated his father's crisis of faith, for he also suggests that the ascendency of materialistic science weighed heavily upon his father:

> My father was obviously under the impression that psychiatrists had discovered something in the brain which proved that in the place where mind should have been there was only matter, and nothing 'spiritual'. This was born out by his admonitions that if I studied medicine I should in Heaven's name not become a materialist. To me this warning meant that I ought to believe nothing at all, for I knew that materialists believed in their definitions just as theologians did in theirs, and that my poor father had simply jumped out of the frying pan into the fire. . . . I was in no danger of succumbing to materialism, but my father certainly was.
>
> (1963)

There is the sense in this passage that Jung is almost ridiculing his father's faith that lacked the strength to be able to assimilate or defend itself against the rise of materialism. Jung regarded modern man as suffering from a deeply divided consciousness so that intellect and emotion, heart and head, science and art are experienced as hostile and antagonistic forces between which we have to choose. The conflict between religion and science is all too evident in the father, and I wonder if this observation informed Jung's understanding of the modern divided consciousness as the source of modernity's suffering. However, this aside I think it is clear that his father's crisis in faith saddened Jung profoundly:

> [I]t was the tragedy of my youth to see my father cracking up before my eyes on the problem of his faith and dying an early death. This was the objective outer event that opened my eyes to the importance of religion. Subjective inner experiences prevented me from drawing negative conclusions about religion from my father's fate, much as I was tempted to do so.
>
> (1951–1961)

Jung's memory of his father was as a:

> Sufferer stricken with an Amfortas wound, a 'fisher king' whose wound would not heal – that Christian suffering for which the alchemists sought the panacea. I as a 'dumb' Parsifal was the witness of this sickness during the years of my boyhood, and, like Parsifal, speech failed me. . . . He had literally lived right up to his death the suffering prefigured and promised by Christ, without ever becoming aware that this was a consequence of the *imitatio Christi*. He regarded his suffering as

a personal affliction for which you might ask a doctor's advice; he did not see it as the suffering of the Christian in general.

(1963)

This wound, in the original German telling of the myth is a severe wound in Amfortas thigh or genital area that prevents him from providing the masculine energy necessary for his Kingdom to flourish. This is very intriguing given that Jung viewed his father as ineffectual and somewhat feminine. Could this referencing to an Amfortas wound point toward a sexual, as well as spiritual, wound? We know that his parents slept apart, and given the very late arrival of his sister, Gertrud (born nine years after Jung) there could be substance to such speculation. However, Jung certainly does not come to look back on the meaning of his life's work as an attempt to heal modern humankind's sexual wound, but rather the *spiritual* wound that conventional Christianity had inflicted upon its followers: his father's failing faith being his first experience of such a wound. Parsifal's task is to become a knight, search for the Holy Grail and eventually, by asking the right question of the ailing fisher king to heal his spiritual wound. Parsifal has the power to heal this wound simply by asking the correct question; ironically, Jung's own questioning only served to provoke his father's anger. And yet the comparison of Jung himself to the 'dumb' Parsifal is a legitimate one, since Parsifal can be considered a figure who encourages a man to develop by improving himself. That Jung regarded Parsifal as a Christian hero therefore strikes me as particularly interesting.

That Jung's attitude towards Christianity was a response to the withered spiritual life of his father is an argument that finds much evidential support in his own writings. His observation that religion can so often be practised superficially without ever being felt or thought is no doubt related to his experience of his father's own sufferings: 'blind acceptance never leads to a solution; at best it leads only to a standstill and is *paid for heavily in the next generation*' (1963). He states often in the *Collected Works* that the first effort of therapy is to connect patients to their previously rejected religious outlooks, since:

> Among all my patients in the second half of life . . . there has not been one whose problem in the last resort was not that of finding a religious outlook on life. It is safe to say that every one of them fell ill because he had lost that which the living religions of every age have given to their followers, and none of them has been really healed who did not regain this religious outlook.

(1932a: par.509)

Does it not follow then that Jung's own personal cure would be found within his reconnection to his father's own loss of faith? And might we speculate that he did indeed pay heavily to correct his father's blind acceptance – one

48   The wounds of the father

is here reminded of Jung's remark that 'the Divine Presence is more than anything else. . . . This is the only thing that really matters. . . . I wanted the proof of a living Spirit and I got it. Don't ask me at what price' (1906–1950). The problematic relationship between formal doctrinal theology and the subjective nature of religious experience would lead Jung to oppose conventional Christianity. But more personally, his years as his father's child left a residue in the form of a negative father complex that would leave a longing for an influential father figure; that is, to a more influential, personal God.

Jung's relationship with Freud can be understood in terms of the positive father complex becoming a negative one. Following his split with Freud, another problematic father relationship, Jung underwent a period of isolation that led to his 'confrontation with the unconscious' described in *Memories, Dreams,Reflections*. Michael Palmer (2003) believes that what had been lacking in the relationship with his own ineffectual father was more than compensated for in Freud's dominant personality, and Jung was happy to fall in with the emotional demands of a surrogate father-son relationship; reciprocating feelings of awed respect and filial devotion. Shortly after their first meeting in 1907, Jung expressed the hope that their friendship would not be 'as one between equals but as that of father and son' – clearly, they undoubtedly had contained for one another disturbing and disruptive elements. For Freud, it became apparent that their relationship was increasingly Oedipal: that the son harbored parricidal feelings towards the father and wished to replace him – to the point indeed that Freud, when Jung spoke of death, fainted on two occasions (at Bremen in 1909 and again in Munich, 1912). Freud's authority, writes Palmer, was robbing Jung of his own intellectual independence, so much so 'that the fantasy of father-murder also required the emasculation of the son'. Things came to a head when during their seven-week trip to the United States in 1909, when they started interpreting each other's dreams. This culminated in Freud stating, 'I cannot risk my authority'. Jung (1963) later recalled that it was at this moment when he realised that Freud was a fraud, 'at that moment he [Freud] lost it altogether. The sentence burned itself in my memory; and in it the end of our relationship was already foreshadowed. Freud was placing personal authority above truth.'

It would seem that central to our understanding of both these individuals as men and as writers, is to understand their relationship to overbearing father figures, or, as in the case of Jung's relationship with Freud, an authority figure that stands in place of the father. It is of no small significance that it was just prior to his father's death that Kierkegaard stopped reacting against his strict upbringing and reconciled with his father and his faith. It was only at this moment that Kierkegaard took to his studies with any seriousness. This reconciliation with his father stimulated the spiritual element of his character, whilst the death of his father was a real source of spiritual

The wounds of the father 49

renewal for Kierkegaard. Just two days after his father's death, Kierkegaard wrote,

> I shall work on coming into a far more intimate relation with Christianity; up to now I have in a way been standing altogether outside it, fighting for its truth. I have borne the cross of Christ in a quite external way, like Simon of Cyrene.[3]

Kierkegaard's father, Michael Pederson Kierkegaard, combined a strict adherence to orthodox Lutheranism with a penchant for formal logic, both of which were enlivened by a captivating imagination. Michael retired early from business and dedicated himself to his youngest, who took him on long exhausting walks through the rooms of their house, visiting foreign countries in their imagination, talking with imaginary people and arguing about the gloomy aspects of religion with hisfavorite son. However, there was a chronic melancholy in the father of which the son was disquietingly aware; he was never able to shake off the influence of his father's overpowering personality. A gifted but melancholy man, Michael Kierkegaard was given to frightening outbreaks of rage. Weiget in her article 'Kierkegaard's Mood Swings' (1960) surmises that this had the effect of reducing the young child to guilt, despair and spiritual impotence. Søren's father had left his home on the Jutland heath for Copenhagen as a boy of twelve. Young as he was, he brought memories with him which were to haunt him to his dying day; hungry, chilled with the wind and rain, and bitter about his loneliness and sufferings he had one day climbed a mound of earth and cried out against the God who had sent him into the world for such misery. Kierkegaard commented in his journal,

> how appalling for the man who, as a lad watching sheep on the Jutland heath, suffering painfully, hungry and exhausted, once stood on a hill and cursed God – and the man was unable to forget it when he was eighty-two years old.
>
> (JP: 1846)

Whilst in his early twenties Kierkegaard writes of the time when he had first discovered his father's guilty secret. He refers to this incident as the great earthquake:

> Then it was that the great earthquake occurred, the frightful upheaval which suddenly drove me to a new infallible principle for interpreting all the phenomena. Then I surmised that my father's old-age was not a divine blessing, but rather a curse, our family's exceptional intellectual capacities were only for mutual harrowing one another; then I felt the stillness of death deepen around me, when I saw in my father an

50 The wounds of the father

unhappy man who would survive us all, a memorial cross on the grave of all his personal hopes. A guilt must rest upon the entire family, a punishment from God must be upon it: it was supposed to disappear, obliterated by the mighty hand of God, erased like a mistake, and only at times did I find a little relief in the thought that my father had been given the heavy duty of reassuring us all with the consolation of religion, telling us that a better world stands open for us even if we lost this one.

(JP: 1938)

Though in real terms what it was that precipitated this earthquake of spiritual crisis remains a mystery, it is commonly thought that this secret concerned his father's sexual indiscretions. Søren's mother had previously been his father's servant before she became his second wife, and it was only four months after this marriage that she would give birth to their first born, Peter Kierkegaard. This impersonal, shadow-like figure of a mother, Kierkegaard would remain entirely silent about. Another possibility involves his father's youthful act of defiance upon that Jutland heath. In later life Michael Kierkegaard would become gripped with the conviction he had committed the unpardonable sin – such feelings of guilt could only have increased following the deaths of five of his seven children within a relatively short time.

The great earthquake awoke in Kierkegaard a lifelong interest, if not obsession, in a theology of authenticity. The tensions between his father's outward piety and inner turmoil gave the character to Kierkegaard's obsession with what it is to be essentially Christian. The parallel here with Jung's early experiences with his own father are remarkable. Kierkegaard surely would have sympathized with Jung's understanding of inheriting a parent's sins as constituting a kind of impersonal karma within a family. Furthermore, this earthquake, like Jung's split from Freud, precipitated an intense preoccupation with the mysteries of the human soul. The great earthquake was the first significant spiritual crisis for Kierkegaard, aged just two. It is not especially surprising that he should have reacted by plunging himself into the decadent lifestyle of the carousing bohemian. The height of Kierkegaard's aesthetic life corresponds, I contend, with his father's revelation. His father's death marked the end of this period of spiritual crisis, whereupon Kierkegaard reflected, 'The powerful religious impressions of childhood acquired a renewed power over me, but softened by reflection' (JP: 1838).

Walter Lowrie (1942) remarked that Michael Kierkegaard's 'profound melancholy impressed upon his religion a character of severity and gloom which was disastrous to his children'. Hannay (2001) who curiously never mentions Lowrie writes that although the Kierkegaard household was not 'fundamentally unhappy' it was 'certainly unhealthy' for a child.

The wounds of the father 51

Kierkegaard himself wrote in a posthumously published *The Point of View for My Work as an Author*:

> As a child, I was rigorously and earnestly brought up in Christianity, insanely brought up, humanly speaking – already in earliest childhood I had overstrained myself under the impression that the depressed old man, who had laid it upon me, was himself sinking under – a child attired, how insane, as a depressed old man. Frightful! No wonder, then, that there were times when Christianity seemed to me the most inhuman cruelty.
>
> (1848/1859)

Kierkegaard was spiritually very much his father's son. In the early 1830s, upon learning of his father's cursing of God and his premarital relations with his mother, he was devastated. His first response seems to have been to embark on a period of mild dissipation. 'May it not', he asked in his journal at this time, 'be best to go through all the dissipations just to experience life?' A few years later, again writing in his journal, he speaks about a man who in an overwrought irresponsible state visits a prostitute:

> now he wants to get married. Then anxiety stirs. He is tortured day and night with the thought that he might possibly be a father, that somewhere in the world there could be a created being who owed his life to him.
>
> (JP: 1843)

Kierkegaard was all consumed with guilt; a 'whole life devoted to God', he confesses in 1939, would 'hardly suffice to atone for my youthful excesses'. Although it would seem that Kierkegaard's exaggerated sense of guilt was indeed inherited from his dominating father, it is clear that it is the analysis of his own depressive moods, and not those of his father, that are most influential in his exposition of the problem of suffering. It could be said that there is a link between these moods and his refusal to marry Regina Olsen, to whom he was engaged: 'My becoming an author', he wrote, 'is due chiefly to her, my melancholy and my money.' Indeed, it is certainly the case that following the broken engagement, Regine would never be far from his thoughts but ultimately it is my belief that the source of Kierkegaard's considerable anxiety is to be found in the figure that he shrouded in silence and secrecy – his mother. However, I digress for it is to his father that we must turn in order to understand his melancholy.

Numerous scholars speak of the unusually strong bond between father and son. Allen (1935a) for instance, surmised that

> he could not speak frankly to Regine either of his own youthful sin, for which he must make atonement, nor could he disclose the secret which

52 The wounds of the father

still bound him to his dead father. *His obligations to the past were so heavy that he could contract none to the* future.

The following quotes serve to highlight the intense emotions surrounding the passing of his father and the severance of his engagement:

> My most difficult period is always from August 9 to September 10. I have always had something against summer. And now, at the time when I am physically at my weakest, come the anniversaries of my father's death and, September 10, of my engagement.
>
> (JP: 1849)

Kierkegaard accords to his father and Regine the privileged title of teachers:

> [A]mong my papers there will also be found a letter about her [Regine] that is intended to be opened after my death. The books will be dedicated to her and to my dead father together: my teachers, an old man's noble wisdom, and a woman's loveable injudiciousness.
>
> (JP: 1849)

What is becoming increasingly apparent in our analysis is just how strongly Kierkegaard's actual experiences and emotional world impacted and constructed his entire philosophy. I do not think it implausible to suggest that Kierkegaard wrote in order to find himself. His writing facilitated a long exploratory search for identity that saw him continually finding himself throughout his work, and nowhere is this more evident than in *Sickness Unto Death*. This work is not the musing of one weathering the stormy identity crises of a prolonged adolescence, but of Kierkegaard's earnest engagement with his own personal and religious development. In 1839 he wrote in his journal:

> The whole of existence frightens me, from the smallest fly to the mystery of the Incarnation; everything is unintelligible to me, most of all myself; the whole of existence is poisoned in my sight, particularly myself. Great is my sorrow and without bounds; no man knows it, only God in Heaven, and he will not console me; no man can console me, only God in Heaven and he will not have mercy upon me.

It is my belief that Kierkegaard's entire thought evolves out of this personal search for identity in the face of his personal experiences and relationships with people closest to him, and his attempts to resolve these to himself though this all-important relationship to God. Such profound anxiety surrounds what he was and had to do in order to attain authentic selfhood. The following quote from Kierkegaard's journal beautifully expresses his

The wounds of the father 53

striving for self-meaning, I have chosen to quote him at length as the following passage serves to capture his sense of religious purposefulness so elegantly:

But when I try now to come to an understanding with myself about my life, things look different. Just as a child takes time to learn to distinguish itself from objects and for quite a while so little distinguishes itself from its surroundings that, keeping the stress on the passive side, it says things like 'me hit the horse', so too the same phenomenon repeats itself in a higher spiritual sphere. Therefore I thought I might gain more peace of mind by taking up a new line of study, directing my energies towards some other goal. I might have even managed for a while in that way to banish a certain restlessness, though no doubt, it would have returned with greater effect like a fever after the relief of a cool drink. *What I really need is to be clear about what I am to do, not what I must know, except in the way knowledge must precede all action. It is a question of understanding my destiny, of seeing what the Deity really wants me to do; the thing is to find a truth which is true for me, to find the idea for which I am willing to live and die.* And what use here would it be if I were to discover a so-called objective truth, or if I worked my way through the philosophers' systems and were able to call them all to account on request, point out inconsistencies in every single circle? *And what use here would it be to be able to work out a theory of the state, and put all the pieces from so many places into one whole, construct a world which, again, I myself did not inhabit but merely held up for others to see? What use would it be to be able to propound the meaning of Christianity, to explain many separate facts, if it had no deeper meaning for myself and for my life? . . .* What use would it be if the truth were to stand before me, cold and naked, not caring whether I acknowledge it or not, and inducing an anxious shudder rather than trusting devotion? Certainly I won't deny that I still accept an imperative of knowledge, and that one can also be influenced by it, but *then it must be taken up alive in me*, and this is what I now see as the main point. *It is this my soul thirsts for as the African deserts thirst for water. This is what I lack, and this is why I am like a man who has collected furniture and rented rooms but still hasn't found the beloved with whom to share life's ups and downs. But to find that idea, or more properly to find myself, it is no use my plunging still further into the world. . . .* Vainly I have sought an anchorage, not just in the depths of knowledge, but in the bottomless sea of pleasure. I have felt the well-nigh irresistible power with which one pleasure holds out its hand to another; I have felt that inauthentic kind of enthusiasm which it is capable of producing. I have also felt the tedium, the laceration, which ensues. I have tasted the fruits of the tree of knowledge and relished them time and again. But this joy was only in the moment of cognition and left no deeper mark upon me. It seems to me that I have not drunk from the cup of wisdom but have fallen into it. . . . My companions have with few exceptions exerted no marked influence upon me. . . . *So I am standing once more at the point where I must begin in another way. I shall now try to look calmly at myself and begin to act inwardly; for only in this way will I be able, as the child in its first consciously undertaken act refers to itself as 'I', to call myself 'I' in a profounder sense. I will hurry along the path I have found and shout to everyone I meet not to look back as Lot's wife did but remember that it is uphill that we are struggling.*

(JP: 1835)

Arguably, a crucial difference between Kierkegaard and Jung is in Kierkegaard's esteem of his father. He wants to hold the father figure aloft and credit him as the basis for his intellectual brilliance and self-maturation. In 1850 Kierkegaard wrote:

Then I came to terms with it religiously [his father's demands upon him]. Humanly speaking it has made me as unhappy as possible, but this pain was the basis on which I developed a brilliant intellectual life as an author. I came to terms with myself in this life. The anguish was frightful but the satisfaction was all the greater. I can never thank God sufficiently for what has been given me.

(JP: 1850)

The following passage could be particularly pertinent here; Kierkegaard in a lucid, raw and real moment following his father's confession wrote:

The most dangerous case is not when the father is a free thinker, and not even when he is a hypocrite. No, the danger is when he is a pious and God-fearing man, when the child is inwardly and deeply convinced of it, and yet in spite of all this observes a deep unrest is deeply hidden in his soul, so that not even piety and the fear of God can bestow peace. The danger lies just here, that the child in this relationship is almost compelled to draw a conclusion about God that after all God is not infinite love.

(JP: 1850)

Søren certainly shared his father's 'silent despair', inheriting from his father both a spirit of melancholy and a profound sense of guilt – by the way of this conviction that he had brought onto his family a terrible curse. Kierkegaard wrote in his journal that sorrow in adulthood can depress the conscious mind, but 'the terrible thing is when a man's consciousness is subjected to such pressure from childhood up that not even the elasticity of the soul, not all the energy of freedom can rid him of it, (of) something which lies as it were beyond the conscious itself. This would seem to suggest that Kierkegaard was well aware that his melancholy had its roots firmly in his childhood. In fact, that this was very much the case is illustrated in the following passage, which makes for sad reading indeed:

> From a child I was in the grip of an immense melancholy, so profound that it could only be adequately gauged by the equally immense ability granted me, of covering it under apparent gaiety and enjoyment of life. From the beginning (as far indeed as my memory reaches back), I found my sole pleasure in letting no one discover how unhappy I felt as a child. . . . I never (even when I stood farthest from it) lost reverence for it, and (especially in the event of my not deciding for Christianity) I had firmly resolved never to initiate anyone into the difficulties which I knew, but of which I had never heard nor read. I never broke with Christianity nor gave it up; it never entered my head to attack it – rather was I firmly resolved, so soon as there could be any question at all of the employment of my powers, to offer my all for its defense, or at any rate for the presentation of it in its true colors . . . so I loved Christianity after a fashion. I reverenced it: humanly speaking, of course, it had made me extremely unhappy. That was of a piece with my relation to my father, the man whom I most dearly loved – and what does that mean? It means in part just that it is he who made me unhappy – out of love! Where he failed was not that he lacked love, but he treated a child as though he was an old man.
>
> (1848/1859)

We might view then the theories of Kierkegaard and Jung as attempts to both understand their own very individual selves, whilst also attempting to heal the spiritual crises of their fathers. Both Paul Jung and Michael Kierkegaard were afflicted by a seemingly incurable religious melancholy. Consequently, their sons carry this enormous burden of having to be the father's savior and so maybe it is not particularly surprising that this shared inheritance becomes a shared sense of predestination. In *Memories, Dreams, Reflections*, Jung candidly confesses that from the very beginning he had a sense of a divinely bestowed destiny:

> From the beginning I had a sense of destiny, as though my life was assigned to me by fate and had to be fulfilled. This gave me an inner security, and, though I could never prove it to myself, it proved itself to me. I did not have this certainty, it had me. Nobody could rob me of the conviction that it was enjoined upon me to do what God wanted and not what I wanted. That gave me the strength to go my own way. Often I had the feeling that in all decisive matters I was no longer among men, but was alone with God.
>
> (1963)

56 The wounds of the father

The image of the savior appears even stronger in the following passage: 'I am, to be sure, a doctor, but even more than that I am concerned with the saving good of man, for I am also a psychiatrist' (1951–1961). And again in 1948, 'I know that my way has been prescribed to me by a hand far above my reach' (1906–1950). Unless he was just waxing lyrical in his 'autobiography' and letters, Jung did believe himself to be following God's plan. Kierkegaard especially felt that it was his divinely directed mission in life to reform bourgeois Christianity, so rigidly steeped in dogmatism and decadence; his religious vocation is woven throughout his entire corpus. Would either Jung or Kierkegaard have pondered the inner experience of religion if it were not for their deep dissatisfaction with the conventional Christianity of their fathers? If it were not for the failing, impassionate faith of their fathers, Kierkegaard and Jung would most likely have never felt compelled to wander from conventional religious paths. The respective relationships with the fathers of these two thinkers clearly colored their life, profession and philosophy. Both wandered from the religious pathways of life owing to the religious melancholy of the father, and came to view their personal solution/salvation as a return/recovery of a previously abandoned religious 'self'. That they both come to view their personal solution as a recovery of an abandoned religious 'self' is surely significant.

Notes

1 'He [God] had even allowed me a glimpse into His own being. This was a great secret which I dared not and could not reveal to my father. *I might have been able to reveal it had he been capable of understanding the direct experience of God*' (1963).
2 'I saw how hopelessly he was entrapped by the Church and its theological thinking. They had blocked all avenues by which he might have reached God directly, and then faithlessly abandoned him. Now I understood the deepest meaning of my earlier experience: God Himself had disavowed theology and the Church founded upon it' (1963).
3 (Luke 23.36) (II A 232).

Part 2

Chapter 6

An unconventional Christianity

It does seem that there is indeed reason to take seriously the suggestion that Kierkegaard and Jung abandoned the conventional religious self because of their fathers. It is important to mention here that it was not just the conventional religious self that is to be left behind but also the entire institution of traditional Christianity. The father-relationship can be subsequently viewed as the foundations of their emphasis on the inner direct and authentic experience of God. Furthermore, the experience of a Christendom that could offer no comfort to their fathers, I believe, leads them to pursue religion on a path of solitude and inner development – it is in this fashion that psychology becomes religiously significant for both Jung and Kierkegaard. Jung felt that Christendom had lost the essential teachings and meanings of Christianity, and had become encompassed instead by objective and dispassionate dogma, and creed. Thus,

> Christian civilization has proved hollow to a terrifying degree: it is all veneer but the inner man has remained untouched and therefore unchanged. His soul is out of key with his external beliefs; in his soul the Christian has not kept pace with external developments. Yes, everything is to be found outside – in church and bible – but never inside.
>
> (Jung: 1844)

Similarly, Kierkegaard complains of the removal of God from Christendom and relates this to the doctrinal element of belief:

> Before Christianity became a doctrine, when it was only one or two affirmations expressed in one's life, God was closer. And with every increase and embellishment of doctrine, with every increase of 'success', God was distanced. When there were no clergy and the Christians were all brothers, God was closer than when clergymen, many clergymen, a powerful ecclesiastical order, came into being. For clergymen are an increase in appearance, and God always relates inversely to outward show.

60 An unconventional Christianity

And:

> This is how Christendom has step by step become so distant from God. Christianity's history is one of alienation from God through the gradual strengthening of appearance. Or it might be said Christianity's history is one of the progressive removal of God tactfully and politely by building churches and monumental buildings, by a monstrous doctrinal system, with an incalculable host of preachers and professors. Established Christianity is about as far away from God as one can possibly get.

There is a sense with both Jung and Kierkegaard that they both differentiate authentic religion from inauthentic institutionalised religion. It would certainly seem the case that both these thinkers rallied and rebelled against conventional Christianity; Kierkegaard calls upon all honest people 'to cease participating in public worship' (Kirmmse 1996). Kierkegaard's philosophy is much more than a protest against the intellectualised religion that had turned away from spiritual ideals and operated in terms of rational reality. From the very beginning of his philosophical works Kierkegaard waged war against what he disdainfully called 'Christendom'; he boldly declared his entire body of works (and not just the overtly religious parts) to be 'related to Christianity, to the problem of becoming a Christian, with direct or indirect polemic against the monstrous illusions we call Christendom' (1848/1859). And so he discovered his vocation of being a missionary to Christendom, of helping people who assumed that they were already Christians to come to some understanding of what genuine Christianity is. In Christendom Kierkegaard saw merely a decadent distraction that served to merely perpetuate the illusion that we are all Christians, that is, more part of the problem than the solution in perpetuating the illusion that we are all Christians. He thought this the most dangerous error of all, for so long as people are lulled into thinking of themselves as true Christians by virtue of being born into Christendom they are prevented from understanding true Christianity and from becoming true Christians. Consequently, Kierkegaard waged a lifelong battle against this kind of complacent, inauthentic Christianity: The contents of this little book [*Point of View*] affirm, then, what I truly am as an author, that I am and was a religious author, that that whole of my work as an author is related to Christianity, to the problem of becoming a Christian, with a direct or indirect polemic against the monstrous illusion we call Christendom, or against the illusion that in such a land as ours all are Christians of a sort.

(1848/1859)

As long as people are lulled into thinking they are already Christians through being born into Christendom, they are prevented from becoming true Christians. It was this very passive acceptance of religion that Kierkegaard spent his lifetime rallying against, he passionately wanted people to

An unconventional Christianity 61

think for themselves, choose for themselves, and not just receive the official religion of their nation. But there is also another, perhaps unhealthy, element here that is revealing of Kierkegaard's positive affirmation of alienation. Despair, anxiety, dread are all symptoms, according to Kierkegaard, that arise in response to alienation from God the psychological consequence of sin; 'sin is: before God, or with the conception of God, in despair not to will to be oneself'. This can be contrasted to faith: 'faith is: that the self in being itself and in willing to be itself rests transparently in God' (1849). And yet his Christianity is itself both alienated and alienating; his desire is for a religion that fights for acceptance that is inherently set against society. His Christian ideal is overwhelmingly isolated. It is not surprising then given the demanding nature of his Christian ideal that Kierkegaard believed genuinely religious persons a rarity amongst his contemporaries. However, he was by no means an elitist and was careful to recognise the possibility that real faith was common among the poor and uneducated. He felt that too many of his peers had substituted an intellectual understanding of Christianity for actually existing as a Christian (Evans 2005). For instance he claimed, 'faith does not simply result from a scientific enquiry' (1846a) and that 'one is deluded in thinking that one could demonstrate that God exists' (1844a). His pious irrationalism seems much akin to Jung's own and would seem to stem from his refusal to elevate reason/intellect (the rational) above all other faculties in the Cartesian manner. In his work *Fear and Trembling* Kierkegaard holds Abraham in high esteem for leaving reason behind and seeking refuge in faith. Furthermore, concluding his Postscript he writes:

> If thought speaks deprecatingly of the imagination, imagination in turn speaks deprecatingly of thought: and likewise with feeling. The task is not to exalt one above the other, but to give them equal status, to unify them in simultaneity; the medium for such unification lies in existence itself
>
> (1846a).

Kierkegaard believed that it was the 'intellectual types' within Christianity that had poisoned and perverted it in their attempt to prove the truth of Christianity. This attempt at supporting faith by rational reasoning was itself, according to Kierkegaard, responsible for fostering religious doubts:

> Some . . . sought to refute doubt with reasons . . . they tried to demonstrate the truth of Christianity with reasons . . . these reasons fostered doubt and doubt became the stronger. The demonstration of Christianity really lies in *imitation*. This was taken away. Then the need for 'reasons' was felt, but these reasons, or that there are reasons, are already a kind of doubt . . . thus doubt arose and lived on reasons . . . the more reasons one advances, the more one nourishes doubt and the stronger it becomes . . . offering doubt reasons in order to kill it is just like offering

the tasty food it likes best of all to a hungry monster one wishes to eliminate. No, one must not offer reasons to doubt – at least not if one's intention is to kill it – but one must do as Luther did, order it to shut its mouth, and to that end keep quiet and offer no reasons.

(1851)

Kierkegaard continually emphasises that Christianity ought to be about imitating Christ, of making Christ the prototype of one's life; that is to say, the key to Christianity is to regard it as a way of life and not as an abstract doctrine. As will be explored later, Jung places a great deal of emphasis on the necessity of balance within the psyche. He certainly endeavored to correct the one-sidedness of the rationalistic tendency that developed with Cartesian philosophy. He reminds us that: 'the rationalistic attitude of the west is not the only possible one and is not all-embracing, but is in many ways a prejudice and bias that ought perhaps to be corrected' (Jung1952a: par.916).

Similarly Jung also warned against exalting the intellect above all faculties, particularly in regards to religion:

Our time has committed a fatal error; we believe we can criticize the facts of religion intellectually. Like Laplace, we think God is a hypothesis that can be subjected to intellectual treatment, to be affirmed or denied. We completely forget that the reason mankind believes in the 'daemon' has nothing whatever to do with external factors, but is simply due to a naive awareness of the tremendous inner effect of autonomous systems.

(1929c: par.51)

Kierkegaard and Jung were both suspicious of any commitment to theological dogma; they rejected the authoritarianism of traditional Christianity, and like Aquinas before them, seemingly declare that reason can only go so far in knowing God for one's ultimate knowledge lies in faith not reason. Simply understood reason will always stumble repeatedly before religion, for it is repugnant to common sense, necessitating the proverbial leap to faith. Jung and Kierkegaard lived uncomfortably in ages of religious decline, warning of the loss of subjective inwardness to unifying power – they both stood beyond their respective ages. Much has been made of Jung's psychologism of religion, his conception of an *Imago Dei* that arises spontaneously in the psyche has led Martin Buber amongst other theologians, including Reverend White, to accuse Jung of creating a new religion of 'pure psychic immanence'. The following section really aims to reach a better understanding of Jung's theorising on religion in order to provide the adequate foundations for appreciating the evolution of Jung's belief that religion provides the energies required for self-renewal and for making life whole by the way of Christian symbols.

Chapter 7

Jung and religion

Jung believed that all psychological theories reflect the personal history of their creators, declaring 'our way of looking at things is conditioned by what we are' (Hannah 1991). Never has this been truer than in the case of Søren Kierkegaard and C. G. Jung. We only need to glance at Jung's *Memories, Dreams, Reflections* in order to gain a sense of just how strongly Jung's actual experiences have shaped his psychology; consequently Jung's psychology is a lived psychology. Barbara Hannah in her biographical memoir of Jung connects the young Jung's puzzlement as to whether he was the boy sitting on the stone or the stone being sat upon with that which was to occupy him nearly 80 years later, 'the thorny problem of the relationship between eternal man' and the 'earth man in time and space'. Quoting Albert Oeri, a childhood acquaintance of Jung, she continues: 'he even said that the decisive question for man is: is he related to something infinite or not? That is the telling question of his life' (Hannah 1991). It is this 'thorny problem' that occupies Jung for the rest of his life; all of Jung's thoughts, as he writes in his autobiography, 'circle around God like the planets around the sun, and are as irresistibly attracted to this force. I would feel it to be the grossest sin if I were to put up any resistance to such' (1963). It is interesting to note that it is just this resistance – the quest for autonomy from God – that Kierkegaard, as already noted previously, specifically defines as sinful. Jung's own personal relation to God is ambiguous to say the least. Best known of Jung's religious pronouncements is his answer to the question whether he believes in God: 'I know. I don't need to believe' (Face-to-Face broadcast 1959). For God to have been present with Jung, God must, for him, exist. However, what Jung means by knowing vis-à-vis believing is scarcely clear. Carved in stone above the door of his house in Kusnacht, Jung chose to have inscribed the words of the Pythian oracle *'vocatus atque non vocatus deus aderit'* ('summoned or not summoned, God will be present'). He explains this inscription's presence as a reminder to himself and to his patients, *'Timor dei initium sapiente'* ('The fear of the Lord is the beginning of wisdom'). Expanding upon this, Jung writes, 'Here another not less important road begins, not the approach to

64 Jung and religion

"Christianity" but to God himself and this seems to be the ultimate question' (1951–1961). Is it possible that 'summoned or not summoned, God will be present' was a conviction that he himself had fought to win following his disappointing early experience of a spiritually stagnant Christianity? He also chose to have the words of the apostle Paul inscribed in stone, 'primus homo terrenus de terra; secundus homo coelestis de coelo' ('the first man is of the earth, a man of dust; the second is of heaven') – I don't think we need have any doubts that this relates to his own first and second personality.

Following Freud, the majority of psychologists have viewed religion with a jaundiced eye. Although religion may have had a role in the spiritual evolution in the past, it is deemed unnecessary, if not harmful, to psychological development of the present mind. In most psychoanalytical writings we find observations that link neurotic symptoms with religious material, and since neurosis was believed to be a psychic sickness that can be overcome, religion finds itself treated in a similar manner. Freud viewed religion as a primitive, if not infantile, attempt to explain things – both obsolete and an obstacle to scientific progress. In this respect Freud was very much a man of his time, a representative of the view that prevailed amongst scientists of the nineteenth century. Jung objected to Freud's reductionistic orientation toward religion. Far from being a primitive attempt to explain things, Jung's understanding of religion affirms the presence of the idea of God; furthermore, he regards it as having healthy elements rather than solely pathological ones. On religion proper Jung has to all appearances only devoted himself wholly to this theme in one very small book, *Psychology and Religion* (1938), whilst his *Answer to Job* (1952) is his only work devoted to the sole discussion of biblical text. However, appearances do indeed prove to be deceptive, for in fact everything Jung wrote is concerned with the religious. Whilst he only deals exclusively with the question of psychology and religion in this one volume of his collected works (Vol. 11), such religious themes resonate throughout everything he ever wrote.

Jung's *Psychology and Religion* has for its main preoccupation the psychological nature of the Christian doctrine of God. He first distinguishes between dogma and religion, defining religion as 'a careful consideration of certain dynamic factors that are conceived as powers: sprits, demons, Gods, laws, ideas and ideals' (1938/40: par.8). Dogma on the other hand involves 'codified and dogmatised forms of original experience' (1938/40: par.10). It therefore transforms religious experience into something much more rigid. Jung writes

> nor has the scientific criticism of the New Testament been very helpful in enhancing the divine character of the holy writings. It is also a fact that under the influence of so-called scientific enlightenment great masses of educated people have either left the church or have become

profoundly indifferent to it . . . if they were all dull rationalists or neurotic intellectuals the loss would not be regrettable. But many of them are religious people, only incapable of agreeing with the actually existing forms of creed.

(1938/40: par.34)

Jung defines religion not by its creed and rituals but by the original religious experiences upon which they depend. That is to say, religion is a 'peculiar attitude of the human mind' in which 'certain dynamic factors' are observed and considered 'beautiful and meaningful enough to be devoutly adored and loved' (1938/40: par.8). This attitude is further characterised as possessing 'the highest or strongest value' and an 'important, even overwhelming, psychic intensity'. He certainly held the belief that the neurosis experienced in the second half of life necessitated the development of a religious attitude, which itself involved a spontaneous revelation of the spirit. 'This spirit', wrote Jung, 'is an autonomous psychic happening, a hush that follows the storm, a reconciling light in the darkness of man's mind, secretly bringing order into the chaos of his soul' (1942/48: par.260).

The religious experience is a numinous experience of the archetypal and eternal foundations of humanity itself and to that extent enables the individual to lift oneself above personal problems and to relate instead to the indestructible and primordial dimension of one's own psychic being. It would be enlightening here for me to quote a passage from Kierkegaard's *Repetition* for it serves to capture beautifully Jung's description of the revelation of spirit:

> I was at the peak and had a presentiment of the dizzy maximum found on no gage of well-being, not even on a poetic thermometer. My body had lost its terrestrial gravity; it was as if I had no body simply because every function enjoyed total satisfaction, every nerve delighted in itself and in the whole, while every heartbeat, the restlessness of the living being, only memorialized and declared the pleasure of the moment. . . . Every thought volunteered itself jubilantly, the most foolish whim as well as the richest idea. . . . All existence seemed to have fallen in love with me, and everything quivered in fateful rapport with my being.
>
> (1843b)

In a letter to Helene Keener, Jung makes several interesting comments concerning religion. He writes:

> Analytical psychology helps us to recognize our religious potentialities. . . . Alll science is merely a tool and not an end in itself. Analytical psychology only helps us to find the way to the religious experience that makes us whole. It is not this experience itself, nor does it bring it

66 Jung and religion

about. But we do know that analytical psychology teaches us that attitude which meets a transcendent reality halfway.

(1951–1961)

Writing of the religious function, Jung claimed the psyche to be a *naturaliter religiosa*, that it possesses a religious function. The religious function serves to reconnect us with the sustaining forces that escape recognition by the ego. The psyche urges us forward, towards the creation of a more complete and whole personality. The individual identifies in Christ archetypal forces that express his own inner psychic need for wholeness and unity. Christ then 'exemplifies the archetype of the self'. This religious or transcendent function is the means of enlarging psychic space in order to make room for coinciding opposites and the creative solution that arises from such a dialogue. The solution or set of symbols that arises from this dialogue addresses us with such compelling authority that Jung likens it to 'the voice of God'. It is this transcendent nature in analysis that takes us beyond ego-consciousness, beyond our whole psyche and into the realm of profound meaning. It would be apt at this juncture to quote a particularly pertinent passage from Gerhald Adler's (1948) examination of Jung's work:

> [T]his regained religious outlook is a fundamental new step in human consciousness. . . . Man's old established superiority of the logos has been decisively challenged by the equally important, but diligently overlooked power of the Eros. Where this challenge is accepted and answered in a constructive sense, a new and active relationship between man and woman as equal partners can be established.

We might reasonably conclude that the goal of therapy for Jung is the provision of a religious experience, or restoring *homo religiosis* to its rightful place in the center of the psyche. The realisation of self is both a collective and archetypal ambition and can therefore be considered as a religious concern. However, the prime reason why Jung considers the individuation goal to be religious in nature is due to the indistinguishable nature of the God and Self-archetypes. In *Mysterium Coniunctionis*, Jung writes,

> the extraordinary difficulty in this experience [of the self] is that the self can be distinguished only conceptually from what has always been referred to as God, but not practically. Both concepts apparently rest on an identical numinous factor which is a condition of reality.

(1955/56: par.778)

Palmer (1997) describes the archetypal God form from which the symbolic archetypal God contents is elevated beyond the world of signs and which gives to every image of God its universal meaning and psychic potency. The symbolic God contents possess the capacity to reveal through its imagery the deepest and most potent level of the psyche, because through it is activated the archetypal and collective dimension of the unconscious mind, which is the archetypal God form. It is through the medium of the God contents that individuals feel they have experienced an aspect of their inner life that transcends their own particularity, an aspect which is timeless, eternal and universal.

The discussions aroused at the time of the reception of *Psychology and Religion* show that theological readers were irritated by his impartiality in bringing religion and psychology together – even though Kierkegaard had done the same some hundred years earlier. This furrow that Jung has undermined religion with his claim that the origins of religious experience in the human psyche is strange, for as Dourley remarks, it supports the contention that human consciousness is in and of itself incorrigibly religious (Dourley 1991). I must confess that I find the disagreement between scholars over Jung's religiosity unwarranted. I would like to take up again the question of whether Jung can be considered a religious writer because I feel it to have so many clinical and ideological implications. Whilst there are those who characterised him as 'unspiritual' (Count Keyserling), others have classified him as an early Christian Gnostic (Martin Buber) but perhaps the most notable examination of his religious belief is to be found in the work of Victor White. Palmer (1997), in agreement with Victor White, the Dominican priest who corresponded and collaborated with Jung, claims that we should be cautious about accepting Jung as a friend of religion. To agree with Jung, writes Palmer:

> Is to adopt a conception of God as an innate human disposition, indistinguishable as anything other than a particular psychic state, and existing only in the sense that anything that works for the psyche will be real. The circularity of this idea is quite apparent – what proceeds from the psyche is validated by the psyche – and provided for Jung, as he took it, with a certain degree of immunity from attack. . . . the trouble with this is that, by setting God within this circle, Jung opens himself up to the charge of psychologism, namely that God has thereby been reduced to nothing more than a subjective experience, on a par with any other experience that one might have and for which one might require treatment, and guaranteed as such in much the same way as say a belief in flying saucers.

The problem as Palmer sees it is that the validity of Jung's God-image requires nothing more than it's being established by psychic effect and thereby renders it indistinguishable from any other image possessing similar powers of transformation. This God-image then is subject to the self-justifying world and internal logic of the psyche. Palmer concedes that whilst this argument helps us to avoid the hazard of elevating the notion of God's transcendence to the point where this idea cannot be correlated with any inner psychological experience, by the same token it has

> So radicalized the notion of God's immanence as an exclusively psychic reality that it becomes equally questionable whether anything has been left of God at all, and thus whether anything distinctive is meant when we speak of religion. Many will regard this as too heavy a price to pay; but it is perhaps the inevitable cost of discarding all questions of metaphysical truth in favor of psychological truth.
>
> (Palmer 1997)

However, as a psychologist, writes Segal, Jung is prepared not merely to identify the function of religion but also to evaluate the worthiness of the function and the effectiveness of religion in fulfilling it. He touts religion for offering perhaps the fullest means of encountering the unconscious short of analysis. Religion provides a most effective, albeit unconscious, vehicle for encountering the unconscious. Jung clearly judges religion to be exceedingly helpful, whether a transcendental God exists or not; however, herein lies the problem. The efficacy of religion depends on the patient's believing religion true, not on its being true:

> I support the hypothesis of the practicing Catholic while it works for him. In either case, I reinforce a means of defense against a grave risk, without asking the academic question whether the defense is an ultimate truth. I am glad when it works and so long as it works.
>
> (1938/40: par.79)

The question that here emerges is whether religious experience is essentially psychological, a product of psyche, constructed and certified by the psyche to be true or as something that exists apart from the psyche as an existential given and which cannot therefore, as Palmer contends, be equivalent to a psychological state. If God is synonymous with the unconscious, how, as Palmer asks, are we to distinguish statements about God from statements about human psychic states? Or 'how are we to avoid the conclusion that a knowledge of God is no more than a form of psychological autobiography, in which we project into our notion of God no more than what we discern in ourselves?' Palmer finds no resolution to these questions in Jung, and this is because 'having once allowed that God can only be understood psychically, he is bound to assert that we cannot speak except by reference to our own psychic condition' (Palmer 1997). However, Kierkegaard may offer us a solution, since he too places paramount importance on subjective knowledge of God. Can we follow Kierkegaard and Jung when they seem to imply that God exists only as and when we believe in him? Such a problem will naturally arise when emphasis is given to subjective existence over and above objective fact, since it leaves us with no criterion by which to determine truth. When the truth has its roots in personal experience there can be no such criterion to distinguish one's truth from illusion. Yet this does not leave Jung's notion of God so radicalised that nothing has been left of God. The function that religion and the God archetype serves is not just helpful but indispensable. I believe Segal to have captured the discontent here in the distinction between function and truth, for as he says religion can be functional yet false or even true yet dysfunctional (Segal 1992). To be functional, religion must only be believed true by believers. With Kant, Jung endeavors to point out the limits of what reason can know and this has the effect of creating a space that can easily accommodate faith. And since Kant there has been a turn away from ascertaining metaphysical truth, as Jung remarks:

> [I]t would be a regrettable mistake if anybody should understand my observations as a kind of proof of the existence of God. They prove only the existence of an archetypal image of the deity, which to my mind is the most we can assert psychologically about God.
>
> (1938/40: par.120)

The archetypal God-image, then, like any other archetype is beyond our rational grasp and so ultimately all we can say with any certainty is that for Jung our experience of God has its roots in the psyche. Such a belief makes no attempt in any way to prove or disprove the existence of God beyond the psyche. Essentially, the archetypal basis of the human experience of God relates us to the only reality of God that it is possible for us to experience, God mediated through the psyche:

> It is only through the psyche that we can establish that God acts upon us, but we are unable to distinguish whether these actions emanate from God or the unconscious. We cannot tell whether God and the unconscious are two different entities. Both are borderline concepts for transcendental contents.
>
> (1952b: par.757)

To say our experience of God emanates through the unconscious does not mean to say that our experience is derived from our own personality. Inner experiences have always been part of a religious individual's makeup. The unconscious is the seat of the religious function; it is the 'inner voice' of revelation. Psychic reality exists over and above personality and ego – it is therefore far removed from all human volition and influence. Jung hypothesised that there is a religious process in every human being and this essential process takes place in the unconscious, having as its goal the actualisation of

70 Jung and religion

the unconscious – the realisation of human potential. In delineating his own intellectual heritage Jung frequently states his indebtedness to Kant. Jung can be considered a follower of Kant in the sense that human interiority and subjectivity are the preconditions and limitations of knowledge. Jung in *The Transformation Symbolism in Mass* (1942) quite explicitly declares the limitations of psychological understanding and clearly prefers to leave the question of God's existence and the realities of faith in the hands of theologians:

> The mass is a still living mystery . . . it owes its vitality partly to its undoubted psychological efficacy, and . . . is therefore a fit subject for psychology. But psychology can only approach the subject from the phenomenological angle, for the realities of faith lie outside the realm of psychology.
>
> (1942/1954: par.296)

Furthermore, Jung retains the Church's interpretation of the transformation rite but then proposes to treat this interpretation as a symbol, stressing once again that:

> Such a procedure does not imply any evaluation of the content of religious belief. Scientific criticism must, of course, adhere to the view that when something is held as opinion, thought to be true, or believed, it does not posit the existence of any real fact other than a psychological one.
>
> (1942/1954: par.376)

The theologian, writes Jef Dehing (1992), should be placated by this argument for Jung clearly does not intend to evaluate the content of religious belief itself. There seems to be two fears about Jung expressed by theologians. Firstly, that Jung reduces religion to psychology, and secondly, that he seeks to replace religion with his psychology. Neither fear is founded. In the first instance, it is clear that Jung has no desire to explain away the ultimate core and meaning of religion. In the second, Jung was quite emphatic in stating that his analytical psychology was not a religion. He thought a person lucky if he or she could be a devout follower of an inherited religion, for then the road would be easy, well planned and secure. Furthermore he often states that his first effort in therapy is to try to reconnect patients to their native religions, since many did not suffer from a sense of the impossibility of coping, but, rather, from a sense of the meaningless, barren quality of life. He held that conventional Christianity had emptied faith of its significance because it had turned symbols into signs. Whilst symbols transmit the all-important immediate experience that addresses itself to the soul, signs point merely to facts – themselves empty of the potential for transformation. He writes, 'we simply do not understand any more what is meant by the paradoxes contained in dogma; and the more external our understanding of them becomes the more we are affronted by their irrationality'(1944: par.19).

And:

> Psychology is concerned with the act of seeing and not with the construction of new religious truths. . . . Since the stars have fallen from heaven and our highest symbols have paled, a secret life holds sway in the unconscious. That is why we have a psychology today, and why we speak of the unconscious. All this would be quite superfluous in an age or culture that possessed symbols.
>
> (1934/1954: par.50)

Religion is then a language that allows us to grapple with archetypal, symbolic contents. However, as Jung viewed it, religion had lost its ability to address the soul owing to the transformation of symbols into signs. We might consider a theologian's focus upon the historical figure of Christ as an example of this reducing of the symbolic to sign. Jung draws the similarity between analysis and religion several times in *The Collected Works*. It is clear that the task of analysis is the task of all religions. Most explicitly he notes that in analysis or the disciplines of religion we try to understand these symbols and thus to absorb and respond to 'the unconscious, compensatory striving for an attitude that reflects the totality of the psyche' (1912/1952: par.346). When Jung declares that 'to gain an understanding of religious matters, probably all that is left us today is the psychological approach' (1938/1940: par.148), I believe he is implying that Christianity is so bereft of its symbolic core that it no longer possesses its own momentum. The question which I suspect is really at the heart of the matter is whether faith is a psychological state or a supernatural endowment; and thus we have the problem of potentiality versus predestination. Whilst we cannot hope to answer such a question within the scope of this work, we can address Palmer's fear that the revelation of God becomes unavoidably reduced to the revelation of man unto himself. For there is a clear distinction between man and God, for man is not part of God, nor is God identified with one function of human nature, even though it is the highest. The relation between the two must always be that in which we are the worshippers and God the worshipped. Jung himself was conscious of such a reductionist over-psychologising of religious experience. Affirming the validity of studying the psychology of religion he writes:

> I am always coming up against the misunderstanding that a psychological treatment or explanation reduces God to 'nothing but' psychology. It is not a question of God at all, but of man's idea of God . . . there are

72 Jung and religion

people who have such ideas and who form such conceptions, and these things are the proper study of psychology.

(1938/1940: par.242)

It is important to understand that Jung does not reduce God to the unconscious. By this I mean to say that he is not identifying the unconsciousness with God which would perhaps mislead us into thinking of God as a mere reflection of self:

This is certainly not to say that what we call the unconscious is identical with God or set up in his place, it is simply the medium from which religious experience seems to flow. As to what the further cause of such experience may be, the answer to this lies beyond the range of human knowledge. Knowledge of God is a transcendent problem.

(1957: par.565)

And again, this time in *The Practice of Psychotherapy* he writes, 'Man is an analogy of God: Man is God, but not in an absolute sense, since he is man. He is therefore God in a human way' (1946: par.537). With regards to the accusation that 'nobody cares whether God exists', it must be conceded that for both Kierkegaard and Jung, God's objective existence is not the most important issue nor should we expect it to be such for two avid followers of Kant. To those who might say of Jung's system that its most important message is to experience an attitude that helps one live, others of a somewhat cynical disposition might simply remark that this is something that could be said of Christianity generally. However, I think it true to say that both Kierkegaard's and Jung's struggle with religion made life for them anything but easier. Kierkegaard similarly emphasises the limitation of ego-consciousness (although he clearly does not express himself in such modern terminology) and the consequent impossibility of acquiring direct knowledge of God. Nevertheless, it would certainly seem the case that Jung, unlike Kierkegaard, is more concerned with God only as a psychological experience.

It is important to bear in mind that religion always relates to our wholeness, a vital component in the process of uniting the disparate parts of the psyche into a living relation. Jung therefore emphasises the compensatory effect of religion. Religion is the medium by which revelation becomes effective for man. Jung associates the religious experience with a forward movement towards balance and unity. Our experience of God 'strives for expression, and can only be expressed "symbolically" because it transcends understanding'. It must be expressed one way or another, for therein is revealed its immanent vital force; 'it wants to step over, as it were, into visible life, to take concrete shape' (1906–1950). Individuation is a journey toward integrity, a natural, innate transcendental orientation of the human person towards a relationship with the numinous, God – the center and source of human wholeness. Ultimately I believe the contention lay in whether the call to individuate issues from within the psyche or externally in the form of a transcendental God figure. Naturally, this is beyond our knowing. Given this, I suggest instead that it is more important to focus on what Jung has to say vis-à-vis integrity and the spiritual dimension that he believed an irreducible part of the psyche. The primary human drives, according to Jung, reflected the very existence of a priori transcendent reality and so he attributed to the spirit a primary instinctive quality equal in power to sexuality. I do not believe that Jung possessed any desire to explain away the ultimate core and meaning of religion.

To reiterate, the workings of the unconscious towards totality is a religious process of religious significance. However, Jung is far from placing all religion on an even footing. As we have previously explored, Jung witnessed first-hand in his father how Protestantism divorces revelation from psychic experience and thus creates a distance between human consciousness and divine reality. Some religious paths are simply more secure than others. For instance, in the case of the Protestant, the individual must withstand what can often be an overwhelmingly powerful experience of the Godly unaided by sacrament or cult. Furthermore, the protestant faith has left the individual completely alone in the face of his or her guilt.[1] The problem with Protestantism, according to Jung's view, was that it had become divorced from its symbolic content. The very symbolic (archetypal) content of religion is capable of not only protecting the ego from dissolution in the unconscious but also protects us from meaninglessness. Speaking at a dinner party, Jung is reputed to have said,

> but today archetypal contents, formerly taken care of satisfactorily by the explanations of the church, have come loose from their projections and are troubling people, questions as to where we are going, and why, are asked on everyside.
>
> (Hayman 2002)

Religion is living and valid only as long as it creates symbols, which include the totality of experience as part of God. When God is made good, then a balance in the personality must be created, in other words an engagement with the devil. This construction, of course, denies the wholeness of God and posits a power that is outside of God. Whilst still symbolically valid, Catholicism too is deemed insufficient in its inability to assimilate femininity and evil. Commenting on the one-sided patriarchal nature of Catholicism, Swanee Hunt (1990) writes; 'theologians, notoriously male in both body and spirit, have created a male God in their image, and this God corresponds to their fantasies about themselves, to the exclusion of the feminine anima' (Hunt 1990). The Catholic Church excluded evil from the makeup of the trinity, holding that God could contain no element of evil, for its presence in him would stand in contradiction to his holiness. In order for the Christian trinity to be made complete, Jung believed a fourth element was

74 Jung and religion

required (1942/1948: par.249). This fourth element consisted of two figures: the Virgin Mary and the devil (femininity and evil) (ibid.par.251–2). Subsequently Jung believed the Catholic Church stood at its zenith during the Middle Ages when the feminine was supplied by the ascendency of Mary. All the major tenets of Christianity were interpreted as instances of archetypes in the collective unconscious. The interpretation of the archetypal dimension of doctrine collapses this distance and frees the ego from the effects of unconscious archetypal influence through changing the relation of the ego to these contents. As a result a new, more integrated relation between ego and the collective unconscious is brought into being – this being the essence of the individuation process.

Jung's view of religion is perhaps most clearly confirmed by delineation of the individuation process found in the *Two Essays on Analytical Psychology* (1917). It is here that he defines the final stage of the individuation as an encounter with a God-image:

> Intellectually the Self is no more than a psychological concept, a construct that serves to express an unknowable essence which we cannot grasp as such, since by definition it transcends our powers of comprehension. It might equally be called the 'God within us'. The beginnings of our whole psychic life seem to be inextricably rooted in this point, and all our highest and ultimate purposes seem to be striving towards it.
>
> (1929a: par.399)

Though it is unclear whether this God self, the "God within us" is a separate archetype to the self is unclear. Jung certainly does not say that they are one and the same. His studies in the phenomenology of the self rely heavily upon an analysis of Christian imagery – these descriptions of the self do not solely evolve around the religious. Many are rather akin to the centers of various systems: the sun in the solar system, the nucleus in the atom, the king in a political system:

> every king carries the symbol of the self . . . king being archetypal anthropos, the original man . . . who not only begets, but himself is the world. The same can be said of Christ. . . . Since Christ as the word is indeed the symbol of the inner complete man, the self.
>
> (1951: par.310)

Candidly addressing the clash between traditional symbols and psychological experience, Jung concluded:

> Although all this sounds as if it were a sort of theological speculation, it is in reality modern man's perplexity expressed in symbolic terms. It is the problem I so often had to deal with in treating the neuroses of intelligent patients. It can be expressed in a more scientific, psychological

language; for instance, instead of using the term God you say 'unconscious,' instead of Christ 'self,' instead of incarnation 'integration of the unconscious,' instead of salvation or redemption 'individuation,' instead of crucifixion or sacrifice on the cross 'realization of the four functions [sic]or of 'wholeness'.

(1956–1957: par.1664)

Jung's portrayal of the individuation process is more than a secularised religious experience. He was adamant that his analytical psychology was not a new religion, neither was he a guru: 'psychology is concerned with the act of seeing and not with the construction of new religious truths' (1944: par.15). At a panel discussion in London organised to consider whether Jung's Analytical Psychology is itself a religion, Segal, Storr and Shamdasani agreed that it was not; although Jung and Shamdasani concur in thinking that the process of individuation can justly be called religion in *statu nascend* (Storr, Shamdasani, Segal 1999). Anthony Storr (1999) makes the very commonsensical remark that:

> whether or not analytical psychology is called a religion doesn't seem to me to matter. It can be a substitute for religion for those who believe in it. It is certainly closer to being a religion than it is to being a medical treatment for neurosis. Turning to the unconscious for guidance through the analysis of dreams is not far removed from praying for God's guidance. As Jung himself said to me: 'Every night you have the chance of the Eucharist.'

God, in Jung's account, seeks to become embodied in one's experience – in one's immediate religious experience. His conception of self seemingly evolves out of the old traditional conception of faith and this imparts to the self a transcendental element. The self becomes then not only uniquely personal but also something that extends infinitely beyond the individual personality. Jung believed there to be no disadvantage to religious tradition to see just how far it coincides with psychological experience. Unfortunately, theologians have not shared such a belief.

Note

1 'The Catholic Church has at her disposal ways and means which have served since olden times to gather the lower, instinctual forces of the psyche into symbols and in this way integrate them into the hierarchy of the spirit. The protestant minster lacks these means, and consequently often stands perplexed before certain facts of human nature which no amount of admonition, or insight, or goodwill, or heroic self-castigation can subdue. In Protestantism good and evil are flatly and irreconcilably opposed to one another. There is no visible forgiveness; the human being is left alone with his sin. And God, as we know, only forgives the sins we have conquered ourselves' (1928:par.547).

Chapter 8

The therapeutic value of faith

In both Jung's and Kierkegaard's work condemnations pertaining to the neglect of religious experience occur in abundance. Kierkegaard's insight into the human person is that we are spiritual creatures, whilst such a concept differentiates Kierkegaard's thought from the vast majority of twentieth century psychological theories, we cannot claim Jung's theories amongst them. Jung was well aware of the crucial part played by a patient's religious attitude in the therapy of psychic illnesses. Also apparent to him was the effect that disregard of the fundamentally religious character of the psyche had in relation to neurosis. The idea of God is certainly believed by Jung to be conducive to psychic health. In *Psychotherapists or the Clergy* (1933) Jung writes:

> all creativeness in the realm of the spirit as well as every psychic advance of man arises from the suffering of the soul, and the cause of the suffering is spiritual stagnation or psychic sterility . . . among all my patients in the second half of life – that is to say, over thirty five – there has not been one whose problem in the last resort was not that of finding a religious outlook on life. It is safe to say that every one of them fell ill because he had lost what the living religions of every age have given to their followers, and none of them has been really healed who did not regain his religious outlook. This of course has nothing whatever to do with a particular creed or membership of a church.
>
> (1932a: par.497)

And:

> It seems to me that, side by side with the decline of the religious life, the neuroses grow noticeably more frequent. We are living undeniably in a period of the greatest restlessness, nervous tension, confusion, and disorientation of outlook.
>
> (1932a: par.514)

The therapeutic value of faith 77

Jung accords to religion the power to produce amongst its followers psychological health and well-being and with such a belief man's religious needs are introduced into psychology. Clearly Jung views the collapse of religion as having instigated this disease of the soul. Religion ministers to psychic health. Jung reaches such a conclusion by way of this observation that none of his patients who are over thirty-five years have yet done with the question of religion. Should one's need for a religious orientation be ignored, neurosis is likely to ensue. In such a case the individual becomes suddenly overwhelmed with the feeling of meaninglessness in his or her life, not merely playing with the idea but experiencing it as a veritable inner paralysis. But if symptoms of this kind fail to appear in persons who have a living religion, particularly in the second half of life, then this is a sure indication of some bond between their religious attitude and their mental health. Conventional religion can have the protective value of a defense mechanism insomuch as it can contain the archetypes that can so significantly influence our behaviour within religious symbols. Any contact with the unconscious is essential and life giving, yet it is also dangerous; the symbols and rituals of a religious system allow one to experience archetypes in a meaningful way, whilst protecting against the 'terrible double aspect' of direct contact with the God within. In short, doctrinal propositions can give expression to symbols that have the effect of releasing things in us, of broadening our horizons and creating order from disorder.

It is therefore not the acceptance of religion that is psychologically damaging but its rejection. This is where Jung's psychology goes beyond Freudian psychoanalysis. For Jung the search for transcendent meaning is the most powerful instinct in human nature alongside the survival instinct. As early as his *Psychology of the Unconscious* (1912) Jung was positing a primary cultural-religious level to the psyche that he believed to be foundational to the sexual and aggressive instincts within man. That he placed such emphasis upon the individual's religious impulse, considering it not just equal to sex and aggression but as foundational to them, marks his split from Freud:

> Religion appears to me to be a peculiar attitude of the human mind, which could be formulated in accordance with the original use of the term 'religio', that is, a careful consideration and observation of certain dynamic factors, understood to be 'powers', spirits, demons, Gods, laws, ideas, ideals, or whatever man has found in his world dangerous or helpful enough to be taken into consideration, or grand and beautiful and meaningful enough to be devoutly adored and loved.
>
> (1932a: par.514)

This religious attitude of mind is an 'instinctive attitude peculiar to man', whose 'manifestations can be followed all through human history' (1957:

78 The therapeutic value of faith

par.512). Certainly, it would seem fruitful to think of religion in light of Jung's writing rather than an accepted ecclesiastical form but of a personal encounter with a stronger spiritual reality that compels examination. The problem with faith, as Jung saw it, is that it is associated with a specific creed, which can only give expression to a particular collective belief. At best, a creed is a confession of faith intended chiefly for the world at large and is thus an intramundane affair, while the meaning and purpose of religion lie in the relationship of the individual to God (Christianity, Judaism, Islam) or to the path of salvation and liberation (Buddhism). Consequently, religion proper must involve an individual and subjective relationship to the eternal. This elevation of the transcendent over the traditional is yet another compelling factor that links Jung and Kierkegaard. Individuation is prompted by immediate personal experience and therein lays the importance of the subjective. Jung strongly warns us against mistaking genuine psychological rebirth for the transformation experienced during group experiences:

> If any considerable group of persons are united and identified with one another by a particular frame of mind, the resultant transformation experience bears only a very remote resemblance to the experience of individual transformation. A group experience takes place on a lower level of consciousness than the experience of an individual. This is due to the fact that, when many people gather together to share one common emotion, the total psyche emerging from the group is below the level of the individual psyche. If it is a very large group, the collective psyche will be more like the psyche of an animal. The group experience goes no deeper than the level of one's own mind in that state. It does work a change in you, but the change does not last.
>
> (1934/1954: par.225)

However, we should not be so surprised by how this similarity underpins both the psychologist who champions individuality and a theologian brought up in a strict tradition of Protestantism who repeatedly gives emphasis to the paramount importance of the individual. What might seem unexpected is Jung's reception amongst theologians, more specifically the sympathetic reception that his work received amongst Catholic theologians. Jung himself remarked in 1935 that though his writings were at one time thoroughly studied and worked over in Catholic circles, as yet no Protestant theologian had taken the trouble even to look into his works (Schaer 1957). Although Catholic philosophers and psychologists for the most part seemed initially unwilling to venture into Jung's analytical psychology, this state of affairs did not last. In 1957 the Jesuit theologian Raymond Hostie published his influential *Religion and the Psychology of Jung*, in which, despite many stringent criticisms, he concluded that Jung had 'rediscovered the religious and the sacred and got rid of an overwhelming rationalism' (Palmer 1997).

It is Hostie who makes the claim that Jung's greatest contribution to theology lies in proving that the symbols, dogma and images of Christianity are archetypal and thus universal to all mankind. This goes someway in explaining the more sympathetic reception of Jung's work amongst Catholic rather than Protestant theologians, which is perhaps not what one might expect. Another possible reason for this initial interest from only the Catholic theologians is related to Jung's belief that the Church places too strong an emphasis on the weakness of man, whose hopes lay entirely on Christ thereby serving to encourage a universal human tendency to remain infantile. This would seem to me to strike at the heart of a psychological interpretation of Protestantism.

We might define religious experience by saying that it tends towards psychic integration; religion is thereby needed for the total development of the personality. Symbolic awareness is necessary in order to bring about the mediation of the inner processes through which integration of the personality is able to take place. Jung described archetypes as 'God's tools' – they facilitate religious healing and we could say that they are the means by which God speaks to us.[1] Is genuine religious experience nothing more than a dialogue with the unconscious and its archetypes? The answer to this depends on whether we view Jung as having located the transcendent 'one' in the psyche.

Having established Jung's view on religion and the role this plays in the formulation of his therapeutic technique, I shall now turn to Kierkegaard in order to explore potential therapeutic aspects of his thinking.

Kierkegaard is no more a therapist than Jung was a theologian; and yet there exists in both their works the notion that faith has considerable therapeutic value. There is a general trend amongst Kierkegaardian scholars dealing with his method of indirect communication. It is assumed that his use of indirect communication reflects his belief that faith is something that cannot be expressed in language, and consequently not capable of direct communication. Thereby it is Kierkegaard's disillusionment with the nature of language to externalise faith and a grappling with this semantic problem that leads him to use various mouthpieces as pseudonyms for his works. However, Jon Stewart (2003) advises caution when dealing with the importance and emphasis of Kierkegaard's pseudonyms, for one must constantly bear in mind that the use of pseudonyms was commonplace in Copenhagen during the early nineteenth century: a common precaution to avoid embarrassment or offense in a small intellectual community where its figures will have been personally acquainted (Stewart 2003). Not only does Stewart's view go against the emphasis that Kierkegaard gives to his method of indirect communication as outlined in such works as *The Point of View for My Work as an Author* (1851), but also runs counter to that which we know of Kierkegaard's character; Kierkegaard simply was no stranger to offense and controversy. Alistair Hannay (1982) draws a comparison between Kierkegaard's indirect communication with

80 The therapeutic value of faith

Wittgenstein's remarks at the end of the tractate about ethics and mysticism, both of which are claimed to be beyond the conveyance of language (Hannay 1982). There can be little doubt that faith for Kierkegaard is beyond language, without expression in language and consequently not capable of direct communication: the domain of 'the universal' (the Symbolic) 'requires speech', but in faith he '*cannot* speak'; he is 'unable to make [him]self intelligible'.[2] His authorial strategy of indirect communication is more than an attempt to express the inexpressible and escape semantics, for it is designed to incite his reader to take responsibility for self-authorship. Kierkegaard's evasive communication, his silence, irony, humor, metaphoric, and poetic style are an indirect way of using language, but yet it is conceivable to view this pragmatically rather than provoked by semantics. Kierkegaard insisted that we cannot force a person into making a choice, or more importantly, you cannot push someone into freedom. It is by turning inward that man discovers freedom; 'and for him freedom is his bliss, not freedom to do this or that, to become king or emperor or the exponent of public opinion, but freedom to know of himself that he is freedom' (1844b). This indirect communication has a pragmatic intention, for it becomes a device intended to engage the reader and subtly lead her or him to an increasing self-knowledge in much the same way, I contend, as the therapist would hope to engage with his patient. His method of communicating indirectly therefore allows him the role of therapist. The problem as he sees it is that one's intellect will always rationalise away all avenues to authenticity: 'for the individual as for the generation no task is more difficult than to escape from the temptations of reflection' (1846b). On indirect communication he writes, 'the art of communication, becomes the art of taking away, of luring something away from someone' (1846a). But what does he want to take away from us? Well, first and foremost as we have already noted the illusion that we are genuine Christians. On this method Kierkegaard's persona, Anti-Climacus, gives an account of normal indirect communication between individuals:

> Indirect communication can be produced by the art of reduplicating the communication. This art consists in reducing oneself, the communicator, to nobody, something purely objective, and then incessantly composing qualitative opposites into unity. This is what some of the pseudonyms are accustomed to call 'double reflection'. An example of such indirect communication is, so to compose jest and earnest that the composition is a dialectical knot – and with this to be nobody. If anyone is to profit by this sort of communication, he must himself undo the knot himself. Another example is, to bring defense and attack in such a unity that none can say directly whether one is attacking or defending, so that both the most zealous partisans of the cause and its bitterest enemies can regard one as an ally – and with this to be nobody, an absentee, an objective something, not a personal man.
>
> (1850)

The therapeutic value of faith 81

Here we see that indirect communication involves forming contradictions through 'composing qualitative opposites into unity', and so one is forced to untie the dialectical knot if one is to accept one side of the contradiction or the other. Ultimately, Kierkegaard wants to transform the reader through this enticement to pursue authenticity, for it is passion for authentic action that will wake us from existential slumber. Merigala Gabriel (2009) discerns in all of Kierkegaard's Edifying Discourses a liturgical pattern, the intent of which is to deepen the reader's inner inwardness. He describes Kierkegaard's writings and commentaries on biblical themes as having 'a quality that induces deep reflection and introspection of the self'. In a journal entry, Kierkegaard writes of strip searching 'the mobs of speakers, teachers and professors'; it would seem fair to assume that he was referring to a fantasised stripping of Hegel. He continues,

> Yes, to strip them of the clothing, the changes of clothing, and the disguises of language, to frisk them by ordering them to be silent, saying: 'Shut up, and let us see what your life expresses, for once let this (your life) be the speaker who says who you are.'

Yet I think it is clear that this deception does not pertain exclusively to the realm of Hegelian philosophy, but to all of us who have forgotten that existence is more than a matter of words or adherence to a set of concepts.

Poul Lubcke (1990) remarks that Kierkegaardian scholars have rather looked upon his communication as an 'interesting text or speech quite capable of being put into biographic framework' and ignored the possibility of engaging with the text and the all-important possibility of making a choice. Kierkegaard far from being disillusioned with language, recognised its therapeutic power, both personally in the way that writing brought him relief (there is the sense that his authorship was an attempt at self-healing), and publicly, as a cure for the engaged reader who grapples with his dialectic knots and begins the process of spiritual maturation. In one journal entry he writes:

> Only when I am productive do I feel well. Then I forget all the unpleasant things of life, all the sufferings; then I am happy and at home with my thoughts. If I stop for just a couple of days, I immediately become ill, overwhelmed, oppressed; my head becomes heavy and burdened. After having gone on day after day for five or six years, this urge, so abundant, so inexhaustible, still surges just as abundantly – this urge is of course also a calling from God.
>
> (JP: 1847)

Referring again to this powerful urge to write, he writes, 'this very work of mine as an author was the prompting of an irresistible inward impulse' (1848/1859). For all his claims concerning the virtue of silence, it would

82 The therapeutic value of faith

seem that only when he was writing and felt a community with his imagined congregation, did Kierkegaard feel well. Kierkegaard renounced all that was finite, constructing a world that most of us would consider to be empty and unlivable. Whatever the reason of the renunciation of his relation to Regine, it surely points towards his attraction to aloneness and the silence of solitude. However, whilst his social network in the real world was severely limited, his many pseudonymous works are populated with a vast amount of characters – the Aesthete and the Judge, Constantine Constantius and the young poet, the seducer and Cordelia, Johannes de Silentio, Johannes Climicaus and Anti-Climacus amongst many others. Remarking on this world that he creates in his pseudonyms, he writes:

> For many years my melancholy has had the effect of preventing me from saying 'Thou' to myself, from being on intimate terms with myself in the deepest sense. Between my melancholy and my intimate 'Thou' there lay a whole world of fantasy. This world it is that I have partly exhausted in my pseudonyms. Just like a person who hasn't a happy home spends as much time away from it as possible and would prefer to be rid of it, *so my melancholy has kept me away from my own self while I, making discoveries and poetical experiences, traveled through a world of fantasy.*
> (JP 1849).

There are those who will say that even though Kierkegaard's work coincides with his attempt at self-healing, it comes at the cost of his unified self. I believe that the act of writing consolidated his religious pathos and gave him a platform upon which to serve Christianity. 'An apostle's task', wrote Kierkegaard 'is to spread Christianity, to win people to Christianity. My task is to disabuse people of the illusion that they are Christians – yet I am serving Christianity' (1851). Yet he also, through his writing, came to understand himself, he confided as much in *The Point of View for My Work as an Author*: 'for my whole activity as a writer . . . was at the same time my own education, in the course of which I have learnt to reflect more and more deeply upon my idea, my task' (1848/1859).

With his pseudonyms Kierkegaard offers us only existential possibilities contrasted with one another. The only place we find an outright endorsement of the religious way of life is in his journals. What we find with these works intended for public reading is a vast array or perceptions that demand the engagement of the reader, who must make a judgement for themselves as to which position feels correct. These pseudonymous characters express their competing and conflicting perspectives on life and this cleverly sets the engaged reader the task of considering a conclusion as to how best to live life. For instance should the reader fall on the side of the aesthete he might then reflect upon the emptiness of his life and feel the despair that invariably accompanies such existence. Consequently then he may strive

The therapeutic value of faith 83

to overcome his sensual nature and thereby begin the process of becoming his own sole creator through creating/recovering his intrinsic self. We might say that there is an element of deception in Kierkegaard's method, that the creation of pseudonymous characters to which we can associate is meant to trick us into seeing our limitations and ourselves more clearly. Such a view resonates with Kierkegaard's understanding of the use of deception in his works in the service of coming to truth: 'To deceive belongs essentially to [my method of] communication,' Kierkegaard writes in his journal, 'and the art consists in . . . remaining faithful . . . to the deception [throughout].'[3] In another journal entry, Kierkegaard goes so far as to give his imagined reader 'advance notice' that he is obligated as an author to 'set between ourselves the awakening of misunderstanding' (JP 1848). And yet, he claims one's deceptions are stronger and more resistant than even the cleverest literary devices and deceits. At best we could rightly say of Kierkegaard's works that they provide the individual with remarkable sources of self-reflection. There can be no doubt that within the prevailing modes of life that Kierkegaard presents us, he is very subtly leading us to adopt their antithesis and thereby encourage us towards a life of authentic faith and selfhood. Essentially, his use of indirect communication is designed so as to lead the reader to take responsibility for his/her self-authorship. And so like the therapist he maintains an impartial silence, allowing the reader to find himself in his text. The indirectness of his approach, his unwillingness to express what it is that he knows, is all to the end of allowing the reader to author himself. However, those of faith would almost certainly claim God's capacity for forgiveness to be far greater than the therapist's mere mortal capacity for acceptance, and yet in Jung, as we have seen, we have a figure that holds these two elements in suspension.

Notes

1 'It as though, at the climax of the illness, the destructive powers were converted into healing forces. This is brought about by the archetypes wakening to independent life. . . . As a religiously minded person would say: guidance has come from God. With most of my patients I have to avoid this formulation, apt though it is, for it reminds them too much of what they had to reject in the first place. I must express myself in more modest terms and say that the psyche has awakened to spontaneous activity: and indeed this formulation is better suited to the observable facts. . . . To the patient this is nothing less than a revelation' (1932:par.534).

2 'Abraham Keeps silent – but he cannot speak. Therein lies the distress and anguish. For if when I speak I am unable to make myself intelligible, then I am not speaking – even though I were to talk uninterruptedly day and night. Such is the case with Abraham. He is able to utter everything, but one thing he cannot say, i.e. say it in such a way that another understands it, and so he is not speaking. The relief of speech is that it translates me into the universal. Now Abraham is able to say the most beautiful things any language can express about how he loves Isaac.

But it is not this he has a heart to say, it is the profounder thought that he would sacrifice him because it is a trial. . . . He [Abraham] is unable to speak, he speaks no human language. Though he himself understood all the tongues of the world, though his loved ones also understood them, he nevertheless cannot speak – he speaks a divine language . . . he "speaks with tongues" '(1843b).

3 'To "deceive" belongs essentially to the essentially ethical-religious communication. "To deceive into the truth." . . . Ethical communication in character always begins with placing a "deception" in between [the teacher and the learner], and the art consists in enduring everything while remaining faithful to character in the deception and faithful to the ethical' (JP 1848).

Chapter 9

Grounding ethics in spirit

The medium of our self-realisation

By claiming that human nature is inherently a moral one, allows both Kierkegaard and Jung to criticise the church and move the religious center within the individual. Whilst the self I am to be is not necessarily determined by the self I have been, it does necessitate the complete acceptance of the latter; this is as true of Jung's psychology as it is of Kierkegaard's theology. There is an inherent danger in such self-acceptance; specifically the empowerment of the autonomy of self, which decides that who and what we are, is acceptable. Consequently, there can be a resignation to justify the lesser self, in other words to wearily resign ourselves to the fact that 'we are who we are'. We might well ask why strive for Authenticity? To this Jung and Kierkegaard may answer that it is in man's nature to strive towards becoming his unique self before God (to ground himself in Spirit) and should this call to authenticity go unheeded, man buries his human potential resulting in psychological symptoms of despair.

In the creation of personal meaning one must first come to terms with the worst and the darkest elements of our psyche, our shadow selves. However, this can only happen once our self-awareness has awoken fully to one's lack of authenticity. This is not a unique attribute of Jung's psychology; in his *Stages on Life's Way* (1845) and *Either/Or* (1843) Kierkegaard depicts the human being as having an actual and an ideal self. In essence Kierkegaard, like Jung, advocates that one must accept one's shortcomings so as to avoid collision between the ideal self and actual self. He writes:

> I am again myself. This self which another would not pick up from the road I possess again. The discord in my nature is resolved, I am again unified. The terrors which found support and nourishment in my pride no longer enter to distract and separate.
>
> (1843b)

For Kierkegaard, ethics requires the passion of faith. His description of an authentic faith corresponds to a passion that enables one to commit oneself to the formation of true selfhood. Authenticity must result from pursuing

86 Grounding ethics in spirit

a lifestyle characterised by creative freedom and decision. Authenticity is a notion identifying among other things a state of integrity between the innermost self and its external manifestations. It is a subjective pathos of inwardness or inward deepening which cannot be judged by any external and objective criterion. Only the individual who strives for authenticity can rightly judge whether his or her search has been successful. However, Kierkegaard says: 'let no one misunderstand all my talk about passion and pathos to mean that I am proclaiming any and every uncircumcised immediacy, all manner of unshaven passion' (Dru 1959). A passion without a definite object consumes the energies of the individual, and forsakes him to an existential blunder, which consequently spells his own annihilation. An unguided, uncontrolled passion means the dissolution of the personality. To fully become our true self, we need to relate to the good; only the good can be willed with purity of heart, no matter how passionately one may will and commit oneself to evil, it cannot make the self whole. It is not simply the case that one must make a choice and take responsibility for that choice, but of making correct ethical choices. Kierkegaard wrote,

> truth, righteousness and holiness are lined up on one side, and lust and base propensities and obscure passions and perdition on other; yet it is always important to choose rightly even as between things which one may innocently choose; it is important to test oneself, lest some day one might have to beat a retreat to the point from which one started.
>
> (1843a)

To this Jung might add the following reassurance:

> in his trial of courage God refuses to abide by traditions, no matter how sacred. In his omnipotence, he will see to it that nothing really evil comes of such tests of courage. If one fulfills the will of God one can be sure of going the right way.
>
> (1963)

At the core of the work of both Kierkegaard and Jung is humanity's desire for a meaningful existence. Simultaneously, Kierkegaard's diagnosis of aesthetic man, and Jung's diagnosis of his neurotic patient can be aptly reduced to an understanding that only the eternal can give meaning and so the aesthete/neurotic is the individual who cannot find within himself the possibility of belief. The result of such thinking is a fixed point of reference for analysing one's own life, at least for those concerned about how they are living and how they might live better. To engage in honest self-scrutinising, ultimately for Kierkegaard and Jung, means to ask oneself 'do I find my life to be meaningful?' As soon as that question is raised, the whole process has already engaged the individual on an ethical plane. For both Kierkegaard and Jung there is a reference point outside of the individual that acts as a guide to non-arbitary answers. So whilst the individual must create his own meaning and sense of purpose he does so with the guidance of a superior 'other' – and as argued earlier whether this 'other' is external or internal to the self is a moot point.

Arguably, the whole of Jung's psychology is ethical. He deals specifically with the ethical in his essay entitled *A Psychological View of Conscience* (1958). This is an interesting essay to look at in terms of a comparison to Kierkegaard. It is here that Jung differentiates a 'moral' form of consciousness from its 'ethical' form, the *vox dei*. The moral form takes its cue from society; it has its basis in generally accepted customs. Whilst the ethical goes beyond the moral so to speak in that ethical acts of conscience arise 'when two decisions or ways of acting, both affirmed to be moral and therefore regarded as "duties", collide with one another' (1958: par.856). Interestingly, for Kierkegaard, ethical choice confronts us at every moment of our fleeting existence and becomes the medium of our self-creation and actualisation. The transition from the ethical to the religious stage is marked by a decisive turn to action and commitment, and an attempt to live an authentic existence. Jung too stresses the importance of action in regards to the relation of ethics and the unconscious:

> I took great care to try to understand every single image, every item of my psychic inventory, and to classify them scientifically – so far as this was possible – and, above all, to realise them in actual life. That is what we usually neglect to do. We allow the images to rise up, and maybe we wonder about them, but that is all. We do not take the trouble to understand them, let alone draw ethical conclusions from them. This stopping-short conjures up the negative effects of the unconscious.
>
> It is equally a grave mistake to think that it is enough to gain some understanding of the images and that knowledge can here make a halt. Insight into them must be converted into an ethical obligation. Not to do so is to fall prey to the power principle, and this produces dangerous effects which are destructive not only to others but even to the knower. The images of the unconscious place a great responsibility upon a man. Failure to understand them, or a shirking of ethical responsibility, deprives him of his wholeness and imposes a painful fragmentariness on his life.
>
> (1963)

Individuation certainly does not relieve the responsibility of living ethically; rather it allows the development of consciousness that enables an ethical standpoint to develop. For Jung, one's ethical responsibility and wholeness are irrevocably linked. The demands of individuation are morally challenging with clear ethical overtones. One can discern in the works of Jung a

88　Grounding ethics in spirit

distinct link between becoming as conscious as possible of ourselves and becoming a higher moral being:

> The only thing that really matters now is whether man can climb up to a higher moral level, to a higher plane of consciousness, in order to be equal to the super human powers which the fallen angels have played into his hands. But he can make no progress with himself unless he becomes very much better acquainted with his own nature. Unfortunately, a terrifying ignorance prevails in this respect, and an equally great aversion to increasing the knowledge of his intrinsic character.
>
> (1952b)

The innate presupposition of the psyche towards maturation is an ethical statement concerning the natural goal of life. Simply understood, choosing oneself becomes an ethical requirement. M.D. Edler in his review of Jung's *Two Essays on Analytical Psychology* suggests that the essence of Jung's therapy is contained in this statement that man is a priori, a moral being. For Jung, as for many priests and religious teachers, this knowledge is vouchsafed. It is the therapist's task to reveal this morality to his patient with a conviction and earnestness that compels his patient to accept himself and thereby enable him to engage with his higher moral self. It is the process of individuation that puts the patient on the path of ethical growth towards the higher moral self.[1]

Writing of our moral nature, Andrew Samuels (1989) refers to Jung's assertion that morality emanates from within; it is a daemon, a voice which we have in us from the start. At times, according to Jung, the moral aspect of man constitutes one of the primal pathways or canals along which, in metaphorical terms, libido may flow, equal in its fundamental status to biology and the spirit (see 1952b: par.100–13). Conscience, writes Samuels, is not a product of education or parental instruction; if it comes from anywhere, it comes from God (1989). It certainly seems to be the case that such an ethical standpoint develops in Jung's theory of individuation, answering critics who accuse his individualism of being to self-serving, Jung informs that:

> It can never be forgotten – and of this the Freudian School must be reminded – that morality was not brought down or taken from Sinai, and forced upon the people. . . . Morality is not forced upon men from without; man has it a priori in himself – not the law indeed, but the moral being.
>
> (1912: par.30)

Self-realisation viewed in such a light becomes a moral problem, insofar as we are responsible for the original potential with which we are endowed. Furthermore, that the God self is at the center of selfhood would seem to imply a very real ethical dimension. Indeed, Palmer remarks that the perception that self-images are religious images is part and parcel of the 'religious outlook on life' that Jung claims is necessary for individuation (1997. This outlook, it should not be forgotten, also has a moral dimension, for in responding to the archetype mediated through the self-image, the personality experiences also what needs to be done for selfhood to be realised. Jung is not as radical an individualist as Kierkegaard, for individual growth in his thinking is intrinsically connected to the collective unconscious. Whereas what defines existence for Kierkegaard is not a relation to others but his awareness of one's own responsibility. He writes:

> A crowd in its very concept is the untruth, by reason of the fact that it renders the individual completely impenitent and irresponsible, or at least weakens his sense of responsibility by reducing it to a fraction . . . for crowd is an abstraction and had no hands: but each individual ordinarily has two hands.
>
> (1848/1859)

It is because of his polemics against the crowd and the evils of mass society that Kierkegaard is often stereotyped as someone who glorified a type of radical individualism.[2] Such crowd behaviour breeds social conformity which prevents a person from becoming an individual. In order to define oneself it is necessary to turn one's back and struggle alone rather than in public opinion. In his emphasis on individuality then it certainly seems reasonable to criticise Kierkegaard on the grounds that he completely underestimated the importance of social interaction in shaping the self. Georg Lukács believes there to be a trend in modern philosophy of turning inwards and away from social concerns, initiated by Kierkegaard and Schopenhauer, that has important implications for philosophers, psychoanalysts and the practice of psychiatry (Chessick 1992). This turning away from social activism, he claims, is accompanied by a despair that cried out for relief from a strong man and a fascist regime. Jung however understood 'the phenomenon of dictators and all the misery they have wrought', to be related to the fact that 'man had been robbed of transcendence by the shortsightedness of the super-intellectuals' and had consequently 'fallen victim to the unconscious' (1963). This aside for a moment, Lukács states that such thinkers as Kierkegaard and his followers, most notably Sartre, created 'a permanent carnival of fetishised inwardness', a carnival which, according to Lukács, continues to 'mesmerize and mislead bourgeois intellectuals' (Hannay 2013). Both Jung and Kierkegaard advocate passionate inwardness (perhaps a fine line between passionate and fetishized) that our answers lay in our innermost depths. In Jung however such inwardness remains connected to the other, for the self is our life's goal: 'it is the completest expression of that fateful combination we call individuality, the full flowering not only of the single individual, but of the group, in which each adds his portion to the whole' (1929a: par.404). Furthermore, as in all therapy, a therapist is necessary, and other people too, but perhaps only as functions of one's inner integration. Jung writes: 'The shadow can be realized only through a relation to a partner, and anima and animus only through a relation to the opposite sex, because only in such a relation do their projections become operative' (1951: par.42). And whilst analysis is essentially an individual matter, possessing no meaning except for the individual, Jung himself was well aware of the need to find some kind of social group or life for his patients in order to prevent them from becoming too isolated and cut off from life, for after all 'you cannot individuate on Mount Everest' (Hannah 1991).

I wonder here if there is a significant social aspect in Kierkegaard that is being overlooked, for it is the refusal of the typical aesthete to bind himself in obligation to others that enslaves the individual to false values. Conversely, the ethical man seeks to bind himself to others in a community, thereby taking upon himself social obligations in friendship, marriage and work.[3] One of the reasons that Kierkegaard feels that it is only in the ethical stage of life that man can develop as a personality is that the ethical life is one defined by a relationship to mutual obligation and responsibility; thus within the community of common need the ethical man finds the sphere and inspiration for the development of personal character.

Although there is a very radical nature to Kierkegaard's individualism, it remains that his ethical standpoint limits the extent of individuality. Casement describes such an ethical stance as living in a reciprocal relationship with one's surroundings so that one will usually enter into marriage, have a job or useful occupation and conduct one's civic duties in a responsible manner (Casement 1998). Such a state can be attained through that which Kierkegaard describes as a qualitative leap to faith, a spiritual and not a rational movement. However, Kierkegaard's faith does not involve just the suspension of the rational, but of the ethical also. The ethical ideal is at the same time the religious ideal, for religion does not supersede ethics but expresses the obligation of the universal in a different form; 'the ethical is the universal, and as such is it is also the divine. It is therefore true to say that all duty is fundamentally duty towards God' (1843b). And yet the whole point of Kierkegaard's *Fear and Trembling* is to illustrate that the greatness of Abraham cannot be understood purely in ethical terms. If there is nothing more to the religious life than moral striving, then Abraham cannot be the paragon of faith that Kierkegaard holds him to be. There is a discernable parallel in Jung's own belief that the individual should not aspire to use a moral code as the 'supreme arbiter' of how to live, as this would usurp the role of God in his or her life. William Kinney wrote to Jung asking about ethics and how one is to find meaning in life. Jung replied that the answers lay in the relationship between man and God:

> live thoroughly and very consciously for many years in order to understand what your will is and what Its will is. If you learn about yourself and if eventually you discover more or less who you are, you also learn

about God, and who He is. . . . So try to live as consciously, as conscientiously, and as completely as *possible* and learn who you are and who or what it is that ultimately decides.

(1951–1961)

Life for both Kierkegaard and Jung is defined from within and not from without. The discovery of the truth that lies at the very core of one's personality is fundamentally a solitary breakthrough. And so, with regards to both these thinkers I think we should tread carefully. We might say of both Jung and Kierkegaard that the most complete expression of individuality involves not just the development of the single individual but of the group. Our ability to cope with the dark sides of our psyche bears directly on our ability to have healthy relationships with others – we must learn to withdraw the projection of parts of ourselves that we have repressed:

> If people can be educated to see the shadow self of their nature clearly, it may be hoped that they will also learn to understand and love their fellow men better. A little less hypocrisy and a little more self knowledge can only have good results in respect for our neighbor; for we are all too prone to transfer to our fellows the injustice and violence we inflict upon our own natures.

(1917/1926/1943: par.28)

Should we be so surprised by the suggestion that greater self-knowledge comes with a greater capability for compassion? After all, the mentally healthy toddler who begins to become self aware at around age three soon after develops empathy. Which of itself would suggest at the very least a tentative link between the two. That Jung understood there to be a relation between one's self-knowledge and compassion is quite evident. The basis of healthy relationships with others is dependent on nurturing this fundamental understanding of the selves that we are and is dependent on the inner growth of the individual. This is not a resigned 'we are who we are' – far from it. Individuation goes beyond resolution of inner conflict, for it impels us towards a more harmonious relation with society as a whole. To give one example: acceptance of our shadow side, of our own hostile and aggressive impulses may in turn unlock other capacities for spontaneous affection, and so enable us to treat those who are hostile to us with greater tolerance and warmth. The psychic harmony that results from acknowledging certain desires and tendencies invariably produces an improved capacity for relationships with others, with for instance, members of one's own family or with the community in general (Palmer 1999). We can detect a similar meaningful contact with the world, dependent upon inner growth and development in Kierkegaard's works. For Kierkegaard, the goal of selfhood is to make true community possible. He describes the religious as 'the transfigured rendering of that which the politician has thought of in his happiest

92 Grounding ethics in spirit

moment, if so be that he truly loves what it is to be a man, and loves people really' (1848/1859).

A sympathetic reading of Kierkegaard and Jung reveals a participation in both spheres of individuality and of common humanity. Certainly Jung's greater transpersonal viewpoint, his acknowledgement that we do not exist in isolation from one another shows itself in his concept of the self that is influenced by, and will influence others. This is an element whose absence is all too apparent in Kierkegaard's work. The notion of relational self is, in real terms, completely alien to Kierkegaard's conception of self, and this is an element of his thought that I shall explore later in relation to the absence of intimacy in Kierkegaard's own life. Binding together the inner transformation of the individual with the transformation with others and of the world itself, Jung writes 'the spirit of the depths in me is at the same time the ruler of the depths of world affairs' (2009). Linking Kierkegaard and Jung quite intimately is this idea that spirituality is the power of a man's understanding over his life.

Notes

1 'Individuation has two principal aspects: in the first place it is an internal and subjective process of integration, and in the second it is an equally indispensable process of objective relationship. Neither can exist without the other, although sometimes the one and sometimes the other predominates. This double aspect has two corresponding dangers. The first is the danger of the patients using the opportunities for spiritual development arising out of the analysis of the unconscious as a pretext for evading the deeper human responsibilities, and for affecting a certain "spirituality" which cannot stand up to moral criticism; the second is the danger that atavistic tendencies may gain the ascendancy and drag the relationship down to a primitive level. Between this Scylla and that Charyb-dis there is a narrow passage, and both medieval Christian mysticism and alchemy have contributed much to its discovery.'

2 A view that Stephen Evans (2006) believes to be shared by both friend and foe of Kierkegaard alike – *Kierkegaard: On faith and the Self, Collected Essays*, (Baylor University Press, 2006). Even writers such as Sylvia Walsh and John Elrod, who would like to read Kierkegaard as putting forward a relational view of self, have difficult finding such a view there. This may well strike us as quite strange since Kierkegaard's Anti-Climacus states clearly that the human self is not an autonomous, contained self, but rather 'a derived, established relation, a relation that relates itself to itself and in relating itself to itself relates itself to another' (*Sickness Unto Death*). However, it is almost certainly the case that this other that the self relates to is restricted to solely God alone.

3 'The person who has chosen and found himself ethically has himself specified in all his concretion. He has himself, then, as an individual who has these abilities, these passions, these inclinations, these habits subject to these external influences, and who is influenced thus in one direction and so in another. He has himself, then, as a task in a way in which the task in essentials is that of ordering, tempering, kindling, repressing, in short bringing about a proportionality in the soul, a harmony that is the fruit of the personal virtues. The aim of his activity is himself, though not arbitrarily specified, for he has himself as a task which is set for him

even though it has become his through his having chosen it. But although he himself is his aim, this aim is nevertheless at the same time something else, for the self that is the aim is not an abstract self which fits in everywhere, and so nowhere, but a concrete self which stands in living interaction with these determinate surroundings, these conditions of life, this order of things. This self which is the aim is not just a personal self, but a social, a civic self. So he has himself as a task for an activity through which, as this determinate personal being, he intervenes in the affairs of life. Here his task is not to mould himself, but to exert an influence, and yet he does at the same time mould himself' (Kierkegaard 1843a).

Chapter 10

Suffering and the pain of personal growth

Perrissem, nisi perissem

Kierkegaard wrote in his journal:

> [P]erissem, nisi perissem (I would have perished had I not suffered) is and remains the motto for my life. Hence I have been able to do and endure what another who was not already dead would have been killed by long ago.
>
> (JP: 1849)

For Kierkegaard, suffering is the essence of religious life. Whilst there are some that would say of him, as they do of Schopenhauer, that he comes dangerously close to proclaiming suffering as a good in and of itself, we must not neglect the fact that such an attitude is typical amongst incredibly pious individuals who rejoice in suffering and demand no compensation for it. Suffering takes us right to the very heart of the mystery of the cross. Kierkegaard would be easier to stomach if he had valued suffering as a creative by-product; however, such is his glorification of suffering that he inevitably strikes us as having championed suffering in and for itself. Suffering for Kierkegaard is the hallmark of Christian existence. It defines the finite individual's relationship to an infinite God: 'in truth there is in suffering a fellowship with God, a pact of tears, which in and for itself is very beautiful'. Whereas Jung's concern was with the eradication of the symbolic life from Christianity, Kierkegaard feared for the erosion of suffering from faith. It was very much his mission to show Christians the true meaning of Christianity. It was his feeling that Christianity had become perverted from its original goal of imitating Christ, of making Christ the prototype of one's life. Being a Christian has everything to do with living as Christ lived and nothing to do with anything else: 'Christianity has been made so much into a consolation that people have completely forgotten that it is first and foremost a demand.' And: 'Christ comes to the world as the example, constantly enjoining: Imitate me. We humans prefer to adore him instead' (Moore 1999).

Suffering is 'the decisive and essential expression' of one's struggle to fully actualise oneself. For those living a predominantly aesthetic existence, suffering is a misfortune to be avoided. But for those for whom the religious conscience has taken precedence, suffering becomes understood as an accompaniment to human freedom. To exist is to suffer. Suffering will always be an integral part of one's relationship to God for it plays an integral role in learning what it means to let God be absolute. As Kierkegaard dramatically phrased it,

> the school of sufferings is a dying to and quiet lessons in dying to the world and worldliness, teaching humility that submits to unavoidable suffering with patience and meekness and courage, submitting freely to this suffering because God sends it. It is also a school of dying from the world into life, for a person must be weaned by sufferings, weaned from the world and the things of this world, from loving it and from being embittered by it, in order to learn for eternity.
>
> (1847c)

Kierkegaard and Jung consistently endorse the power of suffering to develop and deepen inwardness; it is not accidental but essential in the constitution of one's inner being. It is not something to be overcome, but rather a means of acquiring an eternal happiness. Suffering focuses one's attention onto the inner being and therefore teaches us to reflect upon the person we are/are becoming or are to become. Kierkegaard wrote: 'when a person suffers and wills to learn from what he suffers, he continually comes to know only something about himself and about his relationship to God; this is the sign that he is being educated for eternity' (1847c). In a similar, particularly Kierkegaardian fashion, Jung declared:

> Shouldn't we let God himself speak in spite of our only too comprehensible fear of the primitive experience? I consider it my task and my duty to educate my patients and pupils to the point where they can accept the direct demand that is made upon them from within. This path is so difficult that I cannot see how the indispensable sufferings along the way could be supplanted by any kind of technical procedure. Through my study of the early Christian writings I have gained a deep and indelible impression of how dreadfully serious an experience of God is. It is no different today.
>
> (1906–1950)

In his significant later work, Aion (1951), Jung addresses the Christian figure of Christ, noting that the experience of the self and what the New Testament describes as the 'Christ within' are synonymous. The equivalency between 'self' and 'Christ' is strongly evident in the following passage:

> The Self or Christ is present in everybody a priori, but as a rule in an unconscious condition to begin with. But it is a definite experience of

later life, when this fact becomes conscious. It is only real when it happens, and it can happen only when you withdraw your projections from an outward historical or metaphysical Christ and thus wake up Christ within.

(1939a: par.1638)

The figure of Christ remains outside us, when we understand it from a historical – (intellectual) or metaphysical (philosophical) viewpoint because such a figure lacks the symbolic content required to bring transformation into being:

> The crux of this question is: 'Within your own personality.' 'Christ' can be an external reality (historical and metaphysical) or an archetypal image or idea in the collective unconscious pointing to an unknown background. I would understand the former mainly as a projection, but not the latter, because it is immediately evident.

(1939a: par.1648)

The symbolic or archetypal Christ can be viewed as the example par excellence of the potential 'greater personality' in every individual. The life of Christ is the story of a human being transformed by his destiny; 'what happens in the life of Christ happens always and everywhere' (1938/1940: par.146). The individual is far removed from God (the unconscious), and one's ego must die to itself to reach God. Experiencing the self always amounts to defeat for the ego, the ego surrenders to unconscious with all the character of a religious experience; more specifically, a conversion experience of turning one's will over to a higher power. Jung writes:

> the self as a totality is indescribable, and indistinguishable from the God-image, self-realization – to put it in religious or metaphysical terms – amounts to God's incarnation. That is already expressed by the fact that Christ is the Son of God. And because individuation is a heroic and often tragic task, the most difficult of all, it involves suffering, a passion of the ego.

(1942/1948: par.233)

Suffering is an intricate facilitator of consciousness; it possesses a transcendental element, revealing to us a reality greater than one's own private existence. One's wholeness is achieved through enduring a moral suffering of opposites, itself fully equivalent to physical crucifixion – in that one sacrifices the central position of the ego (1942/1954: par.390). This is a necessary step on the way to the reconciliation of opposites in the unity and wholeness of the self. Psychic wholeness is sought through the withstanding and endurance of conflicting emotions – opposites at war – whose very presence

Suffering and pain of personal growth 97

denotes an increase in consciousness. We are not, Jung claims, to repress the painful states of consciousness resulting from the manifestation of the separated opposites but to experience them fully.[1] Only by doing so can we move forward towards the experiencing of the God within and ultimately retrieve one's lost wholeness.

There is the feeling in Jung's writing that far from being the Godly benevolent force, the God self is, in fact, at once one's own biggest help and hindrance. Essential to exploring the significant parallels in their works is to first understand that Jung, like Kierkegaard, is profoundly aware that the way of faith is often the way of despair. The basic choice of oneself, described by Jung and Kierkegaard, is one accompanied inevitably with imperfection, disappointment and disillusionment. It is to will oneself in virtue of the absurd, of willing oneself in virtue of the unknown, the indeterminate and the uncertain. However, resigning that which is most identified with our sense of whom and what we are presents an extreme threat, for there is a narcissistic investment in this self that is hard to be detached from. It is for this very reason that self-transformation and the realisation of one's true potential necessitates suffering. Kierkegaard believed that it is consciousness of sin (what he terms 'dread') that brings fourth suffering; however, the eradication of suffering would consequently abolish the religious life. It is only through an individual's awareness of sin that the possibility of existing as a Christian is made real; 'only the agony of the consciousness of sin', writes Kierkegaard, 'can explain the fact that a person will submit to this radical cure' (JP: 1848). The importance of despair in this journey that facilitates self-knowledge is perhaps best illustrated by the following passage:

> Compared with the person who is conscious of his despair, the despairing individual who is ignorant of his despair is simply a negativity further away from the truth and deliverance. Yet ignorance is so far from breaking the despair or changing despair to non-despairing that it can in fact be the most dangerous form of despair. . . . An individual is furthest from being conscious of himself as spirit when he is ignorant of being in despair. But precisely this – not to be conscious of oneself as spirit – is despair, which is spiritlessness.
>
> (1849)

There are two fundamental ways in which one despairs: firstly, there is the despair at not having a self – spiritlessness – (despair improperly so called) and secondly, despair at not willing to be oneself or in despair at willing to be oneself (despair proper). Whilst the former is a despair of weakness, Kierkegaard holds the latter to be a despair of defiance. Spiritlessness, the lowest form of despair, is that in which one is unconscious of oneself and consequently fails to reflect upon this self. Despair proper involves a degree

98 Suffering and pain of personal growth

of consciousness of self; one either despairingly wants not to be itself (despair of weakness) or despairing wishes to affirm itself as the human self it is, but to do so without recognising the relatedness and ultimate dependence of that human self upon God. The latter constitutes despair in its highest form (despair in defiance). The despairing individual has:

> a consciousness of the infinite self. And it is this self that a person in despair wills to be, severing the self from any relation to a power that has established it, or severing it from the idea that there is such a power. With the help of this infinite form, the self in despair wants to be master of itself, to create itself, to make his self into the self he wants to be, to determine what he will have and not have in his concrete self.
>
> (1849)

Since the individual in the last instance affirms his self-consciousness without acknowledging any transcendent relationship with God, Kierkegaard believes him to still be in despair because he continues to experience God as absent; 'to despair is to lose the eternal' (JP: 1849). Yet, it is in this despair of defiance, which in its most intense form moves one closer to salvation, that an individual comes to understand that despair is something that he had chosen. Common to both forms of despair is the internal disorder of the components of the self. The immediate man is immersed in the earthly and finite; he has no infinite consciousness of the self or of the nature of his despair. He lives on the immediacy of his experience. Kierkegaard's immediate man is left in despair, which can be clinically recognised, I contend, as narcissistic – he is suffering it would seem from a narcissistic neurosis. Such a despairing individual is unwilling to choose himself because he is unwilling to accept his weakness, imperfections and shortcomings. He holds out for something closer to the ideal that he envisions and desires for himself. Kaufmann aptly characterises such a notion of despair as an unfortunate relationship to oneself (Kaufmann 1980). This unfortunate relationship to oneself, Kierkegaard calls 'stoicism'.[2] Such a person can never become a real self for he has buried his desire for God from himself and seeks instead to become his own God in a Nietzschean fashion.

Likewise for Jung, suffering is the foundation of all psychic development; realisation of the self is simply not possible without it. Suffering through the warring of opposites is at the very center of the individuation process; it is a condition of transformation. A central tenet of Jungian theory is that all suffering has meaning. Casement contends that Jung's attitude towards human suffering is one of the defining principles of analytical psychology; it is her belief (and mine too) that Jung endeavored to understand the meaning of suffering without negating or pathologising it (Casement 1998). The same is also true of Kierkegaard. The following quotes capture and briefly summarise Jung's position on suffering:

> We have come to understand that psychic suffering is not a definitely localized, sharply delimited phenomenon, but rather the symptom of a wrong attitude assumed by the total personality. We can therefore never hope for a thorough cure from a treatment restricted to the illness itself, but only from a treatment of the personality as a whole.
>
> (1931a: par.684)

> The principal aim of psychotherapy is not to transport the patient to an impossible state of happiness, but to help him acquire steadfastness and philosophic patience in face of suffering. Life demands for its completion and fulfillment a balance between joy and sorrow. . . . Happiness is itself poisoned if the measure of suffering has not been fulfilled. Behind a neurosis there is so often concealed all the natural and necessary suffering the patient has been unwilling to bear.
>
> (1943: par.185)

Jung understood that suffering accompanies growth and development; for 'there is no birth of consciousness without pain' (1925: par.331). The acceptance of loss, suffering, change and death are necessary for being alive, for enhancing our capacity for unique adaptation, essential for potential creativity:

> I believe that misery is an intrinsic part of human life, without which we would never do anything. We always try to escape misery. We do it in a million different ways and none of them entirely succeeds. Thus I come to the conclusion that a feasible thing would be to try to find at least a way to enable people to endure the inevitable misery that is the lot of every human life. If anybody achieves at least endurance of misery, he has already accomplished an almost superhuman task.
>
> (1951–1961)

In short, it is a hard task, a 'superhuman task', but it is also a vital one. Without it, we lose our way. Kierkegaard linked this very misery to man's aloneness in the world. Indeed we seem to go to elaborate lengths in order to avoid confronting loneliness, he writes,

> in our cowardly time everything possible is done to keep away lonely thoughts by diversions and the Turkish music of loud enterprises, just as

in the American forests wild beasts are kept away by means of torches, shouting, and beating of cymbals.

(1844b)

There seems to be the need to constantly lose oneself through looking at the television for hours, socialising with friends, anything so long as its noise drowns out the silence of solitude. There is in both Kierkegaard's and Jung's writings an emphasis on development as an individual journey, conducted through a profound sense of dis-ease whereby man must wander alone to know himself. Far from being satanic or futile, suffering, misery and loneliness can be creative and fructifying. In the curious work *Psychotherapists or the Clergy*, Jung writes, 'all creativeness in the realm of the spirit as well as every psychic advance of man arises from the suffering of the soul, and the cause of the suffering is spiritual stagnation or psychic sterility' (1932a: par.497).

The mood of helplessness then is not a passive one of weakness but rather a crisis moment attained only after an arduous effort of self-recovery. As we have seen, Kierkegaard argued that there are three basic stages to adult development and that the transition from one to another is always mediated by distinctive kinds of crises. One can get stuck in the first or second of these stages and suffer a corresponding impoverishment or deformation of subjectivity. We have also seen that Jung places such a point of crisis at the midlife stage. The significance of this period of existence lies in Jung's realisation that the first half of life the development of the ego requires expansion in the world; this becomes of lesser importance in the second half allowing for what Washburn (1994) describes as the dark descent into the mysterium tremendum.[3] It is this midlife point that Washburn claims to designate the transitional period between egoic maturity and transegoic awakening. His description of this state of transegoic awakening seems to combine Kierkegaardian and Jungian elements seamlessly, he writes:

> The ego, having completed its development in early adulthood, begins to sense that something is amiss at the very (dualistic) bases of its being. This sense of dis-ease grows into an existential malaise, into as Kierkegaard put it a 'sickness unto death'. The ego begins to 'die in the world' and in doing so is brought slowly to 'the precipice of faith', that is the transegoic possibilities.

(Washburn 1994)

It is at this midlife stage that one's sense of 'I' is a matter of serious significance; this is possibly a consequence of a general erosion of an individual's uniqueness. To undertake the journey of individuation in the first half of one's life is 'almost a sin, or at least a danger' as we discussed earlier in 'Presenting Jung'. Before turning to such fundamental questions concerning one's true personality and life's meaning, one must first have achieved significant ego consolidation and have adapted socially in one's environment. At such a stage we could suggest that it is non-being that is to be faced down, as purposelessness and meaninglessness becomes an issue, along with identity, which is restricted to what one has previously been. It might come as a surprise to mention that Kierkegaard had no doubt that authenticity was very much a second half of life endeavor, for:

> child life and youth life is dream life, for the innermost thing, that which in the deepest sense is man slumbers. The child is completely turned outward, its inwardness is extraversion, and to that extent the child is wide-awake. But for a man, to be awake means to be eternally turned inward in inwardness, and so the child is dreaming, it dreams itself sensuously at one with everything, almost to the extent of confounding itself with the sense impression.

> (1848)

What I hope has been stressed throughout is that the self at this stage of self-development, for both Kierkegaard and Jung, is spurred into activity by dis-ease and rather than constituting a dead end or impasse, it represents a new mode of experience. In Kierkegaard's terms the divided self has arrived at the boundary that serves both as the furthest limit of despair and the precipice of faith. It is at this edge of despair, where all hope in the world has been lost that faith and the numinosity of Mysterium Tremendum lies; on the outermost limits of despair then, in Kierkegaard's account, one is driven to faith, which in turn can lead to the self's calling into the Mysterium Tremendum.

For both Kierkegaard and Jung this process of transformation is preceded by a point of crisis, upon which such development is founded. Jung wrote of neurosis as 'intimately bound up with the problem of our time and really represents an unsuccessful attempt on the part of the individual to solve the general problem in his own person' (1917/1926/1943: par.18). This angst originates from one's awareness of an intimate death and which Casement describes as calling us to make something of our lives. However, although I would be inclined to agree with Casement in her estimation that angst has its roots in one's awareness of death, Jung's description of neurosis as a 'general problem in his own person' is more than a kind of death anxiety; rather it seems a more basic problem related to an individual's willing and choosing of one's self. Jung's emphasis certainly seems to be on the problem of self-perception and the need for knowledge. He writes of the neurotic life as 'usually confined within too narrow a spiritual horizon', lacking in 'sufficient content, sufficient meaning' (1963). Jung offers a particularly enlightening insight into neurosis in Aion:

> When, in treating a case of neurosis, we try to supplement the inadequate attitude (or adaptedness) of the conscious mind by adding to it contents of the unconscious, our aim is to create a wider personality whose centre of gravity does not necessarily coincide with the ego, but which, on the contrary, as the patient's insights increase, may even thwart his ego-tendencies.
>
> (1951: par.297)

If the neurotic develops into a more spacious personality, then the neurosis generally disappears; it is for this reason that Jung claimed that 'the idea of development was always of the highest importance to me' (1963). It would seem to me that the process of analysis acts as a mirror to the self, allowing the facilitation and development of the chosen self. That we can understand Jung's description of the neurotic individual as essentially unable to will oneself in an honest and authentic manner would seem to be given credence in the following passage:

> I have frequently seen people become neurotic when they content themselves with inadequate or wrong answers to the questions of life. They seek position, marriage, reputation, outward success or money, and remain unhappy and neurotic even when they have attained what they were seeking.
>
> (1963)

Neurosis is always a substitute for legitimate suffering, wrote Jung. Jolande Jacobi expanded upon this describing a disingenuous suffering which one feels as senseless and false to life (Jacobi 1999). Conversely, genuine suffering carries with it the feeling of a significance later to be realised. Whilst legitimate suffering is a means to spiritual enrichment, ironically, the substitute suffering that arises when we suppress the legitimate can so often be more painful than one's legitimate suffering in the first instance. It is the process of being made conscious that designates genuine suffering from disingenuous suffering. For instance legitimate suffering becomes the platform upon which one becomes more conscious of oneself, consequently one's self-knowledge increases and this can in turn motivate action that corresponds more to what can be understood as one's true self. Pathological symptoms are therefore understood as an ungenuine suffering since they imprison in the unconscious knowledge that would broaden and deepen one's consciousness to enter. Perhaps in very simplistic terms we could classify ungenuine suffering as pain that remains unprocessed. Jung observed that 'with the decline of religious life, the neuroses grow noticeably more frequent' the result of a loss of faith in revealed faith is the 'shattering of our faith in ourselves and our self worth'; this strikes a resonance with Kierkegaard's understanding of faithlessness (1963).

There is then a similarity, an affinity, between that which Jung describes as neurosis and Kierkegaard's notion of faithlessness; both are moving towards a broader, deeper consciousness, and the sense of a meaningful existence. The search for meaning becomes an innate guiding force. Writing of the meaningless life Jung remarked 'meaninglessness inhibits fullness of life and is therefore equivalent to illness. Meaning makes a great many things endurable – perhaps everything' (1963). Furthermore, he comments:

> However far-fetched it may sound experience shows that many neuroses are caused by the fact that people blind themselves to their own religious promptings. . . . The psychologist of today ought to realize once and for all that we are no longer dealing with questions of dogma and creed. A religious attitude is an element in psychic life whose importance can hardly be overrated.
>
> (1931a: par.99)

It is the very real desire for wholeness, integration and meaningfulness in our lives that is the force driving us through the spheres of existence.

A further area of Kierkegaard's work which finds affinity with analytical psychology is his notion of sin, which, I contend, functions much like a neurosis, in that it makes accessible a self-awareness that, as discussed previously, signifies the beginning of authentic individuality. That sin provokes one's realisation of an incomplete self means it is therefore able to break down persona, allowing one's authentic self to emerge. It is the falseness of self and the inability to will the development of one's individual self that lies at the core of many neurotic difficulties. Towards the end of his life, Jung reflected that many – if not most – of the people who came to see him were not fundamentally, mentally ill per se, but rather that they were in search of a deeper meaning to their lives: 'about a third of my cases are not suffering from any clinically definable neurosis, but from the senselessness and aimlessness of their lives. I should not object if this were called the general neurosis of our age' (1931b: par.83). In short, neurosis is indicative of a lack of self-knowledge – it is understood by Jung to denote a lack of one's sense of 'I'. What is required then, is a critical self-consciousness, the development of considerable clarity about who we are. We could perhaps even go as far as describing such a lack of identity as existential identity. Existential identity is more than dissatisfaction with reality as it is, or the response of an especially sensitive individual who has not yet found a context in which to realise his or her highest aspirations. We might say that Kierkegaard poses the ultimate existential choice for the individual, the ultimate either/or: to become a self-less mass man or to become an authentic Christian individual.

Whether or not the psychological projects of Jung and Kierkegaard actually alleviate suffering is an interesting question. Jung recognised that alleviation of suffering is what the patient strives for and also the point at which the patient will disembark from the individuation journey. However, the eradication of suffering is not Jung's primary concern for the individual; for it is spiritual maturation that is of the upmost importance. As one progresses through Kierkegaard's spheres there is an increasing accumulation of suffering that necessarily reaches its maximum in the sphere of the religious. From Kierkegaard's *Works of Love* we learn that the true Christian must suffer twice:

> the truly Christian struggle always involves a double danger because there is a struggle in two places: first in the person's inner being, where he must struggle with himself, and then, when he makes progress in this struggle, outside the person with the world.
>
> (1847b)

And so rather than an alleviation of one's suffering, what we find in Kierkegaard's model is the gradual intensification of suffering upon the ascent to God. As the individual moves upwards and towards the Christian way of being in the world, 'the ingratitude, opposition, and derision' of the world will increase, and so too will one's suffering, and continually so the more earnest a Christian one becomes. This is what it means to follow in the footsteps of Christ. Christian suffering arises out of the opposition between the ways of Christ and of the world, for as the Christian renounces the world and dies to himself, he awakens the fury of the world, and suffers as if in opposition to it. The double danger then can be summarised as the following: if we love we will fare badly in the world, and good by the same token is rewarded with hate. Christianity comprises suffering; one who takes refuge from Christian suffering is simply therefore not a Christian. Kierkegaard writes, 'only in suffering can the eternal come in contact with the temporal in time; only in suffering can spirit come in contact with worldliness in worldliness' (JP: 1854).

The imitator of Christ essentially lives in opposition to the world and inevitably suffers in collision with the world. In 'The Gospel of Suffering' Kierkegaard retorts 'the truth is hated and its witnesses persecuted', so that 'the good must suffer in the world'(1847c). Again, in *Works of Love* (1847) we see his conviction that Christian love is hated: 'the good is rewarded with hate, contempt, and persecution'. According to Kierkegaard, this manner of suffering is unconditionally required for all Christians. But yet it is when an individual has sought and failed to imitate Christ that he can take refuge in grace.

Whereas, Kierkegaard forthrightly requires the individual to imitate Christ in a very literal sense, Jung himself correspondingly queries the matter thus:

> We Protestants will arrive at this problem: Are we to understand the Imitatio Christi in the sense that we should copy his life and, as it were, ape his stigmata; or in the deeper sense that we are to live our lives as truly as he lived his in its individual uniqueness? It is no easy matter to imitate the life of Christ, but it is unspeakably harder to live one's own life as Christ lived his.
>
> (1928a: par.522)

According to Jung, we are to imitate Christ with the same sacrifice and courage that he bore, but we must ultimately carry our own cross. Kierkegaard perhaps would stand accused, in Jung's eyes, of having forgotten this and out of sheer imitation of Christ failed to realise his own individual, highest meaning. We truly imitate Christ by understanding exactly what is meant by 'the kingdom of heaven is within you'. Whilst Jung treats Christ as an exemplar of individuation, his understanding comes with the added proviso of following one's own path. His *imitatio Christi* does not therefore mean that we are to identify ourselves with the figure of Christ but rather to become Christ-like in our striving to find our own way to an inner spiritual source that is wholly one's own.

Whilst it is unclear whether a Kierkegaardian faith undoubtedly leads the individual away from despair, I think we can assume that there is indeed an absence of despair when the self is the willful participant in the ideal relationship between the infinite creator and creature: so as 'in relating itself to itself and in willing to be itself, the self rests transparently in the power that established it'. To despair is to lack the eternal – it is the refusal to have 'undergone the change of eternity through duty's shall. . . . [It] is not therefore, the loss of the beloved – that is unhappiness, pain, suffering' (1847b). Kierkegaard offers no cure for suffering; he does not seek to relieve us of our sufferings but to encourage the Christian individual to muster the courage to endure genuine religious suffering. Indeed, for Kierkegaard, that we must endure affliction is 'a joyful thought', for in the depths of sorrow the man of faith will find joy:

> When affliction is the way, then is this the joy: that it is hence immediately clear to the sufferer, and that he immediately knows definitely what the task is, so he does not need to use any time or waste his strength, in reflecting whether the task should not be different. . . . Is it not then a joyful thought that it is true that affliction is the way? For then it is indeed immediately clear what the task is? Doubt wishes to make the

sufferer wonder if it might not still be possible for the affliction to be away, and he still continue to walk on the same way – without affliction. But if affliction is the way, then it is indeed impossible for it to be taken away, and the way will still remain the same.

(1847a)

Notes

1 'The process of coming to terms with the unconscious is a true labor, a work which involves both action and suffering. It has been named the "transcendent function" because it represents a function based on real and "imaginary," or rational and irrational, data, thus bridging the yawning between conscious and unconscious. It is a natural process, a manifestation of the energy that springs from tensions of opposites' (1929:par.121).
2 'If a generic name for this despair [of defiance] is wanted, it could be called stoicism, but understood as not referring only to this sect' (1849a).
3 Orginally Otto used the term *mysterium tremendum* to describe the rapturous quality of the numinous. He felt that this term could most accurately describe the simultaneous mystery and awefulness of the numen. Otto's *mysterium tremendum* appealed to Jung who borrowed and broadened the term to capture the character of the 'primitive' religious experience.

Chapter 11

Authenticity

The creation of one's genuine self

As previously conceded neither Kierkegaard nor Jung spoke literally in terms of authenticity or false as opposed to 'true' self; however, that there are such inauthentic ways to exist which carry pathological implications makes the use of such terms relevant and useful. It would certainly seem that Kierkegaard and Jung approach the idea of authenticity in very similar ways. We can deduce from their projects three key similarities – 1. That it is possible to assume an identity which is inauthentic, or not one's own. 2. That we allow others to construct our identities through defining ourselves according to the recognition we gain from them. 3). That one must move to make one's identity more authentic. In this section we will discern in Kierkegaard's psychological philosophy the familiar Jungian themes of psychic harmony, one-sidedness and over-identification.

Conflict is at the core of Kierkegaard's framework and much like the development of personality within Jung's psychology, spiritual development requires the reduction of intrapsychic conflict. Regardless of whether we are conscious of the fact, we are in despair for we have a double nature, comprised of the infinite and the finite, the temporal and the eternal. Whilst Kierkegaard posits a unifying dialectical movement prompting one's 'leap' from one sphere to another, Jung speaks of a self that possesses energy that is 'manifested in the almost irresistible compulsion and urge to become what one is' (1951: par.634). This self with the capacity for unifying parts of the personality is the common engine fueling one's progression to self-reflection, through to personal responsibility and finally personal meaning. The idea that through one's self-awareness the individual can change the nature of his or her existence is one that closely draws Jung and Kierkegaard together.

Kierkegaard and Jung explain God in terms of completion rather than perfection. Jung extends his concept of numinosity beyond moral perfection to human wholeness. Likewise, Kierkegaard sets us a clear teleological purpose of the movement towards a personal whole with ethical connotations. Furthermore, for Jung and Kierkegaard, we are able to accept ourselves by becoming what we genuinely are. What we are according to Kierkegaard are individuals with the potential of receiving God's grace and authentic faith.

108 Authenticity: creation of genuine self

This is achieved through overcoming and acts of the will. 'The chief thing in life', writes Kierkegaard, is to 'win yourself, acquire your own self' (1843a). There is, as we have seen, an important shift from the traditional meaning of truth to one's quest for personal truthfulness. He, who hides himself from his transcendence, alienates himself from genuine selfhood. In both Kierkegaard's and Jung's accounts, wholeness replaces the ideal of perfection and thereby becomes the very hallmark of the healthy personality. A return to a previous original and genuine state of self is characteristic of many thinkers on authenticity.[1] This authentic return is expressed by Kierkegaard through the notion of a corrective, to the return of the early Christian Church. For Jung psychological maturity requires the development of one's shadow – that those parts opposed to our self-styled personality be integrated. Becoming oneself is more than the coming into possession of self-knowledge and resting in self-acceptance. An important aspect in becoming oneself is overcoming one's propensity to self-deceive; it is then a process of the shedding of a false sense of self, facing one's self-deceptions and embracing the unfamiliar and unwelcome aspects of self. This is very much the rationale behind both Kierkegaard's and Jung's call for us to be both creator and the created.

Philosophers, poets, psychoanalysts and writers have all toiled with the idea that there is within us a shadowy Mr. Hyde character. According to Jungian theory, this dark side, the stranger within, is part of ourselves that we fail to see or know. The shadow is a readily dismissed part of us, that which we do not wish to acknowledge. But as well as containing all that we reject in our conscious life, it also is a container of our basic animal nature. Robert Bly offers us a splendid description of one's shadow as a bag that we spend the first 20 years of our life deciding what parts of our self to put in, whilst the rest of our life is consumed with trying to get them out again (Bly 2009). The refusal to deal with the presence of shadow within the personality results in depression, ennui, inner emptiness and the inability to establish mutuality in relationships. When we take our human potential for evil out of the equation and repress the shadow, we lose our capacity for authentic wholeness and selfhood: 'to confront a person with his shadow is to show him his own light. . . . Anyone who perceives his shadow and his light simultaneously sees himself from two sides and thus gets in the middle' (1959: par.872).

Whilst Kierkegaard does not concern himself with shadow projection as such, he does astutely recognise that within every individual there is a shadowy element that prevents us from revealing aspects of ourselves:

> In every person there is something that up to a point hinders him from becoming completely transparent to himself, and this can be the case to such a high degree, he can be so inexplicably intertwined in the life-relations that lie beyond him, that he cannot open himself. But the

person who can scarcely open himself cannot love, and the person who cannot love is the unhappiest of all.

(1843a)

If we allow ourselves to reveal to others our shadow self, we make ourselves vulnerable. According to Kierkegaard, we choose to shrink from revelation because of this very awareness and so the individual has a propensity towards evading authenticity. In 1845, he writes in his journal:

> every man shrinks from becoming personality, from standing face to face with others as a personality; he shrinks from it because he knows that doing so makes it possible for the others to take aim at him. We shrink from being revealed; therefore we live, if not in utter darkness, then in twilight, hoaxes, the impersonal. But Christianity, which knows the truth, know that it means: revelation. That is why Christianity points so decisively at being a personality.

Genuine selfhood depends on a conscious relation to God; however, the individual may substitute a relation to what is less than God:

> And what infinite reality the self gains by being conscious of existing before God, by becoming a human self whose criterion is God! A cattleman who (if this were possible) is a self directly before his cattle is a very low self, and similarly, a master who is a self directly before his slaves is actually no self – for in both cases a criterion is lacking . . . but what an infinite accent falls on the self by having God as the criterion!

(1849)

We cannot possess or develop a strong sense of narrative unity in our life by occupying social roles alone. Purity of heart is to will one thing, but this one thing cannot be the social good, it can only be the eternal – for only the eternal can give life meaning. In the following passage Kierkegaard associates this deepening and broadening of self as something really very torturous:

> One is not tempted to pity you but rather to wish that some day the circumstances of your life may tighten upon you the screws in its rack and compel you to come out with what really dwells in you; that they may begin the sharper inquisition of the rack which cannot be beguiled by nonsense and witticisms . . . do you not know that there comes a midnight hour when everyone has to throw off his mask? Do you believe you can slip away a little before midnight in order to avoid this? Or are you not terrified by it?

(1843a)

110 Authenticity: creation of genuine self

The midnight hour that Kierkegaard refers to is the hour of one's death and when this time comes, one's mask will be thrown aside and man will be revealed for who he has been. Kierkegaard's mask is comparable to Jung's concept of persona in that it captures the sense in which an individual hides and disguises his 'true' self, whilst also emphasising its role in one's relationships with the outside world. It is interesting to note that Jung chose the term persona because it is the Latin word for 'the masks worn by actors in antiquity' (1921: par.800). According to Kierkegaard, he whose life is defined by its relation to others, he who has effectively lived for others will find that in this moment when he finally stands alone that he is no one, that beneath the mask there is nothing. This passage serves also to reflect Kierkegaard's belief that suffering is the gateway to salvation; 'the circumstances of your life may tighten upon you the screws in its rack' – the path to self-realisation is indeed a torturous one. Self-acceptance is not an easy task, nor is it something to be taken for granted. Kierkegaard understood this all too well. We make ourselves victims of false consciousness/selfhood when we fail to acknowledge our own nature, usually the result of fear. Kierkegaard remarks, 'there is nothing with which every man is so afraid as getting to know how enormously much he is capable of doing and becoming' (JP: 1854).

In Kierkegaard's *Either/Or*, the self is portrayed as that which gives unity to an individual; it is 'the unifying power of the personality'; 'the inmost and holiest thing of all'. The problem of selfhood in relation to personal existence as Kierkegaard views it can be understood in terms of integration. Facing existential choice brings the self into existence, when we decisively choose to make choices we integrate the dissociated self – to choose, integrates – 'the choice permeates everything and transforms it'. In his analysis of despair that became *Sickness Unto Death*, Kierkegaard expands his concept of sin, developing a theory of self-deception, which can be seen as a precursor to theories of the unconscious developed by Jung. He believed that truth existed only so far as the individual produces it in action. Thus what is of importance is 'not to cultivate one's mind but to mature one's personality', and this can only be achieved asserts Kierkegaard, through 'decisiveness of spirit . . . self-direction by decision' (1843a). Each moment brings the necessity of choice, and the existing individual is always a learner in the sense that he is always striving towards self-knowledge. Kierkegaard's goal is not knowledge in the traditional sense of the accumulation of wisdom, but of self-knowledge that lends itself to the maturity and development of the personality to its highest potentiality.[2] This can never be attained except as a man chooses to be himself, and if 'another man choose for him a man loses himself', 'not to will deeply and sincerely is a sin and the mother of all sins' (1843a). Human sinfulness appears in Kierkegaard's thought primarily in the phenomenon of self-deception; it becomes a self-defeating force lying within our inner selves. Although Kierkegaard and Jung assert we are spiritual beings made for a relation with God, we all too often rebel against this relationship. Our conscious awareness is often concerned with more superficial relations to further our own one-sided agendas; we all too readily give ourselves over to blind illusions and consequent self-deceptions. This is the reason why individuals are constantly resisting their own true happiness and fighting against their own best interests. Essential in Kierkegaard's theory of development is that a man should choose to be himself. He who restlessly and desperately does not want to be the self he is runs the very real risk of losing himself entirely:

> I have seen men in real life who so long deceived others that at last their true nature could not reveal itself; I have seen men who played hide and seek so long that at last in madness they disgustingly obtruded upon others their secret thoughts which hitherto they had proudly concealed. Or can you think of anything more frightful than it might end with your nature being resolved into a multiplicity, that you really might become many, become, like those unhappy demoniacs, a legion, and you thus would lose the inmost and holiest thing of all in a man, the unifying power of personality?
>
> (1843a)

To despair is to sin and to sin is despair; despair is then the quintessential manifestation of sin. All despair is despair of the self, an expression of one's failure to be the true self for: 'sin is: before God, or with the conception of God, in despair not to will to be oneself, or in despair to will to be oneself', to rebel in such a fashion is to commit oneself to a life of despair (1849). There are two ways in which we may fail the self; we can fail to become the self which God has created – a despair in weakness, or we can attempt to be the self of our own choosing, of our own creation – despair of defiance. Kierkegaard seemingly distinguishes between self-deception, a despair that is essentially passive and self-creation, a despair that is altogether more active. To attempt to self-style, to create one's self is a rebellious and pride-filled attempt at autonomy, since it causes a break in the God relationship and this break becomes psychologically expressed as despair. For Kierkegaard genuine selfhood requires that one stand before God, accepting the self that he is as God given and embracing the task that God has set him. The self therefore that is out of relation to God is not a genuine self; as Judge William of *Either/Or* declares, 'I choose myself; I do not create myself.' The self I should become is viewed as God given; my choice is only to become or not to become what I should be. Additionally we cannot choose the values to which we will commit ourselves; our own inventions could never have this sort of authority over us. Rather, the values must come from outside of ourselves; in short, they must be transcendent:

> The self in despair . . . constantly relates itself to itself only by way of imaginary constructions, no matter what it undertakes, however

vast, however amazing, however perseveringly pursued. It recognizes no power over itself; therefore it basically lacks earnestness and can conjure forth only an appearance of earnestness, even when it gives its utmost attention to its imaginary constructions.

(1849)

Those who fail to establish this relation fail to be themselves in the fullest sense of being oneself. For instance, Kierkegaard's aesthete is concerned with the creation of circumstances for the maximum derivation of pleasure. He is not in the least bit consumed therefore with the need to form his own self; he does not choose himself and therefore he cannot become himself in the fullest sense of Kierkegaard's understanding of true selfhood. As the Judge claims, 'he is immediately what he is' (1843a). What perhaps most significantly characterises this sphere of existence is the absolute non-commitment to anything; man's innate need for transcendence and meaningfulness is therefore repressed. Eventually aesthetic enjoyment will give way to a feeling of estrangement, despair and melancholy, leaving the individual in what Jung refers to as a neurotic state. If the individual, having exhausted and grown dissatisfied with the aesthetic mode of existence should turn to the ethical sphere, he soon finds he is no better off as far as authenticity is concerned. Yet with regards to authenticity one can certainly detect in the ethical sphere an attitude of superiority, an attitude that claims a sincerity of intention and commitment to one object, the good. Regardless of how passionate a commitment one makes to realise high ethical standards, the ethically orientated individual is by his very nature, and because of the ideality of ethics, doomed to fail. And so the individual is confronted by the impossibility of becoming what he ought to be. Deep in despair this individual comes to assume the notion of original sin; hence Kierkegaard's claim that the 'the ethical sphere is a transitional sphere', as it leads one to the religious (1845). When the individual has become conscious of sin, and has negated the possibility of realising the ethical requirement in existence, self-reflection is no longer required since one has become self. With sin comes the possibility of existing as a Christian – 'only the agony of the consciousness of sin can explain the fact a person will submit to this radical cure' (JP: 1849). The individual goes forward in existence precisely by penetrating backward into the self to realise his or her sinfulness. Consciousness of sin brings about a complete alteration of self, so as the existing individual becomes something other than whom he was before. By relating to something that transcends our self we are better able to relate to ourselves. God, in Kierkegaard's account, is the ontological foundation of the self. If we want to become our true selves, we must give ourselves to God:

> Every human existence that is not conscious of itself as spirit or conscious of itself before God as spirit, every human existence that does

not rest transparently in God, but vaguely rests in or merges in some abstract universality (state, nation, etc.) or, in the dark about his self, regards his capacities merely as powers to produce without becoming deeply aware of their source, regards his self, if it is to have intrinsic meaning, as an indefinable something – every such existence, whatever it achieves, be it most amazing, whatever it explains, be it the whole of existence, however intensively it enjoys life aesthetically – every such existence is despair.

(1849)

Faith becomes a matter of being oneself before God and as we have seen to become one's self one must properly relate to God. It is an inner disposition whereby 'the self in being itself and in willing to be itself rests transparently in God' (1849). Resting transparently conjures forth various adjectives; clarity, honesty, openness – might we then speculate that Kierkegaard understood it to be a relationship where nothing is hidden, in terms of relating to another, a perfect honest understanding.[3] Kierkegaard here describes authentic selfhood beautifully:

When all has become still about a man, solemn as a starry night when the skies are clear, when the soul, oblivious of the world, is alone with itself and confronted, not by some distinguished person, but by the eternal power itself. Or rather, it receives itself as something given to it. Then the soul has seen the highest, that which no mortal eye can see, and which can never again be forgotten, then the personality receives the accolade which knights it for eternity. The man who passes through such an experience does not become other than he was before; he becomes himself. As an heir, even were his inheritance the whole world, has nothing of his own so long as he is not of age, so the richest personality is nothing, till it has chosen itself, while on the other hand the poorest personality is everything, when once it has chosen itself. For the great thing is not that one is this or that, but that one is oneself; and that is in every man's power, if he will.

(1843a)

True Christianity is thus a way of being in truth before God, by following Jesus in self-denial, sacrifice and suffering. Kierkegaard was adamant about his own Christian deficiency: 'For my part I do not call myself a 'Christian' (thus keeping the ideal free), but I am able to make it evident that the others are still less than I' (quoted in Bretall 1947). Kierkegaard's strategy was to act as a corrective to the Hegelian rationalism of his day. A note written four years before his death summarises the aims and objectives of his lifetime philosophising: 'My task has continually been to provide the existential corrective by poetically presenting the ideals and inciting people' (JP: 1851).

114 Authenticity: creation of genuine self

Kierkegaard wished to provide this corrective influence to an age that had one-sidedly become one of understanding and reflection, without passion; for 'passion is the real thing, the real measure of man's power. And the age in which we live is wretched, because it is without passion' (JP: 1841). Jung might have viewed this as admirable had Kierkegaard not been a figure who elicited such an emotionally charged negative response from him – a response, I claim, that is most bizarre, given the strong overlaps that I have identified in their projects. Just as Kierkegaard sought to inspire the authentic pathos of faith in those 'who passionately want to be what they ought to be', Jung addresses himself to those who could no longer find their spiritual home within traditional religion:

> In actual life it requires the greatest art to be simple, and so acceptance of oneself is the essence of the moral problem and the acid test of one's whole outlook on life. That I feed the beggar, that I forgive an insult, that I love my enemy in the name of Christ – all these are undoubtedly great virtues. What I do unto the least of my brethren, that I do unto Christ. But what if I should discover that the least amongst them all, the poorest of all beggars, the most impudent of all offenders, yea the very fiend himself – that these are within me, and that I myself am the enemy who must be loved – what then? Then, as a rule, the whole truth of Christianity is reversed: there is then no more talk of love and long-suffering; we say to the brother within us 'Raca,' and condemn and rage against ourselves. We hide him from the world, we deny ever having met this least among the lowly in ourselves, and had it been God himself who drew near to us in this despicable form, we should have denied him a thousand times before a single cock had crowed.
>
> (1932a: par.519–520)

Jung is here perhaps implying that it is often easier for the Christian to accept others than to accept himself. James Hillman interprets Jung's cure as a paradox requiring that 'the moral recognition that these parts of me are burdensome and intolerable and must change and be reconciled with 'the loving laughing acceptance which takes them just as they are, joyfully, forever' (Hilman 1994). What is needed it seems is a loving acceptance of our inferiorities. Revelation says Jung; 'is an opening of the depths of the human soul, a "laying bare", a psychological mode pure and simple, which says nothing about what else it could be. That lies outside the bounds of science' (1938/1940: par.127). This 'laying bare' strikes a chord with Kierkegaard's 'resting transparently'. Although Jung's understanding of revelation is a psychologically immanent interaction of the unconscious with the conscious via the psyche, he does ground man's depths and identity in a divine reality. Frank Bockus (1990) interprets Jung's understanding of God as a force that seeks to become embodied in one's experience, to be incarnated in the world, so as:

> When we know our own depths, our inherent grounding in the divine reality, God becomes effectually and concretely present in human affairs and human experience. Modern individuals must take their potential for self-realization with absolute moral seriousness. Alienated from their own depths, they are alienated from God. And alienated from God, they are estranged from themselves.
>
> (Bockus 1990)

As we saw in the previous chapter, the experience of neurosis often marks the first step in individuation. Jung describes neurosis as 'the suffering of a soul that has not discovered its meaning', 'one-sided development' and also an 'inner cleavage' that arises from the feeling of self-division; of two persons at war with one another (1932a: par.497). Jung never committed himself to a strict definition of neurosis and I suspect this was the result of a recognition that neurosis can appear in many guises. Although he did consistently emphasise the positive aspects and potentiality of neurosis:

> A neurosis is by no means a negative thing, it is also something positive. Only a soulless rationalism reinforced by a narrow materialistic outlook could possibly have overlooked this fact. In reality the neurosis contains the patient's psyche, or at least an essential part of it.
>
> (1934: par.355)

And:

> We should not try to 'get rid' of a neurosis, but rather to experience what it means, what it has to teach, what its purpose is. We should even learn to be thankful for it, otherwise we pass it by and miss the opportunity of getting to know ourselves as we really are. A neurosis is truly removed only when it has removed the false attitude of the ego. We do not cure it – it cures us.
>
> (1932a: par.361)

Contained in this self-division, this 'inner antithesis' is the energy needed to go forward in one's psychological life. Only by accepting and understanding the neurosis can one avoid 'stagnation', 'rigidity', and 'neurotic subterfuge'. Neurosis or any personal suffering for that matter, can open the door to psychological wholeness; by taking responsibility for one's psychological conflict a person is able to develop a greater sense of integrity. Idealising reflections of oneself and a defensive denial of one's darker motives are the *via regia* of the persona. Perhaps the most important aspect of neurosis is its ability to initiate the breakdown of the persona – which at one and the same time can be considered the breakdown of one's inauthenticity. Jung felt that the persona tended to be inauthentic, that it was not in tune with one's inner self. His description of the persona as a mask would certainly seem to confirm this: 'The persona is that which in reality one is not, but which oneself as well as others think one is'(1940/1950: par.221). Furthermore,

> It is, as its name implies, only a mask of the collective psyche, a mask that feigns individuality, making others and oneself believe that one is individual, whereas one is simply acting a role through which the collective psyche speaks. . . . Fundamentally the persona is nothing real: it is a compromise between individual and society as to what man should appear to be.
>
> (1929a: par.245f)

The persona is a defensive structure that permits people to function as individuals prior to understanding (of being aware of) motives, intentions, responsibility, and other aspects of psychological individuality. When the persona is excessively rigid or defensive, the shadow is split off from conscious identity, inaccessible to ordinary awareness; consequently the persona develops into a pathological false self, leaving the shadow entirely out of awareness. We might define the Jungian false self as an identification with persona, or perhaps persona when it functions pathologically. The individual loses authenticity when overinvested in his/her role; Jung denotes this particular inauthenticity of self, one-sidedness. He observed many people who, to their detriment, had identified with their persona, believing themselves to be nothing more than a social position or some other external professional achievement. Persona identification was frequently at the roots of the very psychological troubles that brought patients into his consulting room. Kierkegaard's understanding of despair that arises in response to disequilibrium can be understood as akin to Jung's understanding of one-sidedness. For each despair is characterised by the lack of its opposite, when possibility is not balanced by necessity the self becomes lost in fantasy. However, if necessity is not balanced by possibility then the self becomes lost in a despairing fatalism:

> Possibility and necessity are equally essential to becoming (and the self has the task of becoming itself in freedom). Possibility and necessity belong to the self just as do infinitude and finitude. A self that has no possibility is in despair, and likewise a self that has no necessity.
>
> (1849)

Authenticity: creation of genuine self   117

'Personhood', writes Kierkegaard,

> is a synthesis of possibility and necessity. Its continued existing is like breathing (respiration), which is inhaling and exhaling. The self of the determinist cannot breathe, for it is impossible to breathe necessity exclusively, because that would utterly suffocate a person's self.
>
> (1849)

The despair of necessity is a result of too little possibility and not of too much necessity; we have then a very balanced assessment of despair and personhood that asserts that neither one's immanence nor transcendence should be subordinated to the other. It is possible to view in Kierkegaard's example of the cattleman Jung's theory of over-identification. There is a tendency for those who are over-identified with their social roles to overinvest in the impression they are making on the outside world. In the example Kierkegaard draws upon, this overinvestment in an individual's social role imparts a sense of superiority to one's identity which serves to degrade the self: 'a cattleman who (if this were possible) is a self directly before his cattle is a very low self, and similarly, a slave-owner who is a self directly before his slaves is no self – for in both cases a criterion is lacking' (1849). To ground one's sense of identity in one's social role consequently lacks genuine selfhood.

False or inauthentic existence is the source of psychological conflict; the resignation of this sense of self is thereby required for analytic solution. It would certainly seem to be the case that Jungian analysis involves a continual stripping away of the false components of the analysand's self, along with the motivations behind them. Although both Kierkegaard and Jung focus on the predominately inward: passionately committing themselves to the development of personality to its highest potentiality, Jung alone concerns himself with the archetypical nature of psychical experience. However, though Kierkegaard does not speak in such archetypal terms, his emphasis on the subjective could be said to have its roots in an understanding of the religious attitude that resides in man's deepest depths:

> That was what I lacked in order to be able to lead a complete human life and not merely one of understanding, so that I should not, in consequence, base the development of my thought upon – well, something that is called objective – something that is in any case not my own. But upon something which grows together with the deepest roots of my life.
>
> (JP: 1835)

Kierkegaard views the self as a synthesis of immanence and transcendence, the temporal and eternal – authentic selfhood is to be sought through the

118 Authenticity: creation of genuine self

reconciliation of these conflicting polarities. It is God as that which each self is ultimately grounded upon which is capable of holding these conflicting impulses towards transcendence and immanence in check. Consequently, neither one's sense of transcendence nor immanence can alone define one's existence, when what is required is a stable synthesis between the two. Only by being drawn into a defining commitment, can we achieve that which, while in despair, looked impossible; namely, that immanence and transcendence reinforce each other, so that the more you manifest one, the more you manifest the other (Dreyfus 2001). Self-consciousness is decisive with regard to the self. The more consciousness, the more self; the more consciousness, the more will; the more will, the more self. The person who has no will at all is not a self – Kierkegaardian selfhood is not then an all or nothing (an either/or) affair. The more conscious one is of oneself, the more self one has. There needs to be a balance in the makeup of self between that which is self-styled and that which is accepted as God given. The synthesis is then both a movement of self-transcendence and self-acceptance.

The self that wills to become authentic through becoming transparent before God, receives itself as the gift of divine acceptance. To know God deeper, we must know self deeper. Self-awareness/self-knowledge becomes a prerequisite to this process, whereby we become more authentic through becoming transparent before God. It is when we cultivate our awareness of our self that we arrive at despair: 'he who despairs finds the eternal man', therefore despair is the 'first real choice of the personality' (1843a). The healthy self is free from despair, when precisely by having despaired, it rests transparently in God: 'your emptiness can be transformed into a fertile readiness. Choose despair' (1843a). It is an immanent transformation – choosing to despair whilst being in despair, to despair despairingly, is the double despair that leads to one's choosing the absolute. However, Kierkegaard's conception of the authentic self revolves around more than self-knowledge, although the Socratic person, he claims, does know himself; his

> Knowledge is not mere contemplation (for with that the individual is determined by his necessity), it is a reflection upon himself which itself is an action; and therefore I have deliberately preferred to use the expression 'choose oneself' instead of know oneself. So when the individual knows himself he is not through; on the contrary, this knowledge is in the highest degree fruitful, and from it precedes the true individual.
>
> (1843a)

If we take self-knowledge to be the ultimate goal of Kierkegaard's corpus we grossly misunderstand his earnest attempt to awaken within the individual his capacity for religious passion. This important point is perhaps best expressed in the following except from his prayers:

> Father in Heaven! What are we without You! What is all that we know, vast accumulation though it be, but a chipped fragment if we do not know You! What is all our striving, could it ever encompass a world, but a half-finished work if we do not know You: You the One, who is one thing and who is all!
>
> (Moore 1999)

As we have seen authentic existence, the goal of life is a synthesis of the temporal and the eternal; yet one's ultimate expression of his individual existence through such a synthesis depends upon 'the moment of passion' which by its nature, Kierkegaard asserts, can only be fleeting:

> Only momentarily can a particular individual, existing, be in a unity of the infinite and the finite that transcends existing. This instant is the moment of passion. . . . In passion, the existing subject is infinitized in the eternity of imagination and yet is also most definitely himself.
>
> (1846a)

Kierkegaard's conceptions of subjectivity and inwardness are intrinsically related to his understanding of what it is to be a Christian. Christianity is not external or objective, it is a matter of the heart and the mind, an inward becoming, becoming more like Christ: 'Christianity wants above all to make the infinite change (which is the hidden man of inwardness oriented in inwardness towards the God-relationship' (1847b). Authentic religion, according to Kierkegaard, has everything to do with passion, it was his observation that too many individuals superficially take a little out of religion, and then dispassionately 'have religion'. Authenticity is a function of passion; to be authentic an object must arouse the greatest possible passion. For Kierkegaard this object can only be God. He writes, the 'authentically human factor is passion' (1843b); therefore human wholeness is constituted in the greatest possible energy: passion – the perfect expression of existence. Passion reaffirms subjectivity as the true core of individual existence; importantly it is an inward action that involves the transformation of one's entire existence. And whilst Kierkegaard views self-knowledge as an active reflection, rather than passive reflection, it remains that authentic religion and authentic selfhood requires not self-knowledge but passion. Of course subjective reflection plunges one into inwardness, which in turn culminates in passion, and to this extent self-knowledge becomes a means to a more passionate ends. It is the active moment of passion that is regarded as the source of free action. One's passionate inwardness cannot be acquired in thought, through speculation, divine or otherwise, but by one's actions. The emphasis is always for Kierkegaard in one's actions. Truth, he said, 'exists for the particular individual only so far as he for himself produces it in action' (1844b). The important thing is 'not to cultivate one's mind but to mature one's personality' (1843a), and this is achieved through decisiveness of the spirit. One does not know oneself until one exercises freedom, the freedom of choice to 'decide' who one is. One's subjective truth is to become actualised; it is of little interest to Kierkegaard should one think himself an authentic, loyal follower of faith if his actions are contrary to this. It is only in inwardness that a new self can be born. To choose oneself becomes the repeated refrain throughout *Either/Or*. Wilhelm wrote to the young aesthete, 'you are not to give birth to somebody else – you are simply to give birth to yourself'. At the moment of choice, the self exercises its fundamental freedom – to be or not to be and to choose non-being, is to retreat into unfreedom. Similarly, Jung's advice to us is to descend into the shadowy depths of the soul and become both creator and created. He thus writes:

> To live oneself means: to be one's own task. Never say that it is a pleasure to live oneself. It will be no joy but a long suffering, since you must become your own creator. If you want to create yourself, then you do not begin with the best and the highest, but with the worst and the deepest. Therefore say that you are reluctant to live yourself. The flowing together of the stream of life is not joy but pain, since it is power against power, guilt, and shatters the sanctified.
>
> (2009)

Furthermore, he claims 'the time has come when each must do his own work of redemption. Mankind has grown older and a new month has begun' (2009). Jung's work can be considered redemptive on different levels. Within my research I have concentrated on the restoration of the culturally severed tie between personal and sacred experience, and on one's willingness to take this material as it presents itself instead of reducing it to trauma or biology. I do believe that Jung's individuation, in its demand that one becomes what one really is, is ultimately redemptive: it requires that we take the burden of salvation upon ourselves. Rebirth it would seem is connected with redemption, which necessarily involves the overcoming of the opposing forces of life and death. Consequently, those Gods that die and rise are our redeemer Gods or Gods of rebirth. Jung writes of rebirth in a lecture delivered at the Eranos conference in 1939, stating that it is a purely psychic affair, having two roots: knowledge of the transcendental element in life and the experience of a change in man's own being (terms that echo Kierkegaard's religious psychology). The struggle for rebirth is age old, it voices not only man's wish for a renewal of life in the hereafter but of transformation in the here and now. Nor is it restricted to Christianity

Authenticity: creation of genuine self 121

for the theme of dying and rising again appears in all religions. Individuation is more than just a search for greater wholeness; it is the natural road to rebirth, a constant reminder of one's need for redemption that emanates from our troubling experiences of inner disunity.

The task of self-investigation becomes in Kierkegaard and Jung's hands something altogether bigger. Whilst the clash of opposing forces in Kierkegaard's model find resolution in God, for Jung, the diverse elements of the personality and the clash of opposites are resolved by a transcendent aspect that he calls the 'Self'. He describes this self as the God within. Individuation can then be viewed as the proper relation to this God within. It is to orientate oneself to a wider perspective to life – a God's – eyeview of the world, if you like, that transcends the limited and one-sided prejudice of the ego and its persona. Furthermore, the emergence of symbols in Jung's model can be understood as a gift from God – in essence, an experience of grace:

> It is a fact that symbols, by their very nature, can so unite the opposites that these no longer diverge or clash, but mutually supplement one another and give meaningful shape to life. Once that has been experienced, the ambivalence in the image of a nature-God or creator-God ceases to present difficulties.
>
> (1963)

It is of no small significance that the Holy Spirit was Jung's archetypal symbol of reconciliation: 'an autonomous psychic happening, a hush that follows the storm, a reconciling light in the darkness of mind . . . secretly bringing order into chaos' (1942/1948: par.260). I suspect it is all too easy to underestimate the importance of such an obviously religious concept in the midst of Jung's works; however, I cannot help but think it is the very idea of spirit that forms the basis of such conclusions as 'the sole purpose of human existence is to kindle a light in the darkness of mere being' (1963). The Holy Spirit affects a balance between the opposites paving the way for one's resurrection and incarnation into an authentic self. Jung's notion of authenticity means becoming an individual, and, in so far as individuality embraces our innermost self, we could rightly say of his authenticity that it necessitates a coming to selfhood, a self-realisation. Central to such a process is self-reflection. Emphasising the importance of a reflective life, Jung wrote: 'If ever there was a time when self-reflection was the absolutely necessary and only right thing, it is now, in our present catastrophic epoch' (1917/1926/1943: preface). There is a sense that self-reflection for Jung and Kierkegaard is a fundamentally spiritual act towards self-consciousness. 'God becomes manifest in the human act of reflection' (1942/1948: par.238), wrote Jung, and this can be compared to Kierkegaard's understanding of the genuine Christian – he who has the potential to unleash those powers of transformation, whether these be in the archetypal realm or a transcendental sphere, works toward finding God and ultimately attaining psychic health.

James Hillman (1983) accords to Jung's psychological method, the Socratic overtones of 'know thyself'. He states that to know thyself in a Jungian fashion means to open oneself and listen, to know and discern daemons. It is, writes Hillman 'its own end and has no end. It is a paradoxical hermetic art that is both goal directed and without end'. Similarly, Eva Maria Simms (2004), views 'know thyself' to be Jung's motto. In addition, Colin Wilson (1988) also regarded 'know thyself' to be the guiding principle of Jung's life work. However, whilst self-awareness plays a key role in the descent into one's psyche and with it the scrutinising of one's unconscious, individuation does not rest in one's self-knowledge but in one's sense of wholeness: the becoming of one's self. Only when wholeness is attained shall we have found God. Individuation cannot therefore have as its highest goal self-knowledge. Self-knowledge is for Jung, like Kierkegaard, a secondary factor: a means to the greater end – the attainment of wholeness, the ultimate goal of life. Furthermore, individuation is only complete when one's life has attained the divine, and is in relationship with God. Jung's psychology calls us to become our authentic self, and this carries with it an emphasis to serve one's community with purpose and meaning. Emphasis is on becoming a 'greater personality'. The self is in a constant state of becoming. It is not a static entity; therefore it is not a case of know thyself, but rather become thyself.

To emphasise the extent to which the Christian life is a process Kierkegaard speaks of himself as one who is in the process of becoming a Christian. Whilst Jung likewise wrote, 'no one is justified in boasting that he has fully accepted himself' 1932a: par.521). In the process of becoming there is no final stage, just a succession of superseding selves and so our understanding of ourselves is never the final word on the subject. In this becoming a self, before God, self-knowledge and knowledge of the divine, for Jung and Kierkegaard becomes irrevocably entwined within one another. Goethe (1829) wittily responded to the Socratic injunction to know oneself, 'if I knew myself I would run away' (Hoggart 1995). Warning of a false tranquility that results from pure contemplation, Goethe wrote:

> Here I confess that the great and so high-sounding task, 'know thyself!' has always appeared suspect to me, the ploy of secretly allied priests who wanted to confuse man by making unattainable demands on him, and to lead him away from activity directed at the outer world toward false inner tranquility.
>
> (Beebe 2012)

And both Kierkegaard and Jung would certainly concur in the assertion that pure contemplation, without active engagement, results in the disunity between knowledge and activity. The solely contemplative existence can only, according to Jung's interpretation of authenticity, give rise to a one-sided personality. Similarly, this fundamental lack of correspondence between one's inwardness and one's actions fails to meet Kierkegaard's understanding of truth. Goethe's fear of a false inner tranquility, to my mind at least, finds resonance in the booming and ever so lucrative self-help culture with its mantra of accept your self. This kind of blind self-acceptance gives a dangerous autonomy to the self, and so there is a propensity towards saying the self one is, is fine and complete as it is – regardless of one's actions that may be to the contrary. This is a self-knowledge without the criterion of judgement. Kierkegaard and Jung are able to relieve such fears for at the core of their understanding of authenticity is the very basic truth that what one does either contributes or detracts from the fulfillment of one's self. Ultimately, the choices we make and our approach to life is what matters.

The importance of the process of decision making and responsibility cannot be over-estimated in Kierkegaard's thought. The very creation of the various pseudonyms and the subsequent presentation of various viewpoints force the reader to choose among them. Essential to understanding Kierkegaard is to understand that the key to avoiding the barren quality of his contemporary Christian's spiritual life is to never succumb to passivity. Kierkegaardian ideas of shouldering one's responsibility and engaging in the decision-making process are similarly abundant in Jung. A quarter of a century ago Shelburne (1983) remarked that the ideas of Jung are seldom mentioned in conjunction with existentialism, and it is unfortunate that such a statement is as true today as it was then. It is remarkable that Jung, who had absolutely nothing positive to say about existentialist thinkers, should share such a significant existential perspective. His *Red Book* seems to my mind to have a very existentialist feel to it; for instance his insistence that the individual should not follow a personal or spiritual model but rather assume personal responsibility for his own life is a notable theme of the work, best summed up in his own words: 'If you live according to an example, you thus live the life of that example, but who should live your own life if not yourself? So live yourselves' (2009). The following quote aimed at existentialist thinkers is so reminiscent of Kierkegaard's fantasied strip searching of Hegel, the removal of the 'clothes and disguises' of his language to the ends of letting his life speak for itself: 'this credulity and entrapment in words is becoming more and more striking nowadays. Proof of this is the rise of such comical philosophy as existentialism, which labors to help being become being through the magical power of the word' (1951–1961). This is not just a general lampooning of professors and their word-fetishism but a more poignant reminder of the importance of silence and of naked solitude as the fount of one's healing. Kierkegaard certainly cannot be accused of clouding such issues in philosophical abstraction, since he, much like Jung himself, dealt with essential psychological questions head on by living through them.

However, I suspect that this venom Jung had for Kierkegaard, which indeed does seem more than part of a greater disdain for existentialism, lay in his belief that Kierkegaard did not live through such psychological conflict but rather took refuge in his study, away from the world and its ugliness. The underlying causes of Jung's extreme discomfort with Kierkegaard is something that I should like to explore in more depth in the next chapter. This very comical philosophy, which Kierkegaard pioneered has at its heart the contention that we must choose for ourselves, that we must rely not on objective, universal truth but on that which is true for us – one's subjective truth. The weight of personal responsibility that such a contention carries is echoed in Jung's own work, especially in the previously explored inauthenticity that arises through shadow projection.

Both Jung and Kierkegaard present us with a psychology of presence, by which we mean that each individual has the possibility of experiencing directly, his or her actual wholeness. Interestingly, Tisdell (2003) defines authenticity as 'having a sense that one is operating from a sense of self that is defined by oneself as opposed to being defined by other people's expectations' and whilst we can argue for a certain degree of agreement between Kierkegaard and Jung on this matter, it remains that we must not overlook the limitations that underlie self-creation in Kierkegaard's model. However, both Jung and Kierkegaard agree that authentic existence involves confrontation with truth, not to be defined by others or social norms and is a matter of free will, insomuch as we are choosing possibilities that are uniquely one's own. Furthermore, the existential and Jungian paths to authenticity require self-overcoming; the overcoming of elements in one's life and character that hinder the development of genuine selfhood. Together, our Swiss-born psychologist is a good accompaniment to our spiritual physician. He helps us see these symptoms for what they are and this helps us to move toward greater self-understanding. We can rebel against such self-understanding that reveals our need for God but such an understanding at the very minimum makes faith and an authentic existence a possibility. To live the authentic existence one must choose his own life with the conviction that it can be lived with integrity and meaning.

Notes

1 Nietzsche, Heidegger, Sartre, Camus and Dostoevsky, amongst many other thinkers are notable examples of individuals with a deep concern for existing authentically. I think it's fair to claim that it is in twentieth-century existentialism that the ideal of authenticity really raises to prominence.

2 Knowledge of this kind Kierkegaard calls essential knowledge. Contrasting essential knowledge to accidental knowledge (that which does not inwardly relate itself to subjective existence), Kierkegaard describes the essential as knowledge which has an inward relation to existence. The essential relation means that there is an essential relationship between the knowledge and the knower; 'only ethical and

ethico-religious knowledge has an essential relationship to the existence of the knower'.

3 Perhaps the kind of honest relationship with a complete absence of secrecy that he was unable to have with Regine. Could he have had Regine in mind when he wrote, 'he who cannot reveal himself cannot love, and the man who cannot love is the most unhappy man of all'?

Part 3

Chapter 12

'That Religious Neurotic'

Kierkegaard on the couch

As we have seen, Kierkegaard and Jung sought to expose the very subjective dimension of psychology. Given this, it is curious that Kierkegaard believed that he himself, his own subjectivity and sense of being, could never be found within his work. In 1843, soon after the publication of *Either/Or*, Kierkegaard wrote in his diary,

> After my death no one will find even the least bit of information in my papers (this is my consolation) about what has really filled my life; no one will find that which is written in the core of my being that explains everything, and which often makes what the world would call trifles into exceedingly important events to me, and which I, too, view as insignificance, if I remove the secret note that explains this.

Whether he intended to remove or hide the 'secrets' of his being from his work, or indeed whether this simply exemplifies his attempt to mystify his readers in order to ensure that he remained enigmatic, we will never know. What we can be certain of is that Jung would not have been fooled for a second by Kierkegaard's manipulative attempts to hide or erase himself within his writings; for Jung this is merely an attempt to hide behind the façade or mask of his persona. In 1929, Jung wrote:

> philosophical criticism has helped me to see that every psychology – my own included – has the character of a subjective confession. And yet I must prevent my critical powers from destroying my creativeness. I know well enough that every word I utter carries with it something of myself – of my special and unique self with its particular history and its own particular world. Even when I deal with empirical data I am necessarily speaking about myself.
>
> (1929: cpar.774)

If, as Jung maintains, one's entire existence and subjectivity is written into one's philosophical/psychological reflections and all that one thinks, writes and acts, for Jung there can be no 'secret notes', all is exposed if analysed sufficiently.

If we are to begin to expose the source and cause of Jung's emotive rejection of Kierkegaard, it is necessary to expose aspects of both Jung's and Kierkegaard's personalities and sense of self within their written, theoretical accounts. Inevitably, our analysis will require a speculative approach, an approach that does not lead to definitive answers but often to muddy waters of hypothetical comment; however, in this instance, we shall see it is worth getting a bit dirty. Psychological analyses of Kierkegaard have been predominantly Freudian in their persuasion,[1] and although Kierkegaard was bitterly obsessed with his own early memories (which is particularly apposite for a Freudian approach), the mind and its mechanisms are not of primary significance in his psychology. Kierkegaard is principally concerned with the soul and its relation to God, and for this reason, there is a strong argument to claim that his life and works are better approached from a Jungian, rather than Freudian, position. In this section I redress the balance with a detailed Jungian analysis of Kierkegaard: with the man Jung calls the neurotic 'grizzler'.

It is perhaps telling that whenever Kierkegaard writes of his youth he makes sure to emphasise just how frail, slender, weak and sickly he was; his keenness to do so is both curious and disconcerting. His schoolfellows bear witness to such frailty; they were never in any doubt that he compensated and made up for his physical inferiority with sarcasm, banter and in some instances outright unpleasantries.[2] There is in his constant grievance that, 'alas I was never young',[3] and his repeated lamentations of a childhood that was 'crazy, humanly speaking' something quite pitiful, almost pathetic (Lowrie 2013). His agonising over never having been like other young men, of having ordinary pleasures denied to him, and being tragically aged beyond his years, increases in sheer volume and tone within the later stages of his writing – at a time that coincides with his complete rejection of and isolation from society and its Christendom. That the younger Kierkegaard longed to fit into society is without doubt: we only need to look at letters that he wrote to his physician to ascertain his desire to participate in something that resembled a 'normal' life (JP: 1845). However, along the way this longing becomes transformed into something approaching neurotic hatred and bitterness. I will conclude this section with a thorough Jungian attempt to analyse the personality of Kierkegaard that emerges from his later writings. There I will argue the increased severity of his bitterness together with his Christian idealism is best understood as the compensatory effects of a lifelong suppression of his anima.

In an unpublished foreword to *Concept of Irony*, Kierkegaard describes himself as 'a straggler who has seen nothing in the world and has only taken a journey to the interior within his own consciousness' (Nordentoft 1978). Ever since Kierkegaard sought to encounter the deepest depths of his inner psyche, psychological and psychiatric diagnoses of his very endeavor to do so have been attempted by many. These diagnoses vary greatly. Hjalmer Helweg, whose psychiatric monograph on Kierkegaard was published in 1933, believed Kierkegaard's life expresses a long conflict between the urge toward public activity and the isolating effect of his depression. The purpose of Helweg's work was to establish a manic-depressive diagnosis of Kierkegaard. He argues that Kierkegaard was healthy and normal in his childhood years and that the depressions began in earnest only in 1835, when he was 25 years of age, leading to a psychosis from which he never recovers. Ib Ostenfeld, however, strongly criticises Helweg's diagnosis and takes a particularly dim view of his rendering Kierkegaard a psychiatric patient, as he cannot accept that Kierkegaard's great intellect has at its base a pathological predisposition, that all his great philosophical and religious insights are a mere consequence of his pathology. To suggest that Kierkegaard would not have arrived at his ideas and conclusions had he not suffered from manic-depressive psychosis is a step too far for Ostenfeld (1978). Henning Fenger (1980), however, finds it strange that whilst Ostenfeld himself explains Kierkegaard's father, his brother and the brother's son had each inherited manic-depressive tendencies, he should dismiss without hesitation the possibility that Søren might also. However, despite Fenger's criticism, I contend that Ostenfeld's argument remains convincing, for there is nothing in either Kierkegaard's writing or in his biographical details that substantiates this diagnosis. All the events of his life follow normal psychological patterns of behaviour, and do not indicate manic depression. Likewise, Kierkegaard's work follows a clear and coherent trajectory in its discussion and argument, one that demonstrates itself clearly without break or interruption. And it would seem Ostenfeld is quite correct in his assertion that there is no evidence of these manic-depressive tendencies in Kierkegaard's publications or diaries. Throughout his published works and private journals, we find a continuity and consistency of thought. Even within the late journal entries where we find Kierkegaard's most extreme and emotional expressions that seek to negate the world, we are still able to infer a viewpoint that is consistent with his earlier works.

My issue with a diagnosis of manic depression is that it belittles and misinterprets Kierkegaard's social awkwardness and isolation and his introverted withdrawal into a world of ideas as something pathological. This generalised, almost lazy approach that simply points towards aspects of his introverted personality and diagnoses them instead as schizoid features is all too easy an approach to take. And whilst one may isolate individual quotations or remarks given by Kierkegaard that show his elevated states of excitement, or similarly point to those deeply melancholic passages that are comparable in tone to that written by someone who was truly depressed, it does not mean he is a bone fide manic- depressive. Indeed, more interesting a target and more curious an issue are those aspects of his personality and experience that are ignored by those who attempt to diagnose or analyse his state of body and mind. Thus, what is of interest and relevance to my own Jungian analysis of his personality are these ignored features, such as: Kierkegaard's desire to actively attract contempt from others and his need to be despised; his issues with women (in Jungian terms, with his *anima*), as made clear in relationship with Regine and the notable absence of any allusion to his mother in his works; his weak sexual self; the misrelation in his writings between body and soul; and the fact that he seems fairly stable in the composition of his thoughts. It is these very aspects of Kierkegaard's character and personality that I will draw upon heavily, here in this present chapter.

The very first editor of Kierkegaard's papers, Peter Andreas Heiberg was insistent that Kierkegaard should not be viewed as a medical case history. Heiberg had a very interesting thesis indeed. He saw in Søren's religious development a story of healing – an ongoing attempt at self-recovery (Ostenfeld 1978). Ironically, Fanny Lowtzky (1935), who certainly viewed Kierkegaard as a medical case study, drew the very same conclusion as Heiberg. In her psychoanalytical study she extraordinarily claimed that Kierkegaard was close to resolving his own oedipal complex – which would seem remarkable indeed. For reasons that I shall explore later, this claim has little plausibility. Kierkegaard achieved a great many things, but solving his Oedipus complex was not amongst them. However, his self-understanding, particularly with regards to the repressed contents of his unconscious, what Jung refers to as the shadow, is remarkable, and whilst he never comes to integrate this shadow-self fully (as none of us can), his awareness of his own approach towards this darker and neglected side of the self or spirit is striking, and gives credence to one (but only one) of Jung's criticisms of him. In my Jungian analysis of Kierkegaard I shall focus predominately on his childhood upbringing, which, I argue, forces an unconscious split between real and fantasised parent, and thereby gives rise to Oedipal issues and problems with regards to his anima. To a certain degree I contend that Kierkegaard built his theories of religion around his own problematic experiences of his parents, and, furthermore, that it is in Jung's own unconscious reaction to Kierkegaard's theories and to the psychological makeup of Kierkegaard that underpins these ideas, that we find cause for Jung's emotional dismissal of Kierkegaard and all he supposedly represents for Jung.

Given Kierkegaard adopts pseudonyms in his writings, the task of separating Kierkegaard's intellectual work from his personal life is especially difficult. There simply is no obvious revealing of Kierkegaard in his works, whilst we might point towards a particular character who reminds us of Kierkegaard in terms of historical detail or in personality, care must be taken not to confuse literary fiction for autobiography. Following Jung's claim that every creation is identified with its author, each of the pseudonyms he adopts in his writings are versions of himself; his life is essentially lived out through these characters. This said, the mixing of biography with literary characters is, as we have noted, an intentional ploy on Kierkegaard's part to detract the reader from himself as author. We cannot blindly assume that they are representative of Kierkegaard's own views nor can we rely on the named works to offer a more genuine representation. The distinction between Kierkegaard's life and works is very blurry to say the least, yet, following a Jungian reading, the pseudonymous works are best understood psychologically as direct products of Kierkegaard's personality and experiences. There are scholars who would sooner see his authorship intimately related to his illness; this does not sit comfortably with a Jungian approach, whereby unconscious personalities, as these pseudonyms are, are not necessarily pathological traits but aspects of the wider personality. We ought to take care not to reduce an entire philosophical project into a single cryptic autobiography, making of Kierkegaard a kind of biographical conundrum. Of course there is a process of self-invention throughout his authorship, which combined with a good dose of deception and misdirection (preoccupations that Kierkegaard undoubtedly took pleasure in) certainly creates quite the cryptic autobiography.

Let us now turn to the issue of his authorship before embarking on a Jungian analysis of Kierkegaard that will begin with the issue of Kierkegaard's relation to the feminine, to the anima.

Jung would no doubt see the unconscious as all too evident in Kierkegaard's works given their poetic and unstructured form. Surely Jung would have scoffed at Kierkegaard's gleeful assertion that he himself is totally absent and unfathomable through a consideration of his writing. Indeed, in his letters to Swiss philosopher Arnold Kunzli, having denounced that 'moaner Kierkegaard' together with the philosopher Nietzsche 'who drips with outraged sexuality', Jung continues:

> Philosophy still has to learn that it is made by human beings and depends to an alarming extent on their psychic constitution. . . . There is no thinking qua thinking, at times it is a pisspot of unconscious devils . . . neurosis addles the brain of every philosopher because he is at odds with himself.
>
> (1906–1950)

The mythic Kierkegaard was very much created during Kierkegaard's lifetime by the pen of the great man himself. And it is through his rewriting of history that we catch a glimpse of Kierkegaard, unguarded and real, psychological insufficiencies and all. That supposed 'secret note' that he speaks of (cited at the start of this chapter), which, he says, would allow us to locate him within his work, but which he destroyed, is perhaps not so crucial as he would have us believe. Essentially, Kierkegaard is an actor and the pseudonyms are his roles. It is perhaps fitting that a man so passionate about the theatre (for whom most evenings were spent at the royal theatre) should make of his life a gigantic play, acting out the many roles of his personality. He is as his many roles play out, a seducer, misunderstood genius, victim of the corsair, pious hermit, a preacher sans pulpit and ultimately the self-sacrificing martyr. Kierkegaard writing to Emil Boesen from Berlin in May 1843, described his own ideas as, 'cascading down upon me: healthy, happy, thriving, merry, gay, blessed children born of ease and yet all of them with the birthmark of my personality'. Such a description I contend could equally be applied to his pseudonyms. If this were not the case, his works would surely fail to encourage his readers to think about their own existence, in the way he intended. If Kierkegaard removed himself from his writing, his demand that the reader find his or her own self reflected within it rings hollow and loses its conviction. It is a testament to his ability to weave biography and fiction that we, the reader, are all too often left deeply unsettled by his presence within it. How else would this otherwise dour Dane provoke such devotion from his readers? For those that become well acquainted with his works, Kierkegaard exudes a powerful hold; he has the ability to get close to his readers, under their skin, as if speaking to them personally, directly. To read Kierkegaard is to reflect on one's own existence, and the use of pseudonyms gives him a powerful weapon to this effect. Having briefly acquainted ourselves with the various psychological studies on Kierkegaard and their results, we shall now attempt to redress the balance by offering a Jungian analysis of this suffering and sickly, yet brilliant, individual.

Notes

1 See K. Nordentoft (1978), *Kierkegaard's Psychology*, E. Becker, (1973). *The Denial of Death*, J. Lacan, (1973). *The Four Fundamental Concepts of Psychoanalysis*, J. Preston Cole. *The Problematic Self in Kierkegaard and Freud*, F. Lowtzky, (1935). Søren *Kierkegaard: Subjective Experience and Religious Revelation – A Psychoanalytic Study of a Near Self Analysis*, F. C. Fischer, (1833). *The Zero Point of Existence, As Shown by the Life Form of Kierkegaard* (Munich: C.H. Beck).

2 'He was a strangely dressed fellow, small for his age, thin and freckled' (Edvard J. Anger); 'Søren was a tease and his "foul mouth" cost him many bloody noses' (Frederik Welding); 'He was a skinny boy, always on the run, and he could never keep from giving free rein to his whimsy and from teasing others with nicknames that he had heard, with laughter, and with funny faces, even though it earned him a beating' (Frederik Welding). *Encounters with Kierkegaard: A Life As Seen by His Contemporaries*, ed. Brice H. Kirmmse).

3 'How sad – as I so often had to say of myself in my younger days – alas, I was never young. When I was a youth I was a thousand years older than an old man! Likewise I must also sadly say of myself: I have never actually been a man!' (JP:1854).

Chapter 13

Keeping mum
A powerful silence

Perhaps the most mysterious and commented on facet of Kierkegaard's writing is that throughout his authorship, both published works and in the privacy of his journals, he makes no mention of his mother. For a gifted writer whose attention to the history and the meaning of his own family was obsessive, this textual absence cannot belong to mere happenstance. His mother, Ane, fell seriously ill in May 1834, and died on July 31st, 1834. As far as we know there is no record of Kierkegaard having gone to her bedside. What we do know of Ane comes from Kierkegaard's niece, Henriette Lund and her memoirs published in 1880. Henriette describes Ane as:

> A kind little woman with an unpretentious and cheerful turn of mind. Her sons' development was a bit over her head; their high-flying appeared to her worried heart to be a flight away from the level on which she felt comfortable, and on which she would so much preferred to have kept them. And she was therefore never more in her element than when a passing illness forced them ever so slightly back under her jurisdiction. She was especially gratified when she could get them peacefully into bed, since then she wielded her sceptre with delight, cosseted them and protected them like a hen her chicks. Her motherly inclinations also agreed with the grandchildren in the family. Her plump little figure had only to appear in the doorway of the nursery, and the cries and screams would give way to a hush; the rebellious young boy or girl soon fell sweetly asleep in her soft embrace.
>
> (Kirmmse 1996)

Henriette's description of Ane radiates maternal warmth. Eline Heramb Boisen, a relation by marriage, picks up on Ane's pride and admiration for her sons,

> That winter I was also a visitor several times at the home of the elder Kierkegaard's and those were interesting hours. It was very intriguing

to hear the old man debate with the sons, with none of them giving in, and to see the quiet activity of the old mother, and how she would sometimes listen in admiration and sometimes interrupt to calm things down when they became too heated.

(Kirmmse 1996)

The absence of the mother in Kierkegaard's written recollections is particularly odd, especially given that from what we do know of their relationship, it was one that was far from indifferent. Hans Brøcner retells how his female cousins were warned against the fifteen-year-old Kierkegaard, who was regarded as a terribly spoiled and badly behaved boy with a proclivity to clinging to his mother's skirts (see Kirmmse 1996). Another member of Kierkegaard's extended family, Troels Frederick Troels-Lund speaks of Søren's loss of the two people dearest to him: 'his mother, the mild gentle sunbeam of his childhood home, and his sister, the merry, understanding playmate in her bright new home'.[1] Even more telling is this recollection from Kierkegaard's university tutor and prominent theologian, Hans L. Martensen:

Once he came to us in a state of deep depression and told us that his mother was dead. My mother repeatedly declared that, although she had experienced a good many things in her life, she had never seen a human being as deeply sorrowful as S.Kierkegaard was at his mother's passing, something which caused her to conclude that he must have had an unusually profound sort of spirit.

(Kirmmse 1996)

Clearly, the passing of his mother had left Kierkegaard heartbroken. In his *Works of Love* Kierkegaard, perhaps with his mother in mind, writes: 'I know of no better way to describe true recollection than by this soft weeping that does not burst into sobs one moment – and soon subsides. No, we are to recollect the dead, weep softly, but weep long' (1847b).

Kenneth Greenhalgh in his doctoral thesis, *On Reading Narcissistic Texts: An Object Relations Theory View of the Life and Works of Søren Kierkegaard*, claims the absence of mother in Kierkegaard's *Journals* to be indicative of a profound feeling of shame. Perhaps, he suggests, 'one possible reason is simply social: her lack of obvious intelligence compared with her husband. . . . We are told that her hand had to be guided when making a signature' (Greenhalgh 2008). He arrives at the conclusion that this silence concerning mother equates to her denial and has its roots in shame, for as he writes:

We are not silent about things that make us angry, and we are not always silent about matters of guilt – we wish to expunge the guilt, to rationalise it. But shame speaks from the very centre of being – it is the most private emotion. It is something about which we dare not speak.

Whilst we may bear our shame silently, it is certainly not the only thing that could evoke such silence. Could it be that Kierkegaard had an ordinary relationship with his mother and that there was simply none of the anger-creating, guilt-consuming conflict that would provoke any outbursts or outpourings from Kierkegaard? We need only remind ourselves that he is a man who is not only obsessed with his upbringing but likes to express his bitterness about it. The silence surrounding his mother is, I claim, anything but ordinary. There is something about his mother that he dare not speak, and whereas we might speak of other people's shame, albeit uneasily, the same is not true of our own. Greenhalgh, is, to my mind, perhaps the most insightful commentator about the absence of Kierkegaard's mother from his writings, when he suggests that it has its basis in shame, but his reasons for such an assertion are less compelling. That shame arises in Kierkegaard because, as Greenhalgh contends, his mother has a lowly social status is not a convincing argument. Although Kierkegaard is often accused of being misogynistic,[2] it is most likely that he believed this supposedly inferior gender to still be capable of penetrating the intellectual sphere that he held in high regard. This aside, Greenhalgh does offer a more convincing speculation for the reasons behind Kierkegaard's shame for his mother, concerning her premarital sexual involvement with his father. In his very last journal entry, dated 25th September 1855, Kierkegaard alludes to what he regarded as the sinful conception, through which he was thrust into the world:

> through a crime I came into existence. . . . I came into existence against God's will. The fault, which in one sense, is not mine, even if it makes me a criminal in God's eyes, is to give life. The punishment fits the fault: it is to be deprived of all joy of life, to be brought to the supreme degree of disgust with life.
>
> (JP: 1854)

On this account, we can deduce that his mother's seduction of his father is the root cause of any disposition Kierkegaard has for misogyny, and whilst Greenhalgh views this as the typical behaviour of a male narcissist, I suggest a different, but not unconnected, explanation for this motherly omission. Namely one born of Kierkegaard's outright refusal to engage with his unconscious disposition towards femininity in any shape or form. Understood from a Jungian perspective this would certainly be indicative of Kierkegaard's neglect and inability to integrate anima into his conscious personality. This position is not so much the denial of feminine sexuality by a narcissistic male, but a much more thorough, and deeply unconscious denial of sexuality per se, by a personality that is incredibly fragile in all matters of sexuality. Whilst the mother is surrounded in his feelings of shame and guilt, I will put forward the argument that this shame is Kierkegaard's own, arising from Oedipal issues that instill within Kierkegaard a lifelong sense of guilt. If he feels any shame about his mother, it is projected onto her from his own unconscious feelings of shame that he has about himself in relation to what she, as a woman, represents to him.

Kierkegaard is clearly at home in the world of intellectual ideas and rationality (logos), and since it through his father's world and his relationship with him that he developed his intellectual capabilities, it is hardly surprising that he writes frequently of it. In Jung's writings the feminine is equated with Eros and the masculine with Logos; somewhat controversially, he regards a man as having autonomy and rationality as their primary, conscious qualities (which he designates as Logos), and, as a consequence, their unconscious (which, as we described in Part One of this thesis, is, for Jung compensatory to the conscious mind) anima comprises opposite, supposedly 'feminine', qualities of relationship and feeling (which Jung designates Eros). Essentially, Eros is best understood as a life force that leads us into the world and involvements with others. We could look at his omission of his mother from the perspective of the mother being Eros and the father Logos, such an exaltation of logos over eros in his thought and life simply leaves no room for the mother. When we look closely at the roots of Kierkegaard's fragile sexual self, it would seem that the absence of mother is indicative of a total repression of the feminine. From the little we know of his mother; we know her to be sensual and maternal, like the proverbial 'mother hen' fussing over her chicks: this world of femininity is, I contend, a very uncomfortable place for Kierkegaard. We can perhaps forgive Walter Lowrie for contrasting the 'prodigious impression' of father, to a mother who 'counted for little in the household' (Lowrie 1970). However, what does seem somewhat more surprising, not to mention unjustified, is Lowrie's claim that because Kierkegaard 'had no mother he could adore' he was unable to commit to marrying (Regine); in other words, 'he associated no noble and tender thoughts with woman as mother.' I argue that, on the contrary, the silence surrounding his mother is Kierkegaard's attempt to keep her perfectly preserved, pure and untainted, unchanged and eternal. The perfect preservation of mother (and Regine – who in keeping with Jung's insistence that one's anima originate with one's experiences of mother, before being projected onto every other emotionally valued female – comes to take the place of Ane as a significant anima figure for Kierkegaard) does not lack for tender and noble thoughts, cloaked as it is in complete adoration. Lowrie is certainly not alone with regards to this line of speculation. Patrick Gardiner, for instance, similarly maintains that Ane played a somewhat shadowy part in Kierkegaard's upbringing (Gardiner 1988). All too frequently scholars of Kierkegaard speak of Kierkegaard's father and Regine as the two most significant and influential people for him. Rarely is any significance shown to his mother, that figure shrouded in silence and around which all others orbit.

Ann Casement briefly but significantly suggests that Regine 'may have been an anima figure and inspiring muse who could not be contaminated by the sensualities and everyday aspects of marriage' (Casement 1998). Regine is certainly an inspiring muse and I share Casement's suspicion that strong anima forces are at work in Kierkegaard's successful but ultimately barren wooing of Regine. However, as previously noted, Regine is not the only female whose feminine wiles Kierkegaard has to keep repressed in order to avoid contemplation of his own sexuality and desires as a sexual being. In order to expound on the psychology that underpins the repression of Kierkegaard's sexual desire in the section that follows, I will examine this situation in light of likely oedipal issues that underpin his relationship with his father. But before I do so, I shall explore Kierkegaard's relationship with femininity and sexuality in light of his unconscious anima. Both in regards to the feminine absence that is growing within his unconscious and which, as we will turn to later, overtakes him in later life and in terms of Kierkegaard's claim that woman 'is humble, she is much closer to god than is man'(1843a).

Whilst the persona represents the conscious attitude of a man most acceptable to society's values and is the mask we wish to show others, it is the anima, alongside the shadow, that represents by compensation the inner unconscious attitude. Consequently, the anima contains all those qualities that the persona lacks. And so together with the shadow, the conscious integration of the anima is essential if one is to correct a one-sided persona. In contrast to the engagement with one's shadow, which Jung calls the mere 'apprentice-piece'; the differentiation between one's conscious persona and anima is, Jung says, the 'masterpiece' of analysis (1934/1954: par.61). In order for a man to develop healthily (and achieve 'individuation'), it is necessary for him to identify and engage with his anima, and subsequently to appreciate its unconscious influence over him in the form of the archetypal material and effects it communicates (kast 2006). The anima has its basis within the primordial impressions of the mother (in Jungian parlance, the mother archetype and mother complex) – which is to say that a person's experience of the anima is always shaped by their earliest experiences of their mother, or her absence. Despite mother being the original image and conception of the anima, an awareness of the anima can only come, Jung says, by way of a 'relation to a partner of the opposite sex', because it is 'only in such a relation' that a man can experience his feelings towards it and bring it into conscious realisation. In other words, the anima exists by way of its emotional effect on a man, and this effect is always produced in relation to a woman. Consequently, the first stage of the anima's development within a man coincides with him experiencing sexual or loving feelings with a woman; up until this point the anima has been largely carried by the

140 Keeping Mum: a powerful silence

image and experiences of his mother. In his essay on marriage, Jung writes of the projection of anima as a fascination and falling in love with another (1925). Since it was Jung's belief that the anima is based on the mother archetype it follows that the more influenced one is by one's mother, the more likely one's choice of partner will be a positive or negative unconscious replacement of or substitute for the mother. Jung writes, 'it is the strength of the bond to the parents that unconsciously influences the choice of husband or wife, either positively or negatively' (1925: par.328). The anima whilst initially identified with the mother, is later experienced in the form of a significant other.

In his 1936 text 'Concerning the Archetypes and the Anima Concept', Jung argues that all young men must free themselves from the anima fascination of the mother, and that this is a psychological priority in their first half of life (up until the approximate age of 40). Returning now to Kierkegaard, we can postulate that he is unconsciously fixated on his anima to the extent that he cannot enter into his engagement or union with Regine; and since he cannot sustain an emotional relationship with her at a conscious level, there is no way that the anima can be made conscious through her. Effectively, the anima has not had the chance to develop through his relationship with Regine, but is still grounded within his experiences of mother. That Kierkegaard came to associate Regine as a kind of incarnation of his mother is indicative of the regressive hold that the anima has on his unconscious. In other words, rather than allow the anima to develop by moving from mother onto 'lover', it is stuck in its original, infantile state, within the unconscious attachment to mother. Kierkegaard's inability to free himself from the anima fascination of the mother means he is unable to relate to Regine as the woman she is, or indeed the woman she could be for Kierkegaard: that is to say, wife and sexual partner. Although Kierkegaard is unable to engage with his anima in a developed form, he does not seek to destroy it or to deny its influence, rather he seeks to preserve it in its original form; to keep it pure, he places it upon a pedestal and devotes his entire philosophical/religious project to it. This has the effect that it is placed well out of reach. I suspect that Kierkegaard projects onto Regine an idealised version of womanhood. Like the seducer portrayed in his *The Seducers Diary*, Kierkegaard does not love Regine for who she is, but rather creates an ideal version of her in his imagination. The seducer is not prepared to limit his possible enjoyment of every woman by entering into a relationship with any particular woman. His objectification of women for narcissistic enhancement is indicative of an unintegrated anima. The poetized Regine is similarly objectivised, and so has this aura of otherness about her. For instance, in all his *Journals and Papers* Kierkegaard never mentions Regine by name, but refers to her in the form of the object pronoun 'her'.[3] I do not feel that we can dismiss these references to 'her' simply as an attempt by Kierkegaard to maintain Regine's anonymity; their broken engagement had scandalised Copenhagen society.

Keeping Mum: a powerful silence   141

According to Jung, the anima influences not only a man's interactions with women but also his attitudes towards them. Kierkegaard imagines that the silence of attentiveness to God's word is exemplified in woman (Rae 2010). Arguably, this image of woman stems from and is built around the mother. The most significant qualities that Ane and Regine share, is this uncomplicated, perhaps even simple and pure sense of religiousness, as well as a comforting maternal nature. As we saw, such qualities radiate from the accounts of Ane provided by Kierkegaard's contemporaries. Henriette Lund tells of her surprise at hearing of uncle Søren's engagement, describing Regine as a loving and pretty young girl eager to win their love and affection (see Kirmmse 1996). Troels Frederick Troels Lund has similarly remembrances of Regine describing her as modest and gentle (see Kirmmse 1996). Furthermore, that Regine desired to save Kierkegaard from himself is evident in the letters that the two lovers exchanged. She was as Kierkegaard proclaimed, his 'angel of salvation'.

Throughout Kierkegaard's work he makes several complimentary statements concerning a woman's religious role, in *For Self Examination* he gives this 'eulogy' on feminine silence:

> And you, O woman, for you it is indeed reserved to be able to be the image of the hearer and reader of the Word who is not forgetful. You comply fittingly with the apostle's admonition: Let the woman keep silence in the congregation; it is fitting. Neither does she take up preaching in the home; it is unbecoming. No, let her be silent; let her treasure the Word in silence; let her silence express that she treasures it deeply.
>
> (1851)

And, in a similar fashion, he remarks:

> you simple one, even though you are of all people most limited – if your life expresses the little you have understood, you speak more powerfully than all the eloquence of orators. And you, O woman, even if you are quite speechless in charming silence – if your life expresses what you heard, your eloquence is more powerful, more true, more persuasive than all the art of orators.
>
> (1851)

Kierkegaard is thoroughly preoccupied with this idea of being silent in a deeply religious way; it is this holy silence he believes to be the prerogative of women. According to his understanding, 'every holy feeling which in its most profound depth is good, is silent . . . since the lips are closed and only the heart it opened'. One cannot read these passages without feeling the presence and imagining the doting mother listening diligently to her intellectual gifted husband and her son as they debate matters of the spirit vigorously, and silently welcoming their every word regardless or not whether she understood them. In fact, recalling that Troels Frederick Troels Lund (a relation by marriage) considered Ane to be the 'gentle sunbeam' in Kierkegaard's childhood home, we are encouraged to read the following passage concerning silence somewhat differently:

> Silence is like the subdued lighting in a pleasant room, like the friendliness in a modest living room; it is not something one talks about, but it is there and exercises its beneficent power. Silence is like the tone, the fundamental tone, which is not given prominence and is called the fundamental tone precisely because it lies at the base.
>
> (1851)

Silence and mother are interchangeable here; it is the mother's cheerful disposition that lights a pleasant room; it is she who is not to be spoken of, but whom, rather, exercises her beneficent power. And ultimately, it is she who provides the fundamental tone at the base of everything. Kierkegaard himself does not give any reasons or offer any explanation as to why he attributes this privileged silence to women. I suspect the reason lay in the deeply profound influence of this quiet, cheerful and religiously simple woman, characteristics that he loved and greatly admired. Climacus in *Concluding Unscientific Postscript* remarks, 'how deceptive, then, that an omnipresent being should be recognisable precisely by being invisible' (1846a). I think we might say the same of Ane Kierkegaard. Having given our attention to the anima in relation to Kierkegaard's mother, it is to the father and the Oedipus complex that we shall now turn.

Notes

1 We learn from Troels that the death of Søren's sister was especially tragic. Petrea having zealously cared for her mother whilst pregnant became ill and died four months later, shortly after having given birth to a son (Kirmmse 1996).
2 See Watkin's article 'The Logic of Søren Kierkegaard's Misogyny' for full discussion of this aspect of Kierkegaard's work in *Feminist Interpretations of Søren Kierkegaard*, edited by Céline León & Sylvia Walsh, 1997.
3 'I have bourne the responsibility for her to the point of bearing responsibility for her life'; 'I who in my melancholy had only one wish: to enchant her'; 'If I had not been a penitent I would willingly, more than willingly, have done everything [for her] what happiness for me to be able to make her happy who, though, has suffered much on my account' (JP:1849).

Chapter 14

Søren's spiritual castration

A father's influence

It is a well-established view amongst Kierkegaardian scholars that the father constitutes so much of Kierkegaard's inner being. I have chosen to address the centrality of the mother's influence on Kierkegaard, since it is my belief that the tensions around his relationship to his father and Regine can be traced back to her. However, I do not wish to dispute the importance of the figure of his father that emerges from Kierkegaard's work as the most prominent and dominant conscious force, and to whom Kierkegaard himself attributes a powerful significance:

> It seemed to me that my dead father put this demand to me: You must present Christianity in its utmost rigorousness, but you must keep it poetic, you may attack no one, and on no account may you make yourself out to be better than the most insignificant person, for you know very well that you are not better.
>
> (JP: 1851)

In what follows I will address the influence of Kierkegaard's oedipal battle with his father, which, in psychoanalytic terms, leaves him with an unconscious desire for castration that expresses itself consciously within his desire for spiritual celibacy.

Although the Oedipus complex is most often associated with a Freudian psychoanalytic approach, Jung and Jungian psychology recognise its value, with the important proviso that it, as with all complexes, is not primarily sexual or regressive in its nature (Frattaroli 2008). Jung considered the Oedipus complex an important and necessary focus for the analysis of people in the first half of their life; therefore it demands inclusion when considering Kierkegaard's psychological development here. In his *Symbols of Transformation* (1912), Jung challenges Freud's understanding of the Oedipus complex as focused principally on the infant's 'sexual' attraction to the parent of the same sex, and their aggressive feelings toward the same-sex parent (Sharf 2010). Jung criticised the literal sexual emphasis Freud placed on the incestuous desires of the infant and this stage of its psychological development, and instead understood the oedipal complex as an expression of a spiritual longing for inner unity.

In my reading of Kierkegaard's psychological situation, castration anxiety seems to be a constant, albeit unconscious, presence throughout Kierkegaard's life. In the pre-oedipal stage, the male child feels conflicted between his desire for his mother and his anxiety about the implications of such a desire; notably the fear of the father's aggressive retaliation for the infant's desire for his partner. This fear culminates in a castration anxiety, whereby the father castrates the infant in his retaliation, rendering the infant impotent and unable to satisfy the mother (indeed, making him like her in physical appearance). A resolution of the oedipal complex and the corresponding removal of castration anxiety comes about by repressing the desire for mother. This also allows the anxiety and fear of the father to be abated, thereby allowing the boy to identify fully with his father, and to retain his power and potency, just as he perceives his father as having. Freud maintained that since all men unconsciously desire to rid themselves of the father in order that they may return to the mother, it was necessary for a man to internalise the image of their father (as a moral force, which Freud calls 'superego') so as to avoid this lethal temptation, and all temptations to succumb to those things one should not. And so begins a lifelong servitude to the father as one of the earliest objects of a man's envy. It requires no stretch of the imagination to view Kierkegaard's life as one of servitude to his father; as we discussed earlier, the young Søren bore in himself the burden of his father's salvation. Such a symbiotic identification with a father who has only negative values of life to offer his son becomes a continual source of brooding for Kierkegaard, as evidenced in the repetition of the themes of inherited sin and the sacrificial father/son relationship throughout the corpus of his works.

As noted that Kierkegaard does not even attempt to include mention of his mother within his written recollections is extraordinary for a man who is obsessed with his early memories and identity at this time. To a certain extent all memories are a form of fiction, but in Kierkegaard's case this seems particularly so. There is no doubt in my mind that Kierkegaard was more comfortable in his recollections, in refashioning and reworking them often poetically, than with the facts of real life. This constant flurry of the recreation and rewriting of his experiences is expressive, if not indicative, of a profound repression surrounding some of his experiences. In psychoanalytic terms, Kierkegaard's approach to his experiences is a kind of 'repetition compulsion', which is to say, a need to master unconscious memories of difficult past experiences by revisiting them and refashioning them in creative ways.[1] It is through his recollections that he rewrote his personal history, creating the fictional father in place of the real parent, and immortalising Regine as a fictional muse in place of a potential real-life partner.

Similarly, that he could not engage with either parent on a level that resembled a real relationship perhaps led him to the somewhat cynical view of parenting that he here expresses:

> It is dreadful to see the carelessness, indifference, and unconcern with which children are brought up – and yet by the age of ten every person is essentially what he will become. Yet almost all bear some damage from youth which they do not heal by their seventieth year; furthermore all unhappy individualities usually have a background of a faulty childhood.[2]

Whether his childhood was 'faulty' we cannot know; however, there can be little doubt that Kierkegaard's childhood was, relatively speaking, an oppressive and depressing one. Kierkegaard relates his father's consistently brooding temperament, with the invocation within himself of 'a quiet despair'. In other words, he internalises the negative father within himself, and identifies himself with it. He describes his father as laboring under a secret burden and in relation, himself as a silent confidant, 'upon whom the whole of that melancholy descended in inheritance' (1951). Kierkegaard's symbiotic identification with his father is most evidently apparent in this passage from *Stages on Life's Way:*

> Once upon a time there were a father and a son. A son is like a mirror in which the father sees himself, and for the son in turn the father is like a mirror in which he sees himself in the time to come. Yet they seldom looked at each other in that way, for the cheerfulness of high-spirited, lively conversation was their daily round. Only a few times did it happen that the father stopped, faced the son with a sorrowful countenance, looked at him and said: Poor child, you are in a quiet despair. Nothing more was ever said about it, how it was to be understood, how true it was. And the father believed that he was responsible for his son's depression, and the son believed it was he who caused the father sorrow – but never a word was exchanged about this.
>
> Then the father died. And the son saw much, heard much, experienced much, and was tried in various temptations, but he longed for only one thing, only one thing moved him – it was that word and it was the voice of the father when he said it.
>
> Then the son also became an old man; but just as love devises everything, so longing and loss taught him – not, of course, to wrest any communication from the silence of eternity – but it taught him to imitate his father's voice until the likeness satisfied him. For the father was the only one who had understood him, and yet he did not know whether he had understood him; and the father was the only intimate he had had, but

the intimacy was of such a nature that it remained the same whether the father was alive or dead.

(1845)

This passage can credibly be understood as representing Kierkegaard's own relationship with his father, for in a marginal note to an entry on acedia[3] he remarks again about the internalized despair he acquired from his identification with his father: 'This is what my father called a quiet despair' (1839). Furthermore, in a journal entry from 1844 headed 'Quiet despair; A Narrative' we are presented with a father and son relationship that has obvious autobiographical similarities with Kierkegaard's relationship with his own father:

> There were a father and son. Both were highly endowed intellectually and both were witty, especially the father. Everyone who knew their home was certain to find a visit very entertaining. Unusually they discussed only between themselves and entertained each other as two good minds without the distinction between father and son. On one rare occasion when the father looked at the son and saw that he was very troubled, he stood quietly before him and said: Poor child, you live in quiet despair. But he never questioned him more closely – alas, he could not, for he, too lived in quiet despair. . . . But the father and the son were perhaps two of the most melancholy human beings who ever lived in the memory of man. . . . Whenever the son merely said these words to himself, quiet despair, he always broke into tears, partly because it was so inexplicably moving, and partly because he was reminded of his father's agitated voice. . . . And the father believed that he was responsible for his son's melancholy, and the son believed that he was responsible for his father's melancholy; therefore they never raised the subject. That outburst of the father was an outburst of his own melancholy; therefore when he said this, he spoke more to himself than to the son.
>
> (JP: 1844)

What is most apparent in this passage is this revelation of the father and son's shared and essentially incommunicable melancholy. These are not arbitrary or isolated passages that are taken out of context, but represent a very small proportion of a sheer overwhelming number of references that concern the father in his journals and papers. Together they make clear that Michael Pedersen exerted a powerful influence over his son, Søren. The effect of the old man's melancholy combined with the Christian upbringing he imparted to Kierkegaard, which Kierkegaard describes as stern and serious,[4] instilled in the young Kierkegaard a profound religious melancholy: 'already in my earliest childhood I broke down under the grave impression which the melancholy old man who laid it upon me himself sank under'.

Whilst there is no written evidence pointing towards Kierkegaard's feelings of shame towards his mother, there is an indication of shame felt towards his father's sexual greed. Again we find in *Stages On Life's Way* another narrative that weaves together autobiography and fiction in a literary retelling of the consequences of Michael Kierkegaard's confession. In the piece, entitled, 'Solomon's Dream: When Despair Intensifies, How May It Affect the Whole of One's Existence?' Kierkegaard presents us with Solomon, who is 'blissful in his devotion to his father', and who, upon hearing movement in his father's bedroom and fearing for his life, goes to him and beholds him:

> with a crushed and contrite heart, he hears a cry of despair from the soul of a penitent. Faint at the sight he returns to his couch, he falls asleep, but he does not rest, he dreams, he dreams that David is an ungodly man, rejected by god. . . . While David lay upon the ground with crushed and contrite heart, Solomon arose from his couch, but his understanding was crushed. Horror seized him when he thought of what it is to be God's elect. He surmised that holy intimacy with God, the sincerity of the pure man before the Lord, was not the explanation, but that a private guilt was the secret which explained everything.
>
> (1845)

Solomon imagines he has witnessed the secret guilt of his father and it is this private guilt and not his piety that explains his intimacy with and closeness to God. Here in this parable we have the possible aftermath of Søren's own reflections of his father's sexual indiscretions that had brought him into the world. Kierkegaard had described the discovery of his father's transgressions as 'the great earthquake' (JP: 1838) and it was through this 'terrible upheaval' that he came to suspect that his 'father's great age was not a divine blessing but rather a curse' (JP: 1838) upon the entire family. We cannot be sure exactly where the source of this great revelation lay: perhaps it was to be found in the father's cursing of God for his poor peasant life or, more likely, something altogether more sordid. It is not unreasonable to assume that such transgressions were sexual in nature, and probably pertained to sexual excesses. We do know that by the time of Michael Pedersen's marriage to Kierkegaard's mother (his second marriage) that Ane was already in her fourth month of pregnancy. Claire Carlisle speculates that Michael had likely slept with Ane, who was a servant in the Kierkegaard household at the time, while his first wife was on her deathbed (Carlisle 2006). This affair would have been a great scandal and abhorrent to Kierkegaard, and even more so, given he was the offspring of their unholy union. However, returning to the passage and to the mysterious confession of his father, whatever its content, it takes hold of Kierkegaard and becomes, for him, the cause and meaning of his 'hereditary guilt': a feeling of guilt that he described as 'tragic', and comprising 'the contradiction of being guilty and yet not being

148 Søren's spiritual castration

guilty'(1843a). The discovery of his father's less than pious past was nothing less than catastrophic for Kierkegaard. He laments,

> if there is any pang of sympathy, it is that of having to be ashamed of one's father, of him whom one loves above all and to whom one is most indebted, to have to approach him backwards, with averted face, in order not to behold his dishonour.
>
> (1845)

Lowrie draws upon the following short journal passage to show how Kierkegaard's figure of Antigone (the child of the unholy, incestuous union between Oedipus and his mother Jocasta) was related to Solomon's dream:

> I must again occupy myself with my 'Antigone.' The task will be to develop and explain the presentiment of guilt. It was with this in view I reflected upon Solomon and David.
>
> (JP: 1843)

There is significant resemblance between Kierkegaard's Antigone, and his Solomon and Kierkegaard himself, in terms of their respective realisations that their fathers each have a secret guilt, and also how they each find themselves implicated within their father's guilt (understood within Kierkegaard's theoretical framework as a 'hereditary guilt'). Kierkegaard seems to be projecting himself onto the historical figures of Solomon and Antigone; and this is particularly evident in the case of Antigone, for she must forsake her lover – just as Kierkegaard did Regine – as she cannot entrust to him the secret that constitutes and ravages her identity.[5] Povl Johannes Jensen claims that Kierkegaard, 'has put his own personal relations into the tragedy: in his father's life, too, there was a secret crime, and he, too, sacrificed his betrothed' (Irina.2010). The Greek tragic figure of Oedipus (from whom Freud names his own celebrated 'Oedipus complex') unknowingly killed his father, Lauis, and married his mother, Jocasta, and through their unholy sexual union, brought into the world Antigone (and her siblings, Ismene, Polyneices and Eteocles). Kierkegaard in his essay, 'The Ancient Tragical Motif as Reflected in the Modern' from *Either/Or*, alludes to a revealing twist to his comments about Oedipus. He notes that whilst everyone knows Oedipus killed the Sphinx and consequently freed Thebes, only the daughter, Antigone, knows Oedipus's secret. She must 'silently' keep the knowledge that Oedipus has murdered his father and married his mother and that she herself is the fruit of their unholy marriage. Antigone cannot divulge this secret as this would inevitably bring shame upon her father's memory, and she consequently cannot marry, for she cannot bear to enter into marriage without an open heart. Antigone then is condemned to a lifetime of suffering. Kierkegaard concludes, 'so it is with our Antigone, the bride of sorrow. She dedicates her life to sorrowing over her father's fate, over her own' (1843a). This conclusion is a fitting epitaph for Kierkegaard's own life, for we find in his discussion of Antigone a concession of himself; through her situation, we find his.

Kierkegaard's autobiographical identification with the tragic figure of Antigone is readily apparent. The secret his Antigone carries is the same secret that he himself felt to be carrying: namely, his sinful conception: his coming into existence 'through a crime'. Furthermore, the reason he gives for Antigone's inability to marry could also describe his own inability to marry Regine:

> I could of course end my Antigone by making her into a man. He left his beloved because he could not retain her together with his own sorrow. In order to do so properly he would have had to make his whole love into a deceit towards her; for otherwise she would have shared in his suffering in a quite unjustifiable way. This injury provoked the anger of the whole family.
>
> (JP: 1842)

Significantly, much like our deeply melancholic Kierkegaard, Antigone:

> does not belong to the world she lives in; even though she appears flourishing and sound, her real life is concealed. Although she is living, she is in another sense dead; quiet is her life and secretive, the world hears not even a sigh, for her sigh is hidden in the depths of her soul.
>
> She is my creation, her thoughts are my thoughts, and yet it is as if I had rested with her in a night of love, as if she had entrusted me with her deep secret, breathed it and her soul out in my embrace.
>
> (1843a)

Michael Pederson's mysterious confession was intended to lure the decadent son away from sin and back into the Christian fold. But as Poole remarks, such a confession could hardly have been interpreted by Søren as some sort of enticement back into 'the Christian fold' but rather as a shocking alienation that made inherence in all 'folds' quite impossible from then on (Poole 1993). This last attempt to sway the dandified son away from sin by a father, now deemed sinful himself, would have caused a deep rift between father and son, making inherence into the fold not only impossible but repellent. This 'great earthquake' ruptures Kierkegaard's unconscious and the father with his sexual desires and possible indiscretions bursts into consciousness. We cannot underestimate just how unsettling this would have been for the young Søren. Rarely does Kierkegaard put his cards on the table, but the

150 Søren's spiritual castration

following quote offers a glimpse of Kierkegaard unguarded with regards to the effect that this confession, of one form or another, had upon him:

> If I had had to explain myself then I would have had to initiate her into terrible things, my relation to my father, his melancholy, the external darkness that broods deep within, my going astray, pleasures and excesses which in the eyes of god are not perhaps so terrible, for it was dread that drove me to excess, and where was I to look for something to hold on to when I knew, or suspected, that the one man revered for his power and strength had wavered.
>
> (JP: 1842)

Freud conceived that one's conception of God the father has the same oedipal roots as one's conception of the real father; it thereby emerges from the helpless child's relation to what understandably seems to the child an all-powerful father. 'God', writes Freud, 'is the exalted father and the longing for the father is the root of the need for religion' (1957). The individuals God-image by Freud's reckoning, is therefore always a bearer of residual traces of the Oedipus complex. Essentially, Kierkegaard's conception of God and father has up to now, perhaps as the result of castration anxiety, been intermingled with one another:

> I learned from him what fatherly love is, and through this I gained a conception of divine fatherly love, the one single unshakable thing in life, the true Archimedean point.
>
> (JP: 1840)

This revelation facilitates a split between the real father and the God-image, for it has brought the sexual into the realm of the godly. Such a revelation shatters Kierkegaard's perception of his father as the holy old man, leaving in its place this sensual and sinful old man. And so we have a transition whereby the real father becomes sexualised and has to be repressed (because it is too difficult a fact to accept), and in his place we see the emergence of the divine father, who replaces Michael Pederson as an idealised, perfect father figure, untouched by sexual sin. As Kierkegaard says, 'in all literalness I have lived with God as one lives with a father' (1848). Furthermore, Kierkegaard speaks of:

> The joy of being a child I have never had. The frightful torments I experienced disturbed the peacefulness which must belong to being a child, to have in one's hands the capacity to be occupied etc., to give his father joy, for my inner unrest had the effect that I was always, always, outside myself.

But on not rare occasions it seems as if my childhood had come back again, for unhappy as my father made me, it seems as if I now experience being a child in my relationship to God, as if all my early life was misspent so dreadfully in order that I should experience it more truly the second time in my relationship to God.

(JP: 1849)

Of course we can only speculate when it comes to Kierkegaard's inner being and psychological mindset, but it is not unreasonable to assume that this revelation deeply impressed upon him and shaped his sense of identity. A refashioning of God away from the father image would have been desperately required by Kierkegaard, as a psychological need, in order to keep repressed sexuality and the sin it represents. This man, once revered for his power and strength, had become synonymous with sex.

As I previously explained, Kierkegaard's complex relationship with religion has its basis in his relationship to his father. Kierkegaard notes,

[I]n a way I did love Christianity – to me it was the venerable – to be sure, it had made me extremely unhappy, humanly speaking. It was closely linked to my relationship with my father, the person I have most deeply loved.

(1848/1859)

Whilst Kierkegaard submitted to his father's wish that he study theology, he soon rebelled against this wish, pursuing instead more aesthetic interests, which apparently led to a relatively dissolute lifestyle. This decadent student, not unlike his pseudonym, Johannes from *Either/Or*, was prone to academic laziness. Writing to his brother-in-law, Kierkegaard confesses, 'I am embarked on studies for the theological exam, a pursuit that does not interest me in the least and therefore does not get done very fast' (JP: 1835). It is extremely pertinent that it is only after the father's death that he finishes his theological studies, seemingly without distraction from the Copenhagen's coffee houses, elegant restaurants and theatre that had entertained him previously. We could further speculate that the death of Michael Pederson provides the opportunity for Kierkegaard to successfully and definitively refashion his God-image away from his human father and into his revered holy God.

The death of Kierkegaard's father becomes elevated into an incredibly tragic and narcissistic event. Two days after Michael Pederson's death he writes:

I so deeply desired that he might live a couple of years more, and I regard his death as the last sacrifice of his love for me, because in dying he did not depart from me, but he died for me, in order that something, if possible might come of me.

(JP: 1838)

Kierkegaard is obsessed with sacrifice; notably, the sacrifices of Jesus, of Isaac, of his father's love, and of his own sacrifice of Regine. It is interesting to note that sacrifice is always understood by him in relation to attaining a higher (religious) purpose. This statement concerning the father's sacrificial death is narcissistic, and yet most likely carries some factual truth too. The passing of his father helps him psychologically to consolidate the spiritual aspect of his ego, for the conflict of sacred and profane love can now be put to rest; essentially the sexual instinct no longer threatens as it has disappeared into the unconscious along with his feelings of weakness and shame that he had associated with his real father. Tragically, the possibility of relating to his father has to be kept unconscious so as to keep the reality of sexuality that he associates with his father at bay. And herein, I argue, lies the reason that Kierkegaard could never have overcome his oedipal complex as Lowtzky claims. Whilst the threat of castration has not gone completely, it has been temporarily withdrawn since there is no longer any real physical threat of castration: which is to say, that his father no longer embodies a potent, all-powerful being with authority over Kierkegaard. Kierkegaard wants to be spiritual, he seeks eternal perfection: he meets Regine and makes of her in his mind the perfect partner. However, he cannot allow himself to make her his lover – since this would see him both having to confront the sexual desire surrounding the mother that he has deeply repressed, and also aligning himself with the aspect of his father that he abhors. And so, through cutting Regine off from the real realm of woman by stripping her of the realities of her sexuality and womanhood, Kierkegaard is able to take his fictional muse with him into his religious authorship. We have seen how Kierkegaard refashions his image of God the father away from the image of his real father (in light of the revelation of his father's secret guilt and sexual sin), so that the relationship with the real father and with the sexuality he represents is sacrificed in order to attain an idealised father who is without sexual sin and pure in spirit. And now a similar process can be observed in Kierkegaard's own sacrifice of his partner, Regine, which can be understood as the sacrifice of Kierkegaard's own sexual self, a move necessary for his sustaining the spiritual faith that his father could not do and contaminated instead. Kierkegaard attests to his having neglected the bodily aspect of life, and of having lived in the realm of spirit alone when he writes, 'I had not really lived except in the category of mind and spirit; a human being I had not been, child and youth least of all' (1848/1859). We might view this spiritually motivated castration as Kierkegaard's attempt at staying true and loyal to his father.

Kierkegaard reproached himself over his relationship to his deceased father. Raphael Meyer interviewed Regine in her old age at Regine's request that he listen to what 'an old lady' had to tell. She describes Kierkegaard as having suffered frightfully from melancholia, of having been tormented by the thought that he had failed his father whom he had dearly loved (see Kirmmse 1996). Kierkegaard published no fewer than eight collections of Edifying Discourses with dedications to his deceased father. To quote just a few of these: 'I am indebted to my father for everything from the very beginning'; 'My late father, the person to whom I owe the most, also with respect to my work'; 'My father whom I have loved the most' and 'My beloved, deceased father'. I do wonder if such a multitude of dedications and declarations attesting to his father's importance perhaps hints at overcompensation. Did Kierkegaard feel that he had not loved his father enough? Regardless, it is clear that Michael Pedersen was never far from Kierkegaard's mind.

Notes

1 Freud's use of the concept was described for the first time, in the article of 1914, 'Remembering, Repeating and Working-Through'. Here he noted how a person 'does not *remember* anything of what he has forgotten and repressed, he *acts* it out, without, of course, knowing that he is repeating it. . . . For instance, the patient does not say that he remembers that he used to be defiant and critical toward his parents' authority; instead, he behaves in that way to those he opens himself up to, whether it be his analyst, or, in the case of Kierkegaard, within his writings. (S. E. Freud, 'Remembering, Repeating and Working Through', 12: 147–56).
2 S. Kierkegaard, *Journals and Papers,* Volume 2, ed. and trans. by Howard Vincent Hong, Edna Hatlestad Hong (Indiana University Press, 1978) p. 31.
3 Acedia: an ancient term referring to a weariness of the soul.
4 He writes, 'as a child I was sternly and seriously brought up in Christianity. Humanly speaking, it was a crazy upbringing'. Søren Kierkegaard, *The Point of View for My Work As an Author: A Report to History.*
5 'To Conceal it from such an observant person would be impossible; to wish to have it concealed would be a breach of her love – but with it can she belong to him? Does she dare to confide it to any human being, even to the man she loves? . . . Her life, formerly peaceful and quiet, now becomes violent and passionate, always of course within herself, and her words here begin to fill with pathos. She struggles with herself, she has been willing to sacrifice her life to her secret, but now what is demanded as a sacrifice is her love. She wins – that is to say – the secret wins and she loses' – S. Kierkegaard, *Either/Or.*

Chapter 15

To marry or to martyr

There is a curious relationship between the absence of mother in the works of Kierkegaard and the complete saturation of Regine (albeit as the impersonalised 'Her'). The figure of Regine has appeared in relation to our discussion of the unintegrated anima and unresolved oedipal conflicts, but here she will have the limelight as we delve into Kierkegaard's abandonment of her as his fiancé, and of their impending marriage. In 1840, two years after his father's death, and having just passed his final theological examinations, Kierkegaard proposed to Regine. What follows is a seminal moment in his psychological history, for it is whilst agonising over his engagement that he chooses a poet's existence over that of a husband. 1841 therefore marks not only the creation of philosophy's very own *Romeo and Juliet* but of Kierkegaard's development into the dedicated religious poet. Following this break, Regine becomes a literary creation, immortalized in the corpus of his works, especially his *Either/ Or* and 'Guilty/Not Guilty'. Kierkegaard views his abandonment of Regine a self-sacrifice. My aim is to ascertain whether such sacrifice is born of misrelation[1] (what Kierkegaard refers to throughout his journals as 'the thorn in my flesh'), or from a psychological and spiritual need of his to be a martyr (the call to become the exception) under direction of divine governance.

Jung tells us that the clearest place to witness the effects of archetypal realities is within a person's relationship with others. As I argued earlier, there is good reason to believe that Kierkegaard does not come to recognise the effects of his anima in relation to his mother, and, as a consequence, his anima remains unintegrated, its effects unharnessed, leaving them ripe for unconscious projection on to Regine. If the anima is allowed conscious integration, it brings genuine healing and reconciliation to the ego (Tacey 1997). Thus, by denying the anima, Kierkegaard denies himself the very resource needed to help him develop psychologically, and to remain mentally healthy and stable. For Jung, there are many forms or experiences of the anima, including the mother, the primal feminine, and Eros. Kierkegaard's urge to become hermit-like and remove himself from the social world can be regarded as a failure of eros, as well as anima. Ann Belford Ulanov accords to Jung's concept of Eros, 'the psychic urge to relate, to join, to be in the midst of, to reach out, to value to get in touch with, to get involved with concrete feelings, things, and people, rather than to abstraction or theories' (Ullanov 1971). Jung often stated that Eros, or the principle of relatedness and feeling, is dominant in the female. On the basis of this, it comes as no surprise that the anima was similarly understood to be the archetypal drive in males that governs their capacity for relatedness and relationship. : It is thus the feminine principle of Eros that plays a major role in shaping the anima of a man's sexuality,

> Eros is a questionable fellow and will always remain so. . . . He belongs on one side to man's primordial animal nature which will endure as long as man has an animal body. On the other side he is related to the highest forms of spirit. But he thrives only when spirit and instinct are in right harmony. If one or the other aspect is lacking to him, the result is injury or at least a lopsidedness that may easily veer towards the pathological. Too much of the animal distorts the civilised man, too much civilization makes sick animals.
>
> (1917/1926/1943: par.32)

The consequences of repudiating Eros are profoundly negative, to 'triumph over nature is dearly paid for' ((1917/1926/1943: par.32).

By drawing on the above, I am able to argue not only that this harmony between spirit and bodily instinct is missing in Kierkegaard, but also that Kierkegaard himself recognises it as such. The disharmony between spirit and instinct (soul and body) and its relationship with the oppressive melancholic and agitated introversion that characterises Kierkegaard's work is at its most eloquent in this passage, where he writes:

> I am in the profoundest sense an unhappy individuality which from its earliest years has been nailed fast to some suffering or other, bordering upon madness, and which must have its deeper roots in a disproportion between soul and body; for (and that is what is extraordinary) it has no relation to my mind. On the contrary, perhaps because of the strained relation between soul and body my mind has received a tensile strength that is rare.
>
> (JP: 1846)

It is hard to imagine that Kierkegaard thought of sexual intercourse as anything more than the lowering of oneself to the level of an animal, following the reproductive instinct. That Kierkegaard doubted his role as a sexual male is, I contend, revealed in the following journal passage, in which he alludes to his failure to fulfill his human existence,

> What I lack is the animal attribute. People make use of that against me . . . they take brutish joy in demanding of me what has been denied me and

deriding what has been given me. . . . Give me a body, or if you had given me that when I was twenty years old, I would not have been this way.

(JP: 1850)

That this lack can be adduced to be connected to his relationship with his father is perhaps indicated by Kierkegaard's allusion to the father's guilt prior to him concluding that he is without the body, and its 'physical presuppositions':

In a certain sense all my troubles are due to this: if I had not had a private means, it would not have been possible for me to keep the dreadful secret of my melancholy. (Merciful God, what a dreadful wrong my father did me in his melancholy – an old man who unloads all his depression on a poor child, to say nothing of what was even more dreadful, and yet for all that the best of fathers). But then I would never have become what I have become. I would have been forced either to go insane or to fight my way through. Now I have succeeded in making a *salto mortale* into the life of pure spirit.

But then again as such I am completely heterogeneous to men generally. What I actually lack is the physical and the physical presuppositions.

(JP: 1847)

It seems plausible then to suggest that perhaps there was an issue of sexual impotency underlying Kierkegaard's rejection of marriage (as had been suggested by Georg Brandes in his study of Kierkegaard published in 1877). In any case, that Kierkegaard's thoughts and feelings had circled for years around the issue of whether or not he could hope to realise what he refers to as 'the universal' (which is to say, 'marriage'[2]) is certainly supported by textual evidence. In the following letter written to his physician, Kierkegaard speaks candidly of 'the universal' in a way that gives one the distinct impression that he longs for marriage and union with another as if it would bless him with psychological wholeness:

Although no friend of confidants, although absolutely disinclined to speak with others about my innermost concerns, I nevertheless thought and still think that it is a man's duty not to bypass the court which is available in talking things over with another person, just so this does not become a frivolous confidence but is an earnest and official communication. I therefore asked my physician whether he believed that the structural misrelation between the physical and the psychical could be dispelled so that I could realize the universal. This he doubted. I asked him whether he thought that my spirit could convert or transform this misrelation by willing it. He doubted it; he would not even advise me to set in motion all the powers of my will, of which he had some conception, since I could blow up everything.

(JP: 1846)

It is conceivable that in the early stages of his relationship with Regine, Kierkegaard held the hope that the body could be regained and restored to him through love. The letters sent between the two lovers give the impression that he viewed Regine as his salvation – a role she was naturally suited for, given what we have hitherto argued with regards his psychological makeup. These letters were of great significance to Kierkegaard; he housed these treasured testaments to his love along with other documents related to 'Her' within a custom made 'tall palisander cupboard'. However, since Regine burned the letters she herself had penned to Kierkegaard when the contents of this shrine ('Her tall cupboard') were given to her after his death, it is only Kierkegaard's voice that resonates through these letters and consequently they can tell just one side of the story. We learn from Fenger that following an outburst of loving affection from Regine that Kierkegaard comes to regard her as his 'angel of salvation' (Fenger 1980). In another letter Kierkegaard compares himself to the merman at the bottom of the sea, and according to Fenger, this merman-symbolism was a firm favorite of the two lovers. That Regine was more than happy to play the part of the loving savior is clear from the following lines that she writes on the reverse of a picture enclosed with one of the letters:

And if my arm doth give such pleasure,
Such comfort and such ease;
Then, handsome merman, hasten:
Come take them both – oh, please (Fenger 1980).[3]

Kierkegaard daringly confesses to Regine that she is able to save him with her love. I would like to suggest that Kierkegaard at this time hoped that Regine would heal him in flesh and resurrect him into his body; after all she was his 'angel of salvation'; however this hope disintegrated. To extend our speculation here, we might suggest that oedipal issues revolving around his desire for the mother had once again surfaced consciously thereby preventing the fulfillment of his engagement; in such a situation, to marry would be to affirm the taboo of the infantile incestuous wish; salvation through physical sexual union would have therefore been regarded as forbidden. Furthermore, the temptations of becoming a sexual being would signal to Kierkegaard the potential loss of his God, his idealised father; indeed, the only way he had been able to keep his religious faith following his father's confession was, as we argued, by completely refashioning his image of his father into the pure and unadulterated God-image. In order to consummate any kind of relationship with Regine, Kierkegaard must transform her into

158 To marry or to martyr

something acceptable and non-sexual, and he does so by taking her into his authorship. He writes, 'she has so taken possession of me with her appeals and tears that I have taken her into my relationship to God and keep her there' (JP: 1849).

Fenger presents us with a Kierkegaard who played Regine with an 'unmistakable air of intellectual sadism'; a Kierkegaard who 'transformed their engagement into an epistolary game of a ritual kind'. Reading Fenger's words in our context suggests that Kierkegaard turns their love affair into a game, a mere artifice, in which seduction is replaced with bouts of cruelty. This renders him somewhat like his pseudonym, Johannes, as a man bereft of the capacity to enjoy women and to enjoy sexual relations. This may appear to be a harsh judgement; to talk in this manner gives the impression that the Johannes, the Seducer, is entirely in command of the aesthetic situation, rather than, as Kierkegaard claims is the case, under its control – and the latter is, I contend, closer to Kierkegaard's own situation with Regine. It may be fairer to suggest that Kierkegaard's apparent transition from kind and playful seducer to sadistic ex-fiancé was the result of the conflict he experienced over whether he should distance himself from her, and seek to wean her off him, as it were. Perhaps his more sadistic behaviour towards her was kindness masquerading as cruelty? Irrespective of which explanation is most fitting, we are under no doubt that Kierkegaard sought to lower Regine's own estimation of him. It is fair to assert that Kierkegaard was capable of loving others as a form of social engagement, and that he did indeed love Regine; however, his overriding anxiety and guilt that surrounded his relationship with her forestalled him from experiencing erotic pleasure with her. As we have seen, Kierkegaard attributes his problems to the fact of his finite body and its baser instincts which he has been denied, and it is evident from the following journal passage that he views his lack of sexual relations as the price he must pay for what he construes to be his superior intellect and spiritual sensitivity:

> From that moment I made my choice. I have regarded that tragic misrelation, together with its sufferings (which no doubt would have driven to suicide most of those lacking sufficient spirit to comprehend the utter wretchedness of the agony) as my thorn in the flesh, my limitation, my cross; I have looked upon it as the high price at which God in heaven sold me a mental-spiritual capacity unequalled among my contemporaries. This does not inflate me, for I am crushed; my desire has become a daily bitter pain and humiliation for me.
>
> (JP: 1846)

And yet, it is Kierkegaard who fashions for himself this spiritual-straightjacket that sustains the repression of his sexual desires, and, by the same token, imparts unconscious energy to them, giving them a strong unconscious charge, until his shadow is bloated with them. Sexuality, the erotic, intimacy and marriage threaten and terrify this fragile self that expends so much of its energy in denying their natural existence within the personality as a whole.

It is plausible to suggest that Kierkegaard's deep repression of the erotic has its foundations in the lost or split feminine. My argument has focused predominately on oedipal issues surrounding the mother and their reinforcement by the father as the source of such sexual repression. Indeed, a more explicit fear of the erotic can be traced back to his father, via a fear instilled in Kierkegaard by his father when he was just a young boy. We are told that in the 1820s Michael Pedersen shared a bedroom for a time with his two sons, clearly hoping to keep them from the 'ugly vice of self-pollution' (that is to say, from masturbating) (Fenger 1980). The following journal entry is extremely pertinent here:

> Granted that it was impossible for him to overcome the impressions of childhood. And such a 'leading astray', with respect to what sin is, can very well be caused at times, perhaps, by good intentions. As if a man who had been very debauched, in order to scare his son away from the same thing, came to regard the sexual instinct itself as sin, and forgot that there was a difference between himself and the child, that the child was innocent, and therefore must necessarily misunderstand.
>
> (JP: 1845)

That Kierkegaard's father successfully instilled within Kierkegaard's mind at an early age the notion that sex is sinful is highly likely. The repercussions for Kierkegaard of having such a view instilled within him can be deduced from the following passage, where he writes, 'if one said to a child that it was a sin to break a leg, what anxiety he would live in, and probably break it more often' (JP: 1845). We need not take any fanciful flight of imagination to think that Kierkegaard is referring to himself when he writes 'many a young life has been corrupted because rigorism made it (sexuality) melancholy and sinful' (JP: 1847). Levin astutely remarks that though his body may be calm, Kierkegaard's soul burned with desire (see Kirmmse 1996).

Our argument that the subduing and repression of Kierkegaard's sexuality precipitates a sacrifice of sensual and physical pleasures in order to preserve the perceived purity of the spiritual, finds much support in textual evidence and contemporary reports, but it cannot be considered an exhaustive explanation of matters. There is a grave danger when viewing Kierkegaard from the perspective of psychological diagnosis to want to reduce his entire religious authorship to one complex or another at the expense of other reasonable explanations, or indeed to the view that perhaps there is no viable explanation at all. His parting from Regine cannot be said to be explained totally by his fear of sexuality, and neither can it be said to be triggered by the sole workings of his fear of emotional intimacy. Indeed,

160 To marry or to martyr

the fact that to take a lover and to marry was a position incompatible both theologically and practically to his spiritual aspirations must not be ignored. Kierkegaard's response to his father's death was not only to apply himself more seriously to his theological studies, to pass his exams, and to propose in marriage to Regine, but also to begin training as a pastor. Much has been made of what stopped him from marrying Regine, yet little has been said of what had prevented him from pursuing an ecclesiastical position. Nearing the end of his life, reflective and serene, yet dying in the Royal Fredericks Hospital, Kierkegaard related his inability to marry with his failure to accept an official ecclesiastical position. Kierkegaard reveals to his good friend Emil Boesen:

> Everything looked like pride and vanity, but it wasn't. I am absolutely no better than other people, and I have said so and have never said anything else. I have had my thorn in the flesh, and therefore I did not marry and could not accept an official [ecclesiastical] position. . . . I became the exception instead.
>
> (Kirmmse 1996)

What is evident and striking here is that his important allusion to the thorn in the flesh does not speak of sexuality per se. It is likely that both Kierkegaard's approach to religion and his philosophy are founded upon his insistence on the non-participation in worldly events, and that it is this that prevents him from taking up a bone fide position as a pastor – as that would involve him as a key member of his community. He writes,

> I face a huge obstacle in connection with becoming a pastor. If I undertook it, I would certainly run the risk of causing offense as I once did with the engagement. . . . It becomes more and more clear to me that I am so constituted that I just never manage to realise my ideals, while in another sense, humanly speaking, I become more than my ideals. Most men's ideals are the great, the extraordinary, which they never achieve. I am far too melancholy to have such ideals. Other people would smile at my ideals. It was indeed my ideal to become a married man and make that my whole life. And then, despairing of achieving that, I became an author and perhaps a first-rate one at that. My next ideal was to become a village pastor, to live in a quiet rural setting, to become a genuine part of the little circle around me – and then, despairing of that, it is quite possible that I will again realize something which seems to be far greater.
>
> (JP: 1846)

Again, it is interesting to note that Kierkegaard draws together these two non-events, his becoming a married man and his becoming the rural pastor.

His sacrifice of Regine, along with the hope of a married life and a quiet existence as a rural pastor would seem to have its root cause in Kierkegaard's melancholic constitution. He speaks of a melancholy which 'shadows everything in my life, but that, too, is an indescribable blessing' (JP: 1848). Curiously, it is this very same melancholy that Kierkegaard considers his blessing, 'if I had not found my melancholy and depression to be nothing but a blessing, it would have been impossible to live without her. . . . I always have longed indescribably for her, her whom I have loved so dearly and who also with her pleading moved me so deeply' (JP: 1848).

Of all his concepts his perception of passion is perhaps the most important for making sense of his inner world. Significantly, Kierkegaard believes that passion must be withdrawn and removed from external objects to enable it to fill one's inner being. Certainly in Kierkegaard's own case, such a withdrawal intensifies his spiritual life. Abraham like Kierkegaard perhaps, gives up everything for God.[4] In this sense, we may question whether Kierkegaard gives up Regine – as his greatest sacrifice of love – in order to substantiate his faith as authentically religious. Kierkegaard seeks the authentic religious life, and to do so he believes he must give up the aesthetic lifestyle and concerns with the things of this world, and transcend the ethical code instigated by society.[5]

As we discussed, in his youth Kierkegaard pursued the aesthetic lifestyle, but found it empty, and since then he sought to lock the door to the outside world. Like his famous 'knight of resignation' (who resigns himself to the belief that the finite world and the spiritual world are inherently incommensurable and consequently seeks to lose himself entirely within the world of spirit),[6] Kierkegaard can never be at home in this world – he renounces all earthly pleasures, which includes foregoing any loving human relationships. And like his knight, most tragically of all, he gives up the hope that happiness could be a feature of his human world. Furthermore, like his knight, Kierkegaard is not prepared to renounce the love of and inspiration for his life. There is a parallel between the knight's love for the princess and Kierkegaard's own for Regine:

> the love for that princess became for him the expression of an eternal love, assumed a religious character, was transfigured into a love of the eternal being, which to be sure denied the fulfilment of the love but still reconciled him once again in the eternal consciousness of its validity in an eternal form that no actuality can take from him.
>
> (1843b)

The knight confronts the impossibility of his love's fulfillment by renouncing it outwardly and removing it into the realm of the eternal, and in doing so he protects himself from the wounds of reality. Writing of this resignation, Kierkegaard remarked that 'every man . . . can train himself to make this movement, which in its pain reconciles one with existence' (1843b). There can be no doubt that whilst the infinite resignation portrayed by Kierkegaard's parable of the knight's love for the princess is the final stage one must overcome before achieving true faith, it is not itself overcome by virtue of faith. In contrast to the knight of resignation, Kierkegaard postulates the knight of faith, who, by contrast, is able to maintain his love for the princess in face of its impossibility (that is to say, it cannot be sustained, but must be rejected if one is also to affirm the world of the spirit), and believes in its possibility and fulfillment by 'virtue of the absurd, by virtue of the fact that for God all things are possible' (1843b). Kierkegaard draws an important distinction between the knight of resignation and the knight of faith, and it is this very differentiation between the former as an illustration of the lower form of the religious life, and the completed, more rigorous form of the religious (as exemplified by the latter) that provides the perfect rebuttal to those who accuse Kierkegaard's religious ideal as life-denying. His knight of faith is able to maintain a relationship and live in the finite, whilst the knight of resignation becomes an alien, a stranger to the world, and so 'the knight of faith is the only happy man, the heir to the finite, while the knight of resignation is a stranger and an alien' (1843b).

It is clear that Kierkegaard identified himself with the lower and less rigorous of the two forms of religious life. He writes, 'essentially I belong with the average' (1851), and 'as I have always maintained, I am no apostle, I am a poetic-dialectical genius, personally and religiously a penitent' (JP: 1849). That Kierkegaard was all too aware of his failure to embody the Christian ideal is evident in his description of himself as a poet who does not make himself out to be the ideal but as he who 'must himself first and foremost humble himself under it, confess that he, even though he himself is struggling within himself to approach this picture, is very far from being that' (1848/1859). It would seem that Kierkegaard's knight of resignation is an attempt to deny the bodily whilst seeking the spiritual. This figure personifies Kierkegaard's own pathological position, and expresses in metaphor his own sacrifice of Regine.

When Kierkegaard gives up Regine he becomes his own knight of infinite resignation, for he is not able to make the next step and approach the spirit in such a way that might enable her return to him. He consequently experiences a deficiency of faith within himself; he confesses, 'had I had faith I should have remained with Regine' (JP: 1843). With this confession Kierkegaard was perhaps unconsciously aware that his anima were absent, unintegrated within his ego-consciousness; furthermore, we might reasonably suggest that it is from this point that he devotes the rest of his life to the task of searching for authenticity in faith and being.

We learn from Regine that Kierkegaard himself doubted whether his sacrifice of her issued from the demand of divine governance or from a more pathological desire for self-torture. She recollects, 'I was neglecting a duty not only to him but to God, to whom he sacrificed me – whether it was due to an innate tendency toward self torture (a doubt he himself had), or whether it was an inner call from God' (Kirmmse 1996). Kierkegaard believed that in order to learn true humility one must withdraw from the turmoil of the world, 'for in life either the depressing or the elevating impression is too dominant for a true balance to come about' (JP: 1835). He draws a very sharp distinction between the external/social world and the inner/spiritual world. There is a clear link between his feeling an outsider; of his never quite fitting in and his rejection of conventions so that he could become what he seeks as 'the exception'. Kierkegaard set himself at odds with his contemporaries to an extraordinary extent, of which the '*Corsair*' event of 1845 is a good example. The *Corsair* was a popular newspaper that Kierkegaard sought to undermine. It would seem Kierkegaard, to all extent and purposes, deliberately provoked the *Corsair* into attacking him through their publishing of unfavorable cartoons or caricatures of him. This portrayal irrevocably changed Kierkegaard's private life forever; he had become 'a martyr of laughter' (JP: 1849).

Some might want to say of Kierkegaard's voluntary martyrdom that it was a spiritual sacrifice. This aside, such an act could only consolidate Kierkegaard's desire to separate himself from society, and thereby consolidate the pathological effects of doing so. Arguably, this martyrdom lies at the very heart of his neurosis, perhaps bound up with his egocentric sense of superiority, which with his self-absorption isolates him from community. If we were to judge Kierkegaard according to his own definition of martyrdom we might draw a somewhat milder conclusion. He writes:

> The difference between the person who goes to his death out of devotion to an idea and the mimic who seeks a martyrdom is that whereas the first person lives most fully in his idea of death, the second person delights in the curiously bitter feelings which result from being worsted; the former rejoices in the victory, the latter in his suffering.
>
> (JP: 1836)

In the case of Kierkegaard it is difficult to determine with conviction which camp he falls into. For all his neuroses Kierkegaard's devotion to the Christian ideal is without doubt a very earnest one, and one which occupied him entirely. And yet, we cannot ignore the bitter feelings he exudes or his rejoicing in suffering, which characterises Kierkegaard's later life. Therefore, it would seem, following his own definition, that Kierkegaard is both a martyr and mimic. Regardless of Kierkegaard's afflictions it is important to bear in mind that his insight is fundamentally and genuinely from a 'religious' perspective, in his understanding of the term.

Jung's conception of the shadow, as that which embodies all that we repress and refuse to acknowledge within ourselves, challenges our capacity for self-love; it holds up that which is most perverse and wretched, in order to demand that we not only recognise it as an essential part of ourselves, but more importantly accept it as such. In terms of healthy psychological development, Kierkegaard may well recognise that he is repressing aspects of himself and that he has sought to deny the presence of his anima in his admission of regret that had he attained true faith he would have remained with Regine. Indeed, it is my contention that had he embraced Eros, he would have been able to affirm the shadow side of his personality, and find fulfillment. However, as I understand it, Kierkegaard with his victory over the sexual instinct and his consequent rejection of the body represses Eros, forcing it into the deepest depths of the unconscious, and for this he does indeed pay dearly.

As we have previously discussed eros leads us both into the world and into involvements with others. The shadow cannot be assimilated into consciousness through unconscious acting out, or repression; these simply being two sides of the same coin. It is only through accepting the shadow that one can harness its energies in the service of psychic health and development; once repressed, this dark side or shadow 'remains in the background, unsatisfied and resentful, only waiting for an opportunity to take its revenge in the most atrocious way' (1961: par.1354). Shadow requires Eros – it requires that the individual embrace their shadow, accept all that it represents, even if it repels them in the process. What we see in the Regine saga is the creation of the idealised poet and his lifelong muse; and with this Kierkegaard loses his real self in his own deceptions and fabrications of fantasy. This most solitary of philosophers, who understood profoundly how we so often mistake our deceptions for reality was seemingly blind to his own. His self-imposed isolation, his pathological need to be despised is confused by him for martyrdom, and is perhaps nothing more than a grandiose consolation for the 'misrelation' that we have so often noted him speaking about. That Kierkegaard does not face this problem and govern it himself, but rather ignores it and takes flight into divine governance, perhaps makes his conception of faith slightly problematic; for, as I have discussed at length in Chapter 2, his conception of faith is one that reveals our self-deceptions to us, and that it is through such revelations that we are brought closer to God.

Kierkegaard found in his suffering a great source of consolation; he identifies the precise nature of such consolation in the following quote:

> At times I am buoyed up by the thought that the thorn or spike I have in the flesh, a suffering I try to bear patiently, will itself be or will help me to be a thorn in the eye of the world.
>
> (JP: 1849)

Had Kierkegaard been able to wretch this thorn in his flesh out, he might have been able to marry Regine. Previously, we discussed how castration anxiety was likely to underpin Kierkegaard's mindset as a lifelong presence. If he were to overcome this and thereby allow his sexual nature to evolve, he would have to engage with his anima. This would entail Kierkegaard having first to allow himself to long spiritually for his mother, and then allow it the opportunity to project itself onto the figure of Regine. To do these things would require Kierkegaard to renegotiate his Oedipus complex.

According to Garff, it is Kierkegaard's frenzied writing style that leads to such psychological costs in Kierkegaard's mental state. I cannot accept such a conclusion, On the contrary, it is surely his engagement with his writing – his only source of outward self-expression and engagement with his psychological world – that kept him sane; the psychological cost of not writing, and thereby of failing to engage with his psychological insufficiencies in creative fashion, could have been potentially disastrous. I contend that it is only through his creative activity as a writer that Kierkegaard is able to keep all the conflicting elements of his personality together. As I commented earlier in this chapter, Lowtzsky in her psychoanalytic study of Kierkegaard (1935a) concludes that he came close to solving his own oedipal complex. However, had he actually succeeded in this I suspect he would have been none the better for it. I have grave doubts that it would even have been possible for Kierkegaard to have embarked in a sexual relationship with Regine; to do so would see his conception of God collapse and come crashing down upon him. It is fitting to conclude this section with Kierkegaard's own considered words concerning marriage to Regine:

> Suppose I had married her. Let us assume it. What then? In the course of a half year or less she would have been unhinged. There is – and this is both the good and bad in me – something spectral about me, something no one can endure who has to see me every day and have a real relationship to me. Yes, in the light overcoat in which I am usually seen, it is another matter. But at home it will be evident that basically I live in a spirit world. I was engaged to her for one year, and she really did not know me. Consequently she would have been shattered. She probably would have bungled my life as well, for I always was overstraining myself with her because in reality she was in a sense to light for me. I was too heavy for her and she too light for me, but both factors can very well led to overstrain. Very likely I would not have amounted to anything or perhaps I may have developed just the same, but she would have been a torment to me simply because I would see that she was altogether wrongly situated through her being married to me – then she would have died and all would be over. To take her along into history as my wife – no, it cannot be. It is all right for her to become Madam and Mrs, but no longer may she be maintained in the character of being my beloved; it must be set forth as a story of unhappy love, and for me she

will remain the beloved 'to whom I owe everything'; then history will take her along – on this I will give instructions to history.

(JP: 1849)

Notes

1 Kierkegaard uses this word 'misrelation' throughout his journals to describe the conflict he feels between spirit and body. I, in turn, we also use it as we attempt to clarify the nature of this conflict.
2 Kierkegaard using this term, 'the universal', across several journal entries and since the context for 'the universal' is always one of marriage and procreation, it has been assumed that Kierkegaard always encodes marriage as 'the universal'. See R. Poole, (1993) *Kierkegaard: The Indirect Communication.*
3 Curiously he writes in a journal entry of 1843:
  'I have considered examining an aspect of Agnete and the Merman that has probably not occurred to any poet. The merman is a seducer, but after he has won Agnetes love he is so moved that he wants to belong to her entirely. But, alas, he cannot do so because then he would have to initiate her into the whole of his painful existence, of how he becomes a monster at certain times. The church cannot give them its blessing. Then he despairs and in his despair dives to the bottom of the sea and remains there, but he leads Agnete to believe that he had only wanted to deceive her. . . . If the merman could have faith, then his faith might perhaps transform him into a human being.
  In the character of the merman we see again this conflict between the spirit and the flesh.
4 Kierkegaard openly praises Abraham as a personification of his conception of an authentic religious life, and is therefore a person he would seek to emulate.
5 As Kierkegaard famously notes, 'But in order to find that idea [the idea for which I am willing to live and die]- or, to put it more correctly – to find myself, it does no good to plunge still further into the world. That was just what I did before'.
6 'Spiritually speaking, everything is possible, but in the world of the finite there is much that is not possible. This impossibility, however, the knight makes possible by waiving his claim to it. The wish [for happiness] which would carry him out into actuality, but has been stranded on impossibility, is now turned inward, but it is not therefore lost, nor is it forgotten'. S. Kierkegaard, *Fear and Trembling.*

Chapter 16

The final years of Søren Kierkegaard

A story of archetypal compensation

The final phase of Kierkegaard's life is marked by its lack of human attachment; it is here that his love for God and hatred of humanity reaches its zenith: the 'life-and-death-struggle between what it is to be God and what it is to be man, and to love God is to hate oneself and this world and everything the natural man loves' (JP: 1854). Nearing the end of his short life Kierkegaard's negative view of sexuality, and of all earthly life for that matter, has come to the forefront of his writing. There is simply no denying his rejection of the world, and humanity in the later works; consequently there is in evidence a detachment from reality that manifests in both his writing and personality. After the publications of 1851, Kierkegaard began to lead an increasingly isolated existence, and whilst he continued writing his now vitriolic *Journal* entries, he published very little. For the first time in his life Kierkegaard stopped attending Christian services of worship, and he encouraged others to do the same, by explaining that by staying home people would have one less sin on their souls, since they would no longer be participating in a process that treats 'God as a fool'.[1]

Having looked at how Kierkegaard's engagement to be married affected a real influence on his negative views of sexuality, in the final section of Part Three, I will explore the contention that this negative view of sexuality mutates within Kierkegaard's psyche into a deeper and darker negative view of everything that can be considered 'earthly'. In the context of a Jungian analysis of his psychological situation, it would seem that Kierkegaard's inability to fulfill his engagement to Regine – as I have understood it as a refusal to engage with his anima – becomes the basis upon which he later rejects the sexual drive as a whole, and praises celibacy from the sexual act. There are significant changes in his views towards sexuality and marriage, as indeed there is with Kierkegaard's psyche itself. It is my contention that his increased irritability and anger towards the world and people within it can be understood in terms of the unconscious projections that arise from the anima that has not been integrated into consciousness. The anima, denied its conscious integration, remains in the unconscious as the forbidden feminine. Desperate for conscious expression, as all repressed,

168 The final years of Søren Kierkegaard

material of shadow is, it harasses Kierkegaard with pathological symptoms, of which his increased irritability and anger, and his melancholic depression are examples.

Much that is written in the journals after 1850 conveys an unearthly, cold and almost inhuman rage. The *Journals* entries of 1854–1855, see an unpleasant Kierkegaard speak out with a good deal of disdain against women, sexuality, marriage, reproduction and childbearing. Vernard Eller views Kierkegaard's opinions at this time as 'not merely anti-marriage, nor even misogynist, but deeply and terribly misanthropic' (Eller 1968). Julia Watkin describes the writings of this period as a 'violent attack on women, sex, and marriage' and as exhibiting a 'particularly pronounced misogyny' (Watkin, 2010). Mark Lloyd Taylor offers a wonderful analysis of Kierkegaard's authorship of 1854–1855 that sees the emergence of a stark either/or: 'either New Testament faith in Jesus Christ or women, marriage, family, society, and church' (Taylor 2009). However, it needs to be brought to the reader's attention that there is wide disagreement between Kierkegaardian scholars over not just the issue of misogyny in these latter writings, but whether the later *Journals* and 'attack' literature represent a significant departure from his earlier works. There are even some scholars, who feeling so uncomfortable with the extremism of his thought at this juncture, have opted to discard the later *Journals* and the 'attack' literature as nonsensical, the rantings of an embittered paranoid (León 2008). It is my understanding that these final writings are both misogynistic and depressingly misanthropic. The extreme Christian view assumed by Kierkegaard in the final period of his life represents a significant departure, not in terms of misogyny (since little has changed in his views on women), but through the narrowing of a once enlivened faith. In its place is this monocular focus on the New Testament Christ, whom one is to imitate to the exclusion of almost everything that is earthly. The Kierkegaard of this period is simply not the same man who had ten years previously written *Stages on Life's Way*.

The aggression turned outward that runs like a thread throughout his life, Fenger claims, was a necessary survival tool, a therapeutic effect allowing him to let off steam at appropriate intervals. It is perfectly reasonable to agree that such aggression might well have given Kierkegaard respite from a tremendous inner psychological pressure, and a welcome diversion from his own psychological problems. I suspect that there is more to it than this – namely, the projection of thinly veiled desires and wish fulfilments. His teasing of his schoolmates; his revolt against his older brother; the conflict with his home and his father's melancholy; his sallies against members of the National Liberal Party; his assault upon Hans Christian Andersen[2]; his mocking of the first brood of Danish Heibergians, with Martensen bearing the brunt[3]; his aggressive offensive tirade against Hegel and Goethe[4]; his hysteria in the question of Paul Moller, Goldschmidt and the *Corsair*[5]; his attack on Mynster,[6] and the whole of the Danish State Church – all smack

The final years of Søren Kierkegaard 169

of the desire to participate in something. It is in his final battle with the Church where we arrive at the crescendo of Kierkegaard's bitterness. We could argue that it is the culmination of his lifetime of repression brought about from the conflicts in his personality that lay at the heart of the vicious outbursts that he exhibits at this time. The attacks on women, matrimony, Church and society represent that which he has spent an entire lifetime isolating himself from. Is this the bile of a regretful and envious and alienated old man? As we have seen, personality development in Jung's model requires the reduction of inevitable intrapsychic conflict, a reduction that relies upon being acted out, either in reality or symbolically, so as polarities within us (such as the anima – animus) can be synthesised and resolved – if a resolution cannot be brought to fruition the dialectical process can become destructive.

For the first half of life, young people can bear the loss of the anima, but for the second half of life, the loss of this relationship causes 'a diminution of vitality, flexibility and of human kindness' (1936/1954: par.147). I contend that it is the denied part of Kierkegaard, that which is erotic and sensual, that becomes the source of hostility and aggression. From accounts by Kierkegaard's contemporaries we learn that in his later and final years 'the sickly nature of his profound sensibility . . . increasingly got the upper hand as the years passed' (Kirmmse 1996). And that he

> was noticeably transformed by illness. True, he still walked in the streets a good deal, but I don't think he had his earlier delight in talking with people. At any rate, he never gave me an opportunity to exchange words with him in those days.
>
> (Kirmmse 1996)

Such accounts possibly point towards changes brought about by anima forces, perhaps the result of the subdued and forbidden feminine anima appearing in his irritability and anger.

I believe the change in his view on marriage is a very good example of the change that is brought about by Kierkegaard's unintegrated anima. In *Either/Or*, Judge Wilhelm praises marriage as 'the most intimate, the most beautiful association that life on this earth provides'. Later, when Kierkegaard is overcome with negativity, we read in his journal entries that 'woman is personified egoism. Her burning, hot devotion to man is neither more nor less than her egoism', whereas man 'is not originally as egoist'; he does not become that until 'he is lucky enough to be united to a woman', when he becomes the thorough egoist in the union 'commonly known as marriage . . . the proper enterprise of egoism' (Watkin 1997). The earlier, positive attitude towards marriage becomes consumed by the pessimistic emergence of Kierkegaard's later tendency to depict marriage as state that is both compromised and inferior. And so we see Kierkegaard advocate the withdrawal

170 The final years of Søren Kierkegaard

from social life and the sensuous life of sexuality, marriage and childbearing in a celebration of universal celibacy:

> To love God a man must give up all egoism, and first and foremost the potentiated egoism of the propagation of the species, the giving of life. . . . So God wishes to have celibacy because he wishes to be loved.
>
> (JP: 1854)

His Christianity evolves to become a hatred of worldliness, and so naturally it follows that it must also advocate hatred of woman, marriage and everything that is an affirmation of this human world.

The second half of Kierkegaard's religious authorship includes: the *Sickness Unto Death* (1849); *Training in Christianity* (written in 1848 but held back from publication until 1850) and *For Self Examination* (1851). David Swenson sees present in these works Christian teaching at its most idealised, for they require from the reader no less than 'concession, admission and personal humiliation under the [Christian] ideal' (Swenson 2000). What followed in Kierkegaard's writings was an ever-increasing criticism of the distance between the Christian ideal and the actual life of the Christian world, with the former being praised and the latter belittled.[7] Whilst this period in Kierkegaard's writings is marked by a powerful idealism, Kierkegaard's faith remains seemingly gentle, requiring that the individual accept his or her life in the world as a gift and task from God. It is this notion of a gentle and accepting faith, in contrast to that which he claims requires one to will to be nothing before God, which forms Kierkegaard's later conception of faith. Although, the aim of a faith that wills one is nothing before God is to be rid of self-centeredness, and of oneself, there can be no doubt that Kierkegaard's writings in his final years present the ideal relationship with God as one that is detached from human relationships. The introduction of this idea is, I claim, not so much the result of a natural rational development or progression within his thought, but rather an unhealthy mutation – a corruption that has its basis in his torturous experiences of self and its aggressive projection onto the world that consequently is perceived as something to be hated. Like Nietzsche, whose philosophical outlook similarly isolated him from the mass of humanity, Kierkegaard loses himself in his religious rigorism. Jung held the belief that the individual had to stay in touch with reality:

> You know what my attitude is to the unconscious. There is no point in delivering oneself over to it to the last drop. If that were the right procedure, nature would never have invented consciousness. . . . In my view it is absolutely essential always to have our consciousness well enough in hand to pay sufficient attention to our reality, to the Here and Now. Otherwise we are in danger of being overrun by an unconscious which

The final years of Søren Kierkegaard 171

knows nothing of this human world of ours . . . consciousness must keep one eye on the unconscious and the other focused just as clearly on the potentialities of human existence and human relationships.

(1906–1950)

In regards to the presumption widely held in the Middle Ages that the ascetic withdrawal from the world (and subsequent existence living within a monastery) represents the 'religious life' in its highest form), Kierkegaard denies that the imitation of Christ is meant to promote aesthetic self-torturing. Instead, he claims that the individual need not seek out suffering for suffering will find him who imitates Christ and follows in his example:

> the highest is: unconditionally heterogeneous with the world by serving God alone, to remain in the world and in the middle of actuality before the eyes of all, to direct all attention to oneself – for then persecution is unavoidable.

(1851)

The highest expression of Christian existence for Kierkegaard, therefore, is to suffer as a Christian in conflict with the world; one must exist in tension and conflict with the world. The individual who seeks the religious life will find adequate ascetic trials occurring naturally; he therefore does not need to seek out suffering as a goal in and of itself. Furthermore, prohibition from realising a higher form of religiousness was not to be found in one's external circumstances, but in one's internal relationship with God. That one's worldly circumstances do not prevent one from reaching the ideal relationship with God. However in the period of his spleenful attack on the Church, his conception of the Christian ideal becomes altogether more severe and the torturous asceticism that he previously warned of comes to saturate his ideal.

Whilst I do not wish to dismiss such works, I do feel that we must concentrate on the works that can be rightly designated as being psychologically motivated. Essentially, in his *Concept of Anxiety* and *Sickness Unto Death* Kierkegaard is able to hold the variegated views together without collapsing any of them into the other. Prominent in these works is the dialectical movement of the spheres within each person, the interplay of the multiplicity of selfhood.

There is a very real shift in the religious ideal presented in Kierkegaard's works. We see the embodiment of faith in the knight of faith, who seeks God in and through the world, become in these later works an altogether alienated faith, which is sought by turning away from the world and all it has to offer: 'he lives in the finite, but he does not have his life in it. . . . He is a stranger in the world of finitude'. I do not wish to follow Kierkegaard up to this point in his life, which finds him at his most vulnerable, all too

172 The final years of Søren Kierkegaard

detached from society and estranged from the finite. Whilst the fanatical and idealised Christianity of these later works are important psychologically speaking, and indicative of the major splits that have occurred in his psyche, we must consider Kierkegaard's entire historical life and personage, not merely focus solely upon this Kierkegaard who, living in isolation and dominated by anima, has narrowed his view of faith to such a point that it can only lead to despair and destruction, making of him 'the Pied Piper of Hamelin, pulling everything along with him into destruction' (Fenger 1980). To do so fails to do justice to the positive and liberating Christian faith of renewal exemplified in his earlier works and explored in this thesis.

As we have seen both Kierkegaard and Jung explain God in terms of completion rather, than of perfection – the teleological purpose is the movement towards a personal whole with ethical connotations. There is a gulf between theory and practice as far as Kierkegaard is concerned, for whilst he talks of wholeness, what we see in his life is this obsession for perfection. The split in Kierkegaard's psyche can be seen in his inordinately idealistic conception of marriage. When he speaks of marriage it is always in the absence of the carnal element, that essential part of marriage in the outer world. Kierkegaard, like his Antigone, suffers but kept silent. His morbid preoccupation with his body, and its 'misrelation', seemingly compounds his idealistic concern for spiritual purity, truth and perfection. Consequently Kierkegaard cannot come to accept the realities implicit in being a human animal. He cannot accept his earthly, physical nature. Having explored Kierkegaard from an analytical viewpoint, it is now time to turn to a more specific analysis based upon that which Jung himself has to say about Kierkegaard.

Notes

1 'This has to be said; so be it now said, Whoever thou art, whatever in other respects thy life may be, my friend, by ceasing to take part (if ordinarily thou doest) in the public worship of God, as it now is (with the claim that it is the Christianity of the New Testament), thou hast constantly one guilt the less, and that a great one: thou dost not take part in treating God as a fool by calling that the Christianity of the New Testament which is not the Christianity of the New Testament'. S. Kierkegaard, *Attack Upon Christendom*, 1854).
2 Kierkegaard's *From the Papers of One Still Living* attacked Anderson for allegedly lacking a life view and for having misunderstood the concept of genius. However, this attack was much more than just literary. Kierkegaard personally attacks Andersen, characterising him as having a 'weakly developed temperament'.
3 Kierkegaard's journals from the years 1849–50 are full of criticisms of Martensen's *Dogmatics*.
4 Kierkegaard's disdain for the pretentiousness of Hegel's philosophical system are well known, his criticisms of Goethe less so. The latter is almost certainly motivated by Goethe's link to the Heibergians, whom had celebrated Goethe enormously.
5 Following a frivolous review of Kierkegaard's *Stages on Life's Way* by Moller, Kierkegaard hit back with vehemence in an article entitled 'The Activity of a

The final years of Søren Kierkegaard 173

Travelling Esthetician and How He Still Happened to Pay for the Dinner', exposing Moller's involvement in the publication of *The Corsair* (a publication notorious for gossip and caricature), an association which would ruin Moller's reputation and future career.

6 Mynster, embodied for Kierkegaard the prototypical representative of the official Church of Denmark, which Kierkegaard felt had departed from the Christianity of the New Testament. Following the bishop's death in 1854, Kierkegaard launched a scathing and bitter attack on the man in an article entitled 'Was Bishop Mynster a Witness to the Truth'.

7 For instance, the death of Bishop Mynster in 1853 presents Kierkegaard with the opportunity to attack official Christendom. Martsensen preached a memorial sermon in which he claimed the late Bishop to be 'one more link in the holy chain of witnesses for the Truth, stretching all the way from the days of the apostles to our own times'. This falsification of the Christian ideal Kierkegaard believed symptomatic of the demoralisation to which Christendom as a whole was subject. This riled Kierkegaard considerably, and so he sets upon both a personal attack upon Bishop Mynster (understandably viewed by contemporaries as an attack upon the memory of the dead) and of the legitimation of the established order of the Church which the Bishop had represented.

Part 4

Chapter 17

The nature of a Kierkegaardian neurosis

Jung's reception of Kierkegaard

As we have explored throughout this work, the similarities connecting Jung with Kierkegaard are striking. Kierkegaard's God 'from beneath' stimulates self-renewal in a manner that Jung believed religion and depth psychology ought also to do. As we have seen, for both thinkers, it is through our subjective feelings that we enter these divine depths, and encounter the unconscious. It is through our moods that we feel the effects of the psyche. While we may ordinarily seek to rid ourselves of such moods, Kierkegaard and Jung encourage us to embrace them and to endure even our most painful suffering with a reflective patience. In the course of this thesis we have explored the theories through which both Kierkegaard and Jung emphasise human interiority as the locus for our experience of the divine, and where we can facilitate an increased unity with the God within. And so, given these remarkable similarities and the many reasons why – as I have argued – Jung ought to have found in Kierkegaard a strong, positive influence for the shaping of his own theories, the burning question remains: Why didn't he? Why didn't Jung accept Kierkegaard as a kindred spirit? And, more to the point, why, despite all the evidence to suggest their affinity, did Jung cast him aside as swiftly and strongly as he did?

From a Jungian perspective, we would argue that such a strong resistance in his own dismissal of Kierkegaard is indicative of there being some unconscious reason – some repressed and difficult reason within his psyche that has been cast in there out of an emotional need to forget or disown it. It is there, in his unconscious, desperate to make itself known to conscious awareness, but being forced into silence by the defenses of Jung's ego. As we discussed at length in Part Two of this thesis, when we refuse accountability of the very real contents of repressed material or 'the shadow', we either project the contents onto others (who become the scapegoat for our unowned feelings), or we internalise them as pathological physical or emotional symptoms. The failure to work with repressed material and enable their integration into ego-conscious awareness inevitably leads to the projection of indignation outward onto others; in essence we seek to hang our own stuff onto others, so they find a home elsewhere, we attack those whom we perceive our own unattended shadow. 'Projections', writes Jung, 'change the world into the replica of one's own unknown face' (1951: par.17). I therefore argue that Kierkegaard is a shadow figure for Jung; Jung's hostile reception of Kierkegaard reveals Jung's unknown face. But in order for us to ascertain the nature of his shadow projection onto Kierkegaard, we need to examine that which is similar in these two figures: in other words, determine what it is in Kierkegaard's own personality that lends itself to being a suitable personal 'hook' for aspects of Jung's own. Having attempted to reach behind the Kierkegaardian writings to the perplexed and tortured personality of our melancholy Dane, in what follows I offer an analysis of Jung's dismissal of Kierkegaard, with the hope of better understanding the psychological motivations behind this resistance.

Renowned Jungian analyst Ann Casement (1998) sketches parallels between Kierkegaard and Jung, a brief outline that she describes as a piece of bricolage: an insightful but unstructured musing. In her outline, Casement merely draws on the two references in Jung's *Collected Works* where Jung explicitly refers to Kierkegaard. We have discussed these already, but to reiterate, the passages are as follows:

> There are many Europeans who began by surrendering completely to the influence of the Christian symbol, until they landed themselves in a Kierkegaardian neurosis or whose relation to God, owing to the progressive impoverishment of symbolism, developed into an unbearable sophisticated I-You relationship – only to fall victim in their turn to the magic and novelty of Eastern symbols.
>
> (1934/1954: par.11)

> For [the Western mind] man is small inside; he is next to nothing; moreover, as Kierkegaard says, 'before God, man is always wrong.' By fear, reticence, promises, submission, self-abasement, good deeds and praise, he propitiates the great power which is not himself but *totaliter alter*, the wholly other, altogether perfect.
>
> (1939b: par.772)

Interestingly, Casement cuts the second quote off short, ending it on: 'before God, man is always wrong'. In doing so she misses the most crucially informative statement Jung makes concerning Kierkegaard. For the rest of the passage reveals the Kierkegaardian neurosis to which Jung refers: that is to say, the neurotic projection of all that is positive about Kierkegaard's own sense of self, projected out of him, and put onto or into a being that is wholly other to him. A move that consequently finds Kierkegaard's own self unworthy and ultimately nothing before God, who carries everything

The nature of a Kierkegaardian neurosis 179

positive. Jung summarises this projection elsewhere in essentially Christian terms. He writes, for example,

> The Christian West considers man to be wholly dependent upon the grace of God, or at least upon the Church as the exclusive and divinely sanctioned earthly instrument of man's redemption. . .
> . . . [For the extraverted West] grace comes from elsewhere at all events from outside. Every other point of view is sheer heresy. Hence it is quite understandable why the human psyche is suffering from under-valuation. Anyone who dares to establish a connection between the psyche and the idea of God is immediately accused of 'psychologism' or suspected of morbid 'mysticism'.
>
> (1939b: par.770–1)

Jung knew his ideas challenged the clergy and theologians of his day, as anybody who diagnosed Christian faith in terms of neurotic projection would. Thus he wrote:

> I am not addressing myself to the happy possessors of faith, but to those many people for whom the light has gone out, the mystery has faded, and God is dead. For most of them there is no going back, and one does not know either whether going back is the better way. To gain an understanding of religious matters, probably all that is left us today is the psychological approach. That is why I take these thought-forms that have become historically fixed, try to melt them down again and pour them into moulds of immediate experience.
>
> (1938/1940: par.148)

For Jung, God resides as much within us, within the psyche, as he does outside us. The inner source of life must therefore be acknowledged; otherwise a person is at the mercy of their projections of it onto the world outside. Those who are unaware that the inner deity reveals itself from the depths of the soul are suffering, Jung says, from 'a systematic blindness' (1938/1940: par.100). Although this might include a vast majority of Christian theologians, my argument asserts that Kierkegaard cannot be said to be one of them. Throughout his writings, Kierkegaard often returned to the theme of *inderlighed*, or 'inwardness', which in its most developed form is nothing less than Christian faith. For Jung, it is the concept of 'transcendentalism' (also described as 'uprootedness') by contrast, of Western theological traditions, which he holds responsible for conspiring to uproot humanity from its natural access to its own soul. From Jung's dismissive allusion to Kierkegaard, it would seem that Jung wrongly adduced Kierkegaard to be one of these purveyors of uprootedness. Jung feared what he perceived to be the neurotic aim of Christianity to keep the shadow side of human existence at arm's length and hopelessly relegated to the periphery of religious faith, and it would seem that Jung carelessly attributed such aims to Kierkegaard.

Had Kierkegaard wandered into Jung's consulting room, what would be the subject of their conversation? Well, we know from Jung's letters what Jung would have said to his patient.

> I would have told Kierkegaard straight off: 'it doesn't matter what you say, but what it says to you. To it you must address your answers. God is immediately with you and is the voice inside you. You have to have it out with that voice'.
>
> (1906–1950)

John Dourley interprets this passage as an explicit declaration from Jung that Kierkegaard's thinking stands in need of a corrective to be supplied by a conception of God as both immanent and present within the psyche. Dourley further explains,

> Kierkegaard so distances the realities of God and human beings that they could only be united in the wholly gratuitous and seemingly arbitrary revelation of Jesus Christ for which there was no archetypal basis as the principle of expectation, demand and reception.
>
> (Dourley 1990)

God's presence to man from without, so Dourley believes, underlies what Jung calls the 'Kierkegaardian neurosis'. Dourley here most likely draws upon Jung's critical remarks regarding the notion of the absolute. Thus Jung asserts,

> 'Absolute' means 'cut off,' 'detached.' To assert that God is absolute amounts to placing him outside all connections with mankind. Man cannot affect him or he man. Such a God would be of no consequence at all. We can in fairness only speak of a God who is relative to man, as man is to God . . . that kind of God could reach man.
>
> (1916: note6)

God in the Christian tradition is made absolute; a wholly other being to humankind. The parts of ourselves that we run from and repress within the psyche (symbolised by the shadow, anima/animus) are, however, also missing from God, so Jung claims (1951). However, this Kierkegaardian neurosis is far more complex that Dourley makes it seem, and I contend that there is a strong counterargument to Dourley's assertions that can be made. I find it hard to accept that it is Kierkegaard's refusal to listen to his own inner dialogue that removes him from a life where the divine is truly experienced. Indeed, we have seen that it is principally through a lifetime of engaging with this internal dialogue that we find Kierkegaard removed from the fulfillment of his relationship with Regine, and removed from his community life as a rural pastor. For reasons that will shortly be outlined, I contend that the therapeutic corrective required for Kierkegaard is not found in this God of immanence (which is already present – and perhaps all – too – much for him), but a counterpoint to this inner spiritual voice, and that is the bodily, the sexual, the earthly, and the feminine. Kierkegaard shares Augustine's dictum concerning self-awareness as awareness of God, that asserts: 'in order to know God do not go outside yourself, return into yourself' (Aquilina 2000). And we might go so far as to say that Kierkegaard employs this in his own life in literal terms. Kierkegaard's attempt to share the very truth of his life is, I believe, an entirely earnest one. And it is through his attempts to do so that he sought not only to awaken his readers to their own lives as ones grounded in God, but also, and perhaps moreover, he sought to explain that the central tenet of Christianity is found in dogmatic rules about how one ought to live one's life, and not in how one can live life inwardly, in personal relationship to God.

For Kierkegaard, just as for Jung, God is found within the self, but, unlike Jung, he does not go as far as to imply that 'God is wholly ourselves'. Essentially, I contend Dourley is wrong on two counts. Firstly, Kierkegaard's self is a relational one; Kierkegaard is careful to explain that one can only be a self in relation to God, and if God is wholly other, then it would follow that there is no conceivable way for the self to relate to such a God. Secondly, relating to God through what Kierkegaard supposes is the correct Christian approach, involves resting transparently in the power that created it. Furthermore, Kierkegaard is clear that God is both immanent and absolute.[1]

There could be no movement of synthesis in Kierkegaard's model if God were conceived as an absolute being. For Kierkegaard, God is at one and the same time the absolute other and a love that can be experienced immediately and personally. Climacus's declaration that we should have an absolute relationship with the absolute, and a relative one to what is relative, refutes any attempt to brandish Kierkegaard's God a transcendent one. Kierkegaard as Climacus declares,

> The practice of the absolute distinction makes life absolutely strenuous, especially when one must also remain in the finite and simultaneously relate oneself absolutely to the absolute telos and relatively to relative ends.
>
> (1843a)

This issue over the God of immanence versus the God of transcendence is somewhat of a moot point therefore. If we are to accept that the God-image for Jung is antecedent to an individual's relationship with a transcendent God, then how can Kierkegaard be regarded as a case of 'unqualified'

182 The nature of a Kierkegaardian neurosis

transcendence, when he clearly demonstrates that it is his own inner experience of God that leads to his awareness of a transcendent God? Kierkegaard's religiosity can be considered natural in that it does not solely depend upon a transcendent revelation, but on the kind of knowledge of God that is immanent to human consciousness. Jung and Kierkegaard express different views about the relationship between humanity and God, but this somewhat shrinks into the background when we consider that God is just as much rooted in the inner life of a person as 'He' is for Jung. In addition to this, the focal point for both is the need for religious experience and the immediate relation to God. Jung was strongly critical of the Church for their disinterest in subjective individual experience as a means to God's revelation. He writes:

> I have a real communion only with those who have the same or similar religious experience, but not with the believers in the word, who have never even taken the trouble to understand its implications and expose themselves to the divine will unreservedly. They use the word to protect themselves against the will of God. Nothing shields you better against the solitude and forlornness of the divine experience than community.
>
> (1956–1957: par.1637)

And again he emphasises the demise of authentic religious awareness:

> Christian civilization has proved hollow to a terrifying degree: it is all veneer, but the inner man has remained untouched and therefore unchanged. His soul is out of key with his external beliefs; in his soul the Christian has not kept pace with external developments. Yes, everything is to be found outside – in image and in word, in Church and Bible – but never inside.
>
> (1944: par.12)

In consulting these passages of Jung, we are struck once again by just how remarkable it is that he did not find affinity with the writings of Kierkegaard. How is it that Jung could purport to understand the personality of Kierkegaard, and yet not also have admired Kierkegaard's passionate commitment to an authentic Christian faith? Kierkegaard's emphasis on the authentic Christian existence clearly demands that we not only understand but *experience* the negative determinants of Christian existence (such as consciousness of sin, sacrifice, self-denial, poverty, suffering and adversity) in order to experience the true nature of divine grace. Furthermore, Kierkegaard claims that the very abolishment of this dialectic is itself the 'calamity of Christendom', and in so doing he emphasises the negative aspects of Christian existence. We have then in Kierkegaard's thought a scenario where the movement of faith 'runs counter to ordinary human desires, values, and goals in life' (Walsh 2008). Kierkegaard was especially concerned to empha-sise that Christ embodies both the positive and the negative ideals of Chris-tianity: a concern that is also key to Jung's enterprise. Jung reacted fervently against Christian morality, particularly with regards to what he considered to be the transformation of the erotic into religious activity:

> In the past two thousand years, Christianity has done its work and has erected barriers of repression, which protect us from the sight of our own sinfulness.' The elementary emotions of the libido have come to be unknown to us, for they are carried on in the unconscious; therefore, the belief which combats them has become hollow and empty.
>
> (1912)

Owing to the negative influence of Christian morality, we have, he claimed, become unaware of the primitive emotions of the libido. The repression of such emotions consequently take on an autonomous life of their own in the unconscious. This is why Jung asserts that Christianity is a hot-bed for neurotics and infantile adults. Kierkegaard – perhaps in the libidinous transformation of his unconscious incest wish into socially acceptable reli-gious beliefs – exemplifies this neurotic product of Christian morality for Jung. Yet it is fascinating to note that Kierkegaard's figure of Christ actu-ally embodies a more complete and unified expression of the Godly than Jung allows. In short, Kierkegaard's Christ is far from a one-dimensional embodiment of the *summum bonum* that Jung would assume. According to Kierkegaard, as the redeemer, Christ represents the forgiveness of sins, while as the lowly, suffering servant he represents the possibility of offense. In contrast to Christendom's one-dimensional representation of Christ as triumphant savior, Kierkegaard reminds us that:

> Christ himself willed to be the abased one, this was precisely how he wanted to be regarded. History, therefore, should not go to the trouble of letting him have his due, and we must not in ungodly thoughtlessness presumptuously delude ourselves that we immediately know who he was. No one knows that, and the person who believes it must become contemporary with him in his abasement.
>
> (1850)

From Jung's perspective we repress the notion that evil is part of God, and we do so in the same way that we repress the evil within ourselves (when we repress our shadow-selves). Whilst Kierkegaard does not explicitly attribute to God a dark shadow side, he does, however, avoid attributing to God the *summum bonum* in its absolute and abstract form. His emphasis is on the Christ who is both savior and lowly servant reminds us that God is not an absolute other, that God is within us all, and by accepting Christ we can, in a sense, come to know God. Dourley readily enforces Jung's own distorted view of Kierkegaard, and as a consequence, he unquestionably reinforces the idea that what Kierkegaard lacks and needs is the corrective of the immanent presence of God. Dourley's understanding relies heavily on Jung's proclamation that 'God is immediately with you and is the voice inside you' and that 'You have to have it out with that voice'. Antony Judd concurs with Dourley's thinking, and believes the roots of Jung's dismissal of Kierkegaard lie in their differing attitudes towards religion. Judd notes, 'for it is here that I think we can find, for all their commonalities, the deepest points of contention between them' (Judd 2011). By cutting himself off from his own life, and seeking instead to live solely from within his own introspective life with God and God alone, Kierkegaard actually alienates himself from his own inner dialogue:

> That Kierkegaard was a stimulating and pioneering force precisely because of his neurosis is not surprising, since he started out with a conception of God that has a peculiar Protestant bias which he shares with a great many Protestants. To such people his problems and his grizzling are entirely acceptable because to them it serves the same purpose as it served him: you can then settle everything in the study and need not do it in life. Out there things are apt to get unpleasant.
>
> (1906–1950)

Whilst we cannot ignore the patronising tone Jung adopts here, there is perhaps a shimmer of truth in Jung's words. Yet are we really to believe that Jung is free from the accusations he directs at Kierkegaard? Does he differ significantly from Kierkegaard in this respect? Did he himself settle things outside of his study? Just as an interesting aside, Kierkegaard's Climacus exclaims that, 'it is in the *living room* that the battle must be fought, not imaginatively in church, with the pastor shadowboxing and the listeners looking on' (1846a).[2] Jung's negative and emotional attack on Kierkegaard reveal more than just a difference in religious attitudes – there must be something altogether more personal going on to excite such hostility. Indeed, when considered from the perspective of a Jungian critique there certainly is, although Jung personally is not able to consciously realise the implications of his outward dismissal. To that end, I contend that Jung's problem with Kierkegaard is not found in their theological differences, nor in his philosophical critique of Kierkegaard's ideas, and, furthermore, neither is it to be found in his openly acknowledged psychological diagnosis of Kierkegaard's personality. It is found, I argue, in Jung's unconscious feelings towards all that Kierkegaard represents to him. Although this may seem a tenuous and speculative argument, it is one that can be done with conviction, given the striking evidence available, and not least, using Jung's own psychological theories to do so. It is blatant that Jung pathologises

The nature of a Kierkegaardian neurosis 185

Kierkegaard's personality, and his very attempts to criticise Kierkegaard philosophically are poorly executed, and almost embarrassingly so. A more thorough analysis of Jung's understanding of the neurosis Jung charges Kierkegaard with is required here. Only then can we understand the full meaning and implications of it for Jung's reception (both conscious and unconscious) of Kierkegaard.

As we have already deduced, the 'Kierkegaardian neurosis' is understood by Jung, to be part of a more general 'theological' or Christian neurosis. This point is further supported by the following emotionally charged comment Jung, writing to Rudolf Pannwitz in a letter dated 27th March 1937, makes: 'that you find Kierkegaard "frightful" has warmed the cockles of my heart. I cannot understand, or rather, I understand only too well, why the theological neurosis of our time has made such a fuss over him' (1906–1950). Jung, writing of neurosis in general, observed that:

> Hidden in the neurosis is a bit of still undeveloped personality, a precious fragment of the psyche lacking which a man is condemned to resignation, bitterness, and everything else that is hostile to life. A psychology of neurosis that sees only the negative elements empties out the baby with the bath-water, since it neglects the positive meaning and value of these 'infantile' i.e., creative-fantasies.
>
> (1934: par.355)

Following Jung's line of thinking, if Kierkegaard is indeed neurotic (and my argument so far suggests that, from a psychoanalytic-Jungian perspective, he certainly is) then one precious fragment that is missing from his psyche is, as I noted earlier, the feminine; culturally speaking we might say that the repression of the feminine is the prime cause of neurosis. That Jung can see nothing of positive value in Kierkegaard's neurosis is of great significance, given that his theories emphasise the positive element in neuroses. For instance in his Tavistock lectures:

> Dr. Dicks: I understand, then, that the outbreak of a neurotic illness, from the point of view of man's development, is something favourable?
>
> Professor Jung: that is so . . . that is really my point of view. I am not altogether pessimistic about neurosis. In many cases we have to say: 'Thank heaven he could make up his mind to be neurotic.' Neurosis is really an attempt at self cure. . . . [Neurosis] is an attempt of the self-regulating psychic system to restore the balance, in no way different from the function of dreams – only rather more forceful and drastic.
>
> (1935a: par.388–9)

Kierkegaard's entire philosophical corpus is construed by Jung to be a symptom, if not the product, of his neurosis. Jung is nothing but pessimistic about

Kierkegaard's Christian neurosis, which, as I have argued is completely out of step with Jung's thoughts concerning the healing potential of neurosis. We know Jung understood neurosis to be the result of self-division; that is to say, the symptom of inner discourse and unbalance within the psyche, giving rise to further disunion and discord within the self. Following this, we can deduce Kierkegaard's decidedly Christian neurosis to involve a disunity and imbalance of spirit and body, whereby the spirit is sought and promoted over and above the body to its detriment and rejection. This is further reflected in the desire for the God, who is separate from the body, and promoted over and above the wants and desires of the all-too-human ego. The projection of everything of positive value onto the external deity creates a psychological one-sidedness that can only impede growth and maturation of the total personality.

Kierkegaard's religious faith therefore becomes diametrically opposed to bodily life; it lacks the power of self-renewal, becoming destructive and tyrannical. Writing specifically of Christian theology, Jung levies the accusation that 'it proclaims doctrines which nobody understands and demands a faith which nobody can manufacture' (1942/1948: par.285). Kierkegaard's personal faith does indeed demand a faith that no human can manufacture. There is in Kierkegaard's thinking a very real awareness of the need to acknowledge one's individual self, but there is also in evidence the need to deny the worth of one's personal life experiences, and notably those of the human flesh, and relations with women (exemplified by his failed relationship with Regine and the oddity that surrounds his relationship with his mother, as discussed in Part Three: 'Keeping Mum'). Indeed, the feminine aspect that we find willingly sacrificed by Kierkegaard is also that which Jung believed to be missing in Protestantism generally, and one of the prime causes of it being an unhealthy approach to life. From Jung's perspective, Kierkegaard has nailed himself to the patriarchal line of the Old Testament, and in doing so removed himself from the essentially maternal and feminine experience that is inseparable from immediate contact with the unconscious (Dourley 1990). Kierkegaard rationalises the symptoms of his neurosis in theological terms, so that it appears to be his Protestant theology that makes him a sick man. Furthermore, Kierkegaard is so preoccupied and wrapped up in the development of his own thinking and the expectations of his faith that he inadvertently sacrifices the very aspect that Jung would surely reckon was fundamental to faith: love. As Jung writes:

> The woman is increasingly aware that love alone can give her full stature, just as the man begins to discern that spirit alone can endow his life with its highest meaning. Fundamentally, therefore, both seek a psychic relation to the other, because love needs the spirit, and the spirit love, for their fulfilment.
>
> (1929a: par.269)

The most scathing comments Jung makes about Kierkegaard are not in his theoretical works, but in his personal correspondence. Jung writes in a letter to Willi Bremi, 26th December 1953:

> I was once again struck by the discrepancy between the perpetual talks about fulfilling God's will and reality: when God appeared to him in the shape of Regina he took to his heels. It was too terrible for him to have to subordinate his autocratism to the love of another person.
>
> (1951–1961)

With this not so subtle aside, Jung clearly identifies not only Kierkegaard's failure to embrace his anima, but also, in employing the Latinised form 'Regina' he would appear to be emphasising Kierkegaard's broken engagement with Regine as indicative of Kierkegaard's failed attempts at individuation (i.e. to flourish psychologically). It is well known that Jung was keen to explain his theories of individuation in alchemical terms, and here we note that the alchemical partnership between rex (animus) and Regina (anima) is essential for the individuation process to occur; without an intense relationship between the contra-sexual components within the psyche, individuation simply cannot take place. Since Jung intimates that one encounters anima once the shadow has been engaged successfully, Kierkegaard's apparent failure to relate to his anima would imply an inability to progress beyond the encountering of his shadow, what Jung refers to as the 'apprentice-piece' in the work of one's individuation. We might then make the assumption that for Jung, Kierkegaard falls considerably short of taking up the task of healthy development.

It is difficult to gauge just how much of Kierkegaard's life and works Jung was familiar with. He obviously knew of his love affair and the broken engagement. And his quoting of 'before God, man is always wrong' would suggest that he had perhaps read or was at least acquainted on some level with Kierkegaard's work, *Either/Or*, specifically the sermon, 'The Upbuilding that Lies in the Thought That in Relation to God We Are Always in the Wrong'. However, evidence strongly suggests that Jung did not read Kierkegaard's work seriously. As we note in his letter of December 10th 1945 to Pastor Buri, he writes, 'Kierkegaard's view that animals have no fear is totally disproved by the facts. There are whole species which consist of nothing but fear. A creature that loses its fear is condemned to death' (1906–1950). This is of course a terrible misreading of Kierkegaard, for it is not *fear* that Kierkegaard believes to be absent in animals, but *anxiety*: a distinction Jung would certainly be familiar with in his own field. According to Kierkegaard, animals do not experience anxiety, only human beings do; for Kierkegaard, anxiety is the defining characteristic of man. Kierkegaard draws a very clear distinction between fear as something knowable and

188 The nature of a Kierkegaardian neurosis

definite from anxiety, which has no concrete object but is a rather a fear of nothing – a fear of the effects of our own fear:

> Anxiety is a qualification of dreaming spirit, and as such it has its place in psychology. Awake, the difference between myself and my other is posited; sleeping, it is suspended; dreaming, it is an intimated nothing. The actuality of the spirit constantly shows itself as a form that tempts its possibility but disappears as soon as it seeks to grasp for it, and it is a nothing that can only bring anxiety. More it cannot do as long as it merely shows itself. The concept of anxiety is almost never treated in psychology. Therefore, I must point out that it is altogether different from fear and similar concepts that refer us to something definite, whereas anxiety is freedom's actuality as the possibility of possibility. For this reason anxiety is not found in the beast, precisely because by nature the beast is not qualified as spirit.
>
> (1844b)

Thus Kierkegaard uses the figure of the beast as that which, lacking the possibility of spirit, also lacks anxiety and the possibility of sin; 'if a human being were a beast or an angel, he could not be in anxiety. Because he is a synthesis, he can be in anxiety' (1844b). Anxiety reveals the possibility of the self in relation to itself. In anxiety we are not our true/authentic self; rather it is through anxiety that we become ourselves – this is the meaning of one's anxiety. That which both fears and repels is one's freedom; the potential of becoming, possibility, the future – it is this potential for an individual's spiritual transformation that awakens anxiety. He continues,

> The nature of original sin has often been explained, and still a primary category has been lacking – it is anxiety; this is the essential determinant. Anxiety is a desire for what one fears, a sympathetic antipathy; anxiety is an alien power which grips the individual, and yet one cannot tear himself free from it and does not want to, for one fears, but what he fears he desires.
>
> (JP: 1842)

Interestingly, we have with his work *The Concept of Anxiety* (1844) a shift from thinking about creation in the past tense to thinking about creation in the present tense. Rather than look to the past and to the origin of sin in Adam and Eve's disobedience, he calls us to look within ourselves, to our own individual sinful flight from God. Instead of looking primarily toward the past, Kierkegaard's thought leads us to find the roots of our problems in our attempts to evade the call of God, the call of the future. Interestingly, is this not the fundamental difference between Jung and Freud? After all, Jung looks inwardly and upwardly towards the future and posits the

The nature of a Kierkegaardian neurosis 189

development of the self from what it currently lacks, whilst Freud has us looking outwardly and towards the past, and posits the development of the self from out of our past, repressed experiences from childhood. For Kierkegaard, anxiety is an incredibly important and fundamental dynamic of the human condition. It is crucial here to emphasise the great extent to which Kierkegaard's thinking is in accord with Jung's own views about the transformative potential of neurosis (the core feature of neurosis being anxiety): 'a man is ill, but the illness is nature's attempt to heal him, and what the neurotic flings away as absolutely worthless contains the true gold we should never have found elsewhere' (1934: par.361). Jung's proposition is that pathology has an unconscious purpose, for 'there is no illness that is not at the same time an unconscious attempt at cure' (1939c: par.68). We must therefore endure anxiety; to flee anxiety is not only cowardly but destructive to the self as it leads to an imbalanced and one-sided personality. In similar vein to Jung, Kierkegaard maintains that anxiety is an unconscious driving force that leads one into action:

> There is an anxiety in him, but this anxiety is his energy. It is not an anxiety which is subjectively reflected in him; it is a substantial anxiety. . . . When one throws a pebble so that it skims the surface of the water, it can skip along for a while in little hops, but as soon as it stops skipping, it instantly sinks into the abyss. In the same way, he dances upon the abyss, jubilant in his brief span.
>
> (1843a)

Anxiety for Kierkegaard denotes a psychological possibility; it is this potentiality that lies at the center of Kierkegaard's understanding of the personality. We are free to ground ourselves in what is less than God, but if we are to flourish and realise our psychological and religious potential we must ground ourselves in relationship with God. Far from a pathology per se, anxiety is integral to one's human self; it enables the realisation of one's potential, and for transformation. This notion of anxiety as an energy and potential for experience is a key point linking both Kierkegaard and Jung. Anxiety possesses creative communication, rather than presenting an emotional state that we would do well to be rid of – both thinkers emphasise the crucial role of anxiety for restoring us, and for helping us to realise our potential; anxiety then has a good deal to tell us about ourselves. However, Kierkegaard tells us that if anyone is a stranger to anxiety it is only because he is spiritless: 'in spiritlessness there is no anxiety, because it is too happy, too content, and too spiritless for that' (1844b). This clearly runs counter to Jung's own view that neurotic symptoms often manifest when an individual is spiritless. Nevertheless, Kierkegaard's profoundly psychological understanding of anxiety adds yet another instance of Jung's misunderstanding of him, and raises again the need to question the underpinning motivations

190 The nature of a Kierkegaardian neurosis

for his unwarranted dismissal of him. Could the motivations be, as I claim, the result of Jung's unconscious need to distance himself from Kierkegaard's thought?

There are no works of Kierkegaard to be found in Jung's library today, nor are there any works listed in the 1967 library catalogue. However, there are two copies of a PhD thesis on Kierkegaard's notion of angst by Arnold Künzli, entitled *Die Angst Als Abendlandische Krankheit: Darges-Tellt Am Leben Und Denk en Soeren Kiergaards* (Anxiety as an Occidental Disease: The Life and Thought of Søren Kierkegaard). If we consult this, we find, according to Künzli, that Kierkegaard's life was one of severe neurotic anxiety. Künzli explores Kierkegaard's life in great detail, leaning heavily upon Jung's analytical psychology and Freudian psychoanalysis for his analysis of it. He explores Kierkegaard's philosophical system as a protest against intellectualised religion and contemporary culture; finding motivation for this protest philosophy issuing from Kierkegaard's personal life. Even a cursory look at the blurb of this book would have shown Jung that the anxiety-laden division in Kierkegaard's own breast was a true mirror reflection of the modern age, resulting (according to Künzli) from an overvaluing of the intellect to the expense of all other mental/soul functions. Through the excessive culture of understanding the modern spiritual Westerner has lost the earth under his feet and consequently over intellectualised Christianity. In this respect, Künzli holds that Kierkegaard was very much a child of his time and overcome in dogmatic intellectualism; he remained in his lifelong unhealthy division (a debilitating life anxiety) which preached water and drank wine. It would seem that Jung did not actually get round to reading this thesis or at least had not reflected on its contents in any useful depth. Had he done so he would have discovered a number of important facts and ideas that may have dispelled his fantasy projections onto Kierkegaard. For example, he would have read that Kierkegaard felt that he had the head of an old man; that he hated his mother (seeing in her the purely one-sided aspect of primitive drives and sexual object) but loved his father (whom he associated religious feelings as expressions of fatherly love), and as a consequence, Kierkegaard gradually rejected the world of the maternal toward that of the paternal God. Jung would have also read of how Kierkegaard was equally as obsessed with healing the split between Christianity and modern man as he himself was; that Kierkegaard felt that he had to reform bourgeois Christianity, which had become rigidly steeped in dogmatism. Künzli portrays Kierkegaard as one who searched for individual freedom; for the ability to find one's self and be one's self regardless of dogma and tradition. To Kierkegaard selfhood meant an individual's capacity to face anxiety and to live in spite of it. Had Jung read this work, one wonders whether he would have seen in Kierkegaard a kindred spirit and brother-in-arms. And yet Jung clearly does not feel this way: this in itself would lend a degree of credibility to the idea that Jung unconsciously distances himself from Kierkegaard.

The nature of a Kierkegaardian neurosis 191

Scholars, notably Paul Bishop and Lucy Huskinson, have documented Jung's outright failure in his understanding of Nietzsche's philosophy, unconsciously motivated by his need to distance himself from the insane Nietzsche by exaggerating Nietzsche's neurosis at the same time as promoting his (Jung's) own psychological health.[3] And yet, whilst Jung recognised the need to distance himself from Nietzsche owing to his fear that he might be 'another one in the same mould' (1963) and therefore suffer the same fate, Jung had a lifelong fascination and deep respect for Nietzsche. As we have discerned through the course of this chapter, Jung construes Kierkegaard's philosophical corpus to be a product of his neurosis and given his outright pathologising of Kierkegaard's personality combined with his poor attempt to criticise Kierkegaard philosophically, we might similarly conclude that Kierkegaard, like Nietzsche, was a figure that Jung felt necessary to distance himself from. It is interesting to note that Jung is eager to come to the defense of religion where Nietzsche is concerned, and yet bears nothing but hostility for Kierkegaard. Clearly, Jung was keen to explore Nietzsche's situation in depth, both his life and works, yet he bypasses the works and personality of Kierkegaard, despite their strong similarities with regards to their religious ideas. Could there be something in the figure of Kierkegaard that resonates so deeply within Jung's own psyche? Does Kierkegaard become, for Jung, a more volatile figure than Nietzsche? In the following chapter I will contrast the neurotic 'one-sidedness' that Jung attributes to Nietzsche with the one-sidedness that is evident in Kierkegaard. By doing so I will elucidate the nature of what Jung refers to as the 'Kierkegaardian neurosis'.

Notes

1 See for instance, 'He is in the creation, everywhere in the creation, but he is not there directly, and only when the single individual turns inward into himself (consequently only in the inwardness of self-activity) does he become aware and capable of seeing God' (1846a).
2 And yet, Kierkegaard clearly did not take on the fight in his own childhood living room, nor the one he once shared with his beloved Regine.
3 See L. Huskinson, Nietzsche and Jung: The Whole Self in the Union of Opposites (Routledge, 2004).

Chapter 18

Kierkegaard and Nietzsche

Polar opposites in the mind of Jung

If we are to believe, as Dourley (1990) suggests, that Jung's resistance to Kierkegaard is the latter's one-sided emphasis on God's transcendence (at the expense of his immanence), does this really provide enough fuel to provoke such scathing remarks about Kierkegaard from Jung? Contrary to Dourley, I contend that Jung's emotional dismissal of Kierkegaard originate from the latter's denial of the sexual and feminine, for it is these elements that are so evocative for Jung. The influential philosopher of religion and psychiatrist Karl Jaspers considered Kierkegaard alongside Nietzsche as the greatest figure of 'intuitional psychology' (Jaspers 1997), but interestingly, Jung, however, perceives both to be deeply troubled and divided personalities, with each suffering a neurosis that is revealed in their religious writings.

Having already examined Jung's belief that religion provides the energies required for self-renewal, we now have to pause a moment to consider the pathological phenomena that he sees evident in religious experience. Whilst Jung does not put religion and neurosis in the same psychological swag bag as Freud, he certainly did assert that religious feelings can easily succumb to pathological distortions. As we discussed in Part Two, especially in the chapter pertaining to the value of suffering, Jung believed we are essentially religious, in so far as our lives are felt to be meaninglessness without the symbolic life provided it by religion. Where there is no acknowledgement of a higher power in the form of a God or guiding ideal, Jung proposes that something inappropriate will come in to take possession of the personality in this role. His primary warning is of the mystical tendency to unite with God, and he understands this as representing a dangerous psychological desire to identify with the unconscious:

> That is one of the great difficulties in experiencing the unconscious – that one identifies with it and becomes a fool. You must not identify with the unconscious; you must keep outside, detached, and observe objectively what happens . . . it is exceedingly difficult to accept such a thing, because we are so imbued with the fact that our unconscious is our own – my unconscious, his unconscious, her unconscious – and our prejudice is so strong that we have the greatest trouble disidentifying.
>
> (Jung 1932a)

The philosopher Friedrich Nietzsche was Jung's most detailed case study of the pathologies of the personality,[1] and in the course of it Jung outlines his diagnosis of Nietzsche's insanity and its cause as Nietzsche's personal identification with the autonomous complex of God:

> If you knew what reality that fact possesses which has been called God, you would know that you could not possibly get away from it. But you have lost sight of it; you don't know what that thing means and so it gets you unconsciously, and then without knowing it you are transformed into God almighty, as happened to Nietzsche. It got into him to such an extent that he went crazy and signed his letters 'the dismembered Zagreus' or 'Christ Dionysus', because he became identical with the God he had eliminated.
>
> (1934–1939: p.903)

And:

> One cannot feel a presence if one is God, because it is then one's own presence and there is no other. If all is conscious, one knows of no presence because one is everything, so long as one is identical with the deity there is no presence.
>
> (1934–1959: p.1174)

According to Jung, Nietzsche's very denial of this divine presence as autonomous to him, led to his owning the psychological fact of God for himself; that is to say, Nietzsche finds the religious and divine presence of God within himself *as* himself, *as* his ego-personality, so that he inadvertently becomes 'responsible for all that God once was' (ibid. p. 50). This denial of God and displacement of God's psychological value into Nietzsche's conscious personality causes an imbalance within the psyche as a whole. That is to say, locating the very source of life and meaning in the ego-consciousness creates a lop-sided and grandiose personality, one that lacks depth, and the capacity for self-critique. In response to such a fully-loaded consciousness, the psyche initiates a compensatory drive to try to rectify the imbalance, but given Nietzsche's identification with God is so strong, the counterpunch from the unconscious is similarly strong. So strong in fact that Jung claims that it caused a breakdown in Nietzsche's personality, and finds its expression in Nietzsche's conscious personality through his believing himself to be the *crucified* Christ, and the Greek god, Dionysus (who, in traditional Greek myth was ripped apart by the Titans):

> As is well known, Nietzsche's psychosis first produced identification with the 'crucified Christ' and then with the dismembered Dionysus. With this catastrophe the counteraction at last broke through the surface.
>
> (1916/1957: par.162)

Jung's seminar on Nietzsche's most favored work, *Thus Spoke Zarathustra* (a work that parodies the Bible with the teachings of Zarathustra, who has come to teach the death of God) reflects Jung's appetite and desire to create a role for religion in response to Nietzsche's claim of God's death – an appetite that Paul Bishop (1967) describes as 'his post-Nietzschean agenda for the transformation of faith into a secular, psychological religion' (Bishop 1995). In response to Nietzsche's proclamation, 'God is dead', Jung reassures us that 'God is a fact that has always happened', 'a very definite psychological fact' (1934–1939). In Nietzsche we have the religious psychotic 'whose deification of the body', writes Lucy Huskinson (2004), 'is merely, according to Jung, the deification of consciousness'. Conversely, in his acknowledgement of a higher power and complete surrender to the Christian symbol, Kierkegaard becomes a figure that can be considered an inverse of Nietzsche, and thus, a religious neurotic.

In *Memories, Dreams, Reflections* (1963) Jung writes:

> I was held back by a secret fear that I might perhaps be like him, at least in regard to the 'secret' which had isolated him from his environment. . . . I feared I might be forced to recognize that I too, like Nietzsche, was 'another one in the same mould' . . . I must not let myself find out how far I might be like him.
>
> (1963)

Jung was convinced that his life, like Nietzsche's, would become unbearable if he allowed himself to be one-sidedly guided by the aesthetic attitude (Tjeu Van den Berk 2012). Kierkegaard captured this same sense of one-sidedness, when he writes; 'Infinitude's Despair is to lack Finitude' and 'Finitude's Despair is to Lack Infinitude' (1849). From Kierkegaard's perspective, the individual is caught between two modes/spheres of existence. There is the here and now, immediacy, of the aesthetic world and the 'ethical' transcendent, eternal world. Neither world is capable alone of fulfilling all our needs for 'the self is composed of infinitude and finitude' (1849). Theoretically, Kierkegaard's view is identical to that which Huskinson identifies in relation to Jung's rejection of Nietzsche:

> The notion of 'body' is not to be equated with 'soul', it is simply 'the guarantee of consciousness' and 'a biological function' that the self directs to its own purpose . . . the body can only enable the physical outward manifestation of the self. It is not the totality of the Self, for the Self is also identified with an 'inner spiritual manifestation'. In other words, it is both conscious and unconscious.
>
> (Huskinson 2004)

Nietzsche with his proclamation that 'God is dead' adopts the role of a God-like being becoming the originator of truth and of his own self. Both

Kierkegaard and Jung would agree that this Nietzschean eradication of the self's dependency on a power outside of the individual ego can only lead to despair and ill health. Jung believed Nietzsche to have lost his self to finitude. I contend that we can reasonably speculate that Jung's accusation that Kierkegaard 'can then settle everything in the study and need not do it in life' hints at Kierkegaard's loss of self to infinitude. There can be little doubt that Jung held Nietzsche's aesthetic view of life responsible for his insanity and ill health. The body is part of the concrete expression of one's animal aspect, of all those instincts that we consider our base desires; it is these powerful instincts that Jung believed to be part of the shadow side of civilised humanity. Jung accuses Nietzsche of having over-identified with Dionysus at the expense of Apollo, thus becoming one-sidedly over-balanced on the side of the unconscious which sees him descending into madness. In his 1913 essay 'A Contribution to the Study of Psychological Types', Jung associates the Dionysian impulse with extraversion (the directing outward of libido), since the Dionysian involves the investment of libido in as many objects in the world outside the self as possible in a 'plunging into the multiplicity of the objective world'. Whilst the Apollonian is defined by a withdrawal of the libido into oneself, a 'shut up within oneself' and therefore pertains to the introverted character type (whereby the libido is turned inward). Apollo is generally associated with thinking and intuition whereas Dionysus is generally associated with feeling and sensation. In Nietzsche we have absolute obedience to one's instinctual drives and self-transcendence. What we see in Kierkegaard is the absolute denial of one's instinctual drives (which is equivalent in Jung's reading of Nietzsche to the 'Dionysian') and a transcendence that Jung likely suspects to subsume the individual self. We might go as far as to suggest that Kierkegaard abandoned the Dionysian and sought self-annihilation in the absolute Godhead. For Kierkegaard, nothing meaningful can exist outside the spirit; therefore there is no room in his model for the body as an active and productive force. Nietzsche's *Ubermensch* and Kierkegaard's knight of faith consequently suffer from one-sidedness, and thus lack the unity each requires for the compensation of the other, and for the realisation of the wholeness Jung requires for healthy flourishing. Kierkegaard's model, just as the Nietzschean model, thereby fails to unite the opposites because it promotes one opposite element at the expense of the other. With Nietzsche and Kierkegaard, Jung has at his hands useful figures upon which to pin his own psychological analysis of religious experience and a pathological analysis of religious experience. We also have perfect candidates for Jung's transcendent function as well as the Nietzschean antinomy of the Dionysian and the Apollonian in the mediation of opposites. Like two minus figures making a whole, perhaps a neurotic Kierkegaard with a neurotic Nietzsche similarly makes for a whole self, the ultimate in psychic health. If Nietzsche represents 'the Dionysian experience *par excellence*' (1934–1939), Kierkegaard is surely the prime representative of the Apollonian era of Christianity. Kierkegaard is after all the pin-up boy *par excellence* for Christianity's ascetic denial of sexuality.

Palmer, in his *Freud and Jung on Religion* (1997), explores both Freud's claim that religion is an obsessional neurosis and Jung's assertion that it is the absence of religion that presents a neurosis, as the defining points in their different philosophies. In contrast to Palmer, we might argue that Jung's view of religion and neurosis is far more complex than this; that his is a more subtle, dialectical understanding of the ability of religion to have both a positive, and wholly destructive or negative effect upon the self. There is, therefore, both a neurosis that can occur as a consequence of an unrecognised absence of religion (as we find in Jung's most general thinking about neurosis) and that which occurs as a result of a fervent religious presence, that which he deems a 'Kierkegaardian neurosis'. This can be illustrated through the figures of Kierkegaard and Nietzsche; both exemplify Jung's one-sided 'sick animals',[2] whose illnesses can be understood as the result of an imbalance between body and spirit. Nietzsche invests in the bodily; Kierkegaard invests his life in that which Nietzsche rejects, the spiritual. However, for Jung the outcome is the same: an one-sidedness that leads to illness. In Nietzsche's case there is an overestimation of the conscious, ego-personality, and in Kierkegaard's an underestimation of it – an underestimation that Jung identified as a symptom of Christianity in general. Nietzsche's overwhelming focus on the body has the effect of relegating the spiritual counterpart to the unconscious where it becomes autonomous and seeks continual expression (Huskinson 2004). Whilst Kierkegaard's overwhelming focus on the spirit has the effect that the here-and-now of earthly experience becomes relegated. And so it is one-sidedness then that emerges as the hallmark of the unhealthy psyche in Jung's thinking. The here-and-now of earthly existence is likewise something that Jung found Christianity to be lacking:

> It must be admitted that the Christian emphasis on spirit inevitably leads to an unbearable depreciation of man's physical side, and thus produces a sort of optimistic caricature of human nature.
>
> (1912/1952: par.60)

Kierkegaard alienates the body; for him nothing meaningful can exist outside of spirit. He renounces everything, including this fundamental bodily identity, in order to pursue spiritual perfection and so it is spirit that becomes the essence and cornerstone of his masculine life. Kierkegaard brings our attention to his one-sidedness in his own writings, to his inhumanly working as spirit – without body – that is, in the third person:

> Now I am able to say that Christ has come in this way to reveal to me that saviour is to be understood as one who helps a person out of his misery and not simply one who helps a person bear it. But the

point is that I have never been able to take command of myself in the ordinary human sense because of my unfortunate melancholia, which at one point was a kind of partial madness. Thus my only possibility was to function as spirit, and that is why I could be only an author. At last I was ready to stake everything (the consequence of working in this way) and then of my own volition retire, again because I inhumanly have been able to work only as spirit, that is, in the third person . . . now governance has intervened and required me in self denial to abandon that bold but also demonic idea. It will help me if God enable me to work more humanly so that I do not always need to make myself a third person, that I personally may enter things.

(JP: 1849)

If we combine this insight with those diagnoses he makes of his partial madness (which he accounts for by the disproportion – the 'misrelation' – between his soul and body), we have an incredibly profound self-diagnosis.

Jung was certainly very aware of the Christian hostility to the feminine as a threat to male spiritual perfection.[3] Previously we explored Jung's insistence that the religious impulse is a motivating psychic force that is on a par with other basic drives to life, such as sexuality. Now we have to consider the inseparable nature of the sexual and spiritual. Sexuality has a special position in regards to the other passions:

We could call sexuality the spokesman of the instincts, which is why from the spiritual standpoint sex is the chief antagonist, not because sexual indulgence is in itself more immoral than excessive eating and drinking, avarice, tyranny, and other extravagances, but because the spirit senses in sexuality a counterpart, like every other instinct, into its service, so sexuality has an ancient claim upon the spirit, which it once – in procreation, pregnancy, birth, and childhood – contained within itself, and whose passion the spirit can never dispense with in its creations.

(1928b: par.107)

However, it is not just the sexual or feminine element that Jung finds lacking in Christianity, but also the Dionysian. Jung hints as much when he wrote,

The meaning of my existence is that life has addressed a question to me. That is a supra-personal task, which I accompany only by effort and with difficulty. Perhaps it is a question which preoccupied my ancestors, and which they could not answer? Could that be why I am so impressed by the problem on which Nietzsche foundered: the Dionysian side of life, to which the Christian seems to have lost the way?

(1963)

I think we can make a compelling case for linking the Dionysian, the feminine and sexuality that Jung feels to be absent in Christendom with the Dionysian, feminine and sexual elements that are denied by Kierkegaard. As we previously discussed, Jung draws together extraversion and the outward directing of libido, feeling and sensation with the Dionysian impulse. The bodily, sexual and instinctual are, I contend, all Dionysian elements:

> I have an idea that the Dionysian frenzy was a backwash of sexuality, a backwash whose historical significance has been insufficiently appreciated, essential elements of which overflowed into Christianity but in another compromise formation.
>
> (FJL: pp.279–80)

> The dying and resurgent God (Orphic mysteries, Thammuz, Osiris [Dionysus], Adonis, etc.) is everywhere phallic. At the Dionysus festival in Egypt the women pulled the phallus up and down on a string: 'the dying and resurgent God'.
>
> (ibid., p. 263)

The one-sided spiritual emphasis of Christianity relegates the body, the instinctual and the sexual; it is precisely these elements that Jung identifies as absent in Christendom's figure of Christ.[4] In this sense Christ has opposing characteristics to Dionysus. By ascribing the dark side of the human totality to the antichrist, Christ is made one-sidedly perfect; consequently 'the Christ-symbol lacks wholeness in the modern psychological sense since it does not include the dark side of things, but specifically excludes it in the form of a luciferian opponent' (1951: par.74). However, it is not just good and evil that become split and dissociated in the Christ figure but spirit from bodiliness:

> the psychological concept of the self, in part derived from our knowledge of the whole man, but for the rest depicting itself spontaneously in the products of the unconscious as an archetypal quaternity bound together by inner antinomies, cannot omit the shadow that belongs to the light figure, for without it this figure lacks body and humanity. In the empirical self, light and shadow form a paradoxical unity. In the Christian concept, on the other hand, the archetype is hopelessly split into two irreconcilable halves, leading ultimately to a metaphysical dualism.
>
> (1951: par.76)

Christ rises in spirit and acts as a source and inspiration for those who wish to follow in his spirit. Jung's redemption of the human body, the here-and-now of earthly existence can be viewed as an attempt to ground the individual, to prevent him from losing his footing in pursuit of spiritual perfection. Jung writes:

> We should emphasize the body, for thus we give body to concepts, to words. . . . We should return to the body in order to create spirit again: without body there is no spirit because spirit is a volatile substance of the body. The body is the alembic, the retort, in which materials are cooked, and out of that process develops the spirit, the effervescent thing that rises.
>
> (1934–1939: p.368)

We must return to the body in order to recreate the spirit and integrate 'the other [i.e. repressed] face of God' through understanding that sexuality has a fundamental spiritual aspect:

> It is a widespread error to imagine that I do not see the value of sexuality. On the contrary it plays a large part in my psychology as an essential though not the sole-expression of psychic wholeness. But my main concern has been to investigate, over and above its personal significance and biological function, its spiritual aspect and its numinous meaning . . . sexuality is of the greatest importance as the expression of the chthonic spirit. That spirit is the 'other face of God,' the dark side of the God-image.
>
> (1963)

Jung maintained that 'there can be no doubt that the original Christian conception of the *image dei* embodied in Christ meant an all embracing totality that even includes the animal side of man' (1951: par.74). Only one's confrontation with the shadow, that deposit of animality, instinctuality and energetic dynamism, can facilitate a movement towards psychological and spiritual wholeness. Jung offers through his psychological model then, that which he perceived to be lacking in the Christian model. For Jung, wholeness is only attained through the union of opposites; it cannot be achieved through suppression or negation of one at the expense of the other:

> The superior thing can only be created if it is built upon the inferior thing. The inferior thing must be accepted in order to build the superior . . . You must not be afraid of the dirt; one has to accept the ugliest man if one wants to create.
>
> (1934–1939: p.1006)

Religion becomes life-constricting when it reduces the human totality to a part of itself; in short, when it fails to embrace wholeness. Following this, we might then suggest the 'Kierkegaardian neurosis' opposes the deepest energies of the psyche; that it is Kierkegaard's very sense of religiousness that ultimately leads him to hold fast to his Christian faith, despite the sickness it causes him. It is not an immanent God that Kierkegaard needed in order to correct the one-sidedness of his personality and the theories that underpinned his theological ideas, but the integration of the feminine and the Dionysian. An integration that revolves around the bodily, the elements which Kierkegaard himself believed had been denied him (as we saw in Part Three). The ideal for Jung could very well be in the unity created through what Kierkegaard and Nietzsche represent for him: for a Kierkegaardian, one-sided spiritual emphasis requires the compensation of the Nietzschean deification of the body. In his letter to Freud, dated 11th February 1910, Jung writes:

> I think we must give it time to infiltrate into people from many centres, to revivify among intellectuals a feeling for symbol and myth, ever so gently to transform Christ back into the soothsaying God of the vine, which he was, and in this way absorb those ecstatic instinctual forces of Christianity for the *one* purpose of making the cult and the sacred myth what they once were – a drunken feast of joy where man regained the ethos and holiness of an animal. That was the beauty and purpose of classical religion, which from God knows what temporary biological needs has turned into a Misery Institute. Yet what infinite rapture and wantonness lie dormant in our religion, waiting to be led back to their true destination!
>
> (FJL: p.294)

Jung's solution to the problem that he believed Nietzsche had failed to find is in the transformation of Christ back into Dionysus. For both Jung and Kierkegaard, the imitation of Christ has the potential to transform one's character; however, it is in their very different conceptions of Christ that the greatest point of contention between them is evident. For Kierkegaard, the solution to the paradox of human existence is found in the figure of Christ, who being both a finite and infinite being embodies this very paradox. The resolution that Jung offers comes in the form of the individuated human being, as represented in the figure of Christ: 'the drama of the archetypal life of Christ describes in symbolic images the events in the conscious life – as well as in the life that transcends consciousness – of a man who has been transformed by his higher destiny' (1942/1948: par.233). Jung advises the withdrawal of projections of Christ, essentially when an individual's attempt to imitate the life of Christ detracts from his or her own unique individuation. Jung remarks, 'if you live according to an example, you thus live the life of that example, but who should live your own life if not yourself? So live yourselves' (2009). Conversely, Kierkegaard's task is to describe

Kierkegaard and Nietzsche: opposites 201

what a life in Christ is like; authentic faith follows quite literally in the footsteps of Christ. In contrast to Jung's joyous, life-affirming archetypal Christ, Kierkegaard's emulation of the historical Christ becomes inevitably and overwhelmingly life-denying.

Kierkegaard remarks that Christ did not suffer 'in order to introduce a few doctrinal propositions'; God 'has his sights on something else: the transformation of character'. Kierkegaard's Climacus observes that everyone in Denmark is presumed to be Christian simply by virtue of being born within a Christian society (1846a). Such a viewpoint can be considered Kierkegaard's own since he writes in his journal:

> My Christian position is: Christianity does not exist at all. I speak of Denmark and, of course, within the limits of what is humanly possible to know. Christianity does not exist; but through having the objective doctrine, we are more or less captivated in the fancy, trapped in the illusion, that we are Christians.
>
> (JP: 1853)

The religious impoverishment of his day is characterised by superficiality; Kierkegaard viewed his fellow Christian as infused with Christianity from 'the outside' when one must exude Christianity from within. According to Kierkegaard, the individual must take up their cross and, like Christ, suffer persecution at the hands of a hostile world:

> In today's Christianity we take ordinary human suffering and turn it into a Christian example. 'Everyone has a cross to bear.' We preach unavoidable human trials into being Christian suffering. How this happens is beyond me! To the contrary, the difference between them is infinite. If I happen to lose everything, this is one thing. But if I voluntarily give up everything, choose danger and difficulties, this is something entirely different. When this happens it is impossible to avoid the trial that comes with carrying Jesus' cross. This is what Christian suffering means, and it is a whole scale deeper than ordinary human adversity.
>
> (1850)

Suffering becomes the hallmark of the authentically Christian life, the absence of which signifies the absence of religion:

> Inwardness is the individual's relation to himself before God, its reflection within himself, and that it is exactly from here that suffering comes, but also has the fact of its essential appertaining to religion based in this, so that its absence signifies the absence of religiousness,
>
> (1846a)

In his discourse 'What Meaning and What Joy There Are in the Thought of Following Christ' (1847a) Kierkegaard continues this line of thought and begins by citing Luke 14: 27: 'Whoever does not carry the cross and follow me cannot be my disciple'. Christ is the prototype whom we are to follow and live our life by:

> There is only one name in heaven and on earth, only one road, only one prototype. The person who chooses to follow Christ chooses the name that is above every name, the prototype that is supremely lifted up above all heavens, but yet at the same time is human in such a way that it can be the prototype for a human being, that it is named and shall be named in heaven and on earth, in both places, as the highest name.
>
> (1847c)

It is clear that the cross that we are to carry is not our own but that of Christ; the Christian individual must walk by 'the same road Christ walked in the lowly form of a servant, indigent, forsaken, mocked, not loving the world and not loved by it' (1847c). His understanding of discipleship then necessitates being in irrevocable conflict with the world that imparts an incompatibility between divine love and earthly joy. Kierkegaard assumes that because Christ suffered that Christianity must run contrary to the natural pursuit of happiness. To be a Christian in the Kierkegaardian sense is to stake one's life on the absurdity of the risen Christ, to commit to an ethical standard which no human can reach. This is a constant and in some ways hopeless effort at perpetually becoming what you can never fully be. Ultimately Kierkegaard is unable to maintain the dialectical tension between divine love and earthly joy; instead he ends up preaching his world-denying rhetoric of ascetic renunciation.[5] Kierkegaard's religious faith for all its radicalness still revolves around the traditionally one-sided imitation of Christ. Kierkegaard attempts a more fully embodied image of *imitatio* by emphasising the human aspect of Christ, but Kierkegaard's divine savior is still only capable of affirming the absurd, offensive, painful and dangerous aspects of the truly religious life. In a letter to Freud, Jung writes, 'must we not love evil if we are to break away from the obsession with virtue that makes us sick and forbids us the joys of life?' It will not come as a surprise to learn that Kierkegaard's understanding of joy consists in the increasing intensity of one's suffering, since this signifies that one has chosen correctly and is advancing along the divine path that Christ had gone before, in preparation for his disciples (1847c).

Jung is critical of this very kind of imitation; one should in Jung's reckoning pursue one's own unique path to individuation:

> Christ is an exemplar who dwells in every Christian as his integral personality. But historical trends led to the imitatio Christi, whereby the

individual does not pursue his own destined road to wholeness, but attempts to imitate the way taken by Christ.

(1963)

Jung draws the distinction between Christianity's 'Christ' and the archetypal 'Christ', a distinction that essentially marks the difference between historical fact and symbolic truth. Modern day Christendom had so elevated the literal element that the symbolic content of Christianity has become completely denigrated.

> if one inclines to regard the archetype of the self as the real agent and hence takes Christ as a symbol of the self, one must bear in mind that there is a considerable difference between perfection and completeness. The Christ image is as good as perfect (at least it is meant to be so), while the archetype (so far as known) denotes completeness but is far from being perfect. It is a paradox, a statement about something indescribable and transcendental.

> (1951: par.123)

This conception of Christ as a symbol of the self could be seen as a challenge to the Church to recover its lost symbolic life. For Jung, the imitation of Christ should not be understood as the torturous attempt to 'ape his stigmata', rather than this literal imitation, Jung urges the individual to attempt the 'unspeakably harder' task of living his or her *own* life:

> We Protestants must sooner or later face this question: Are we to understand the 'imitation of Christ' in the sense that we should copy his life and, as if I may use the expression, ape *his* Stigmata; or in the deeper sense that we are to live our own proper lives as truly as he lived his in its individual uniqueness? It is no easy matter to live a life that is modelled on Christ's, but it is unspeakably harder to live one's own life as truly as Christ lived his.

> (1928a: par.522)

Kierkegaard's understanding of Christ is literal and one-sidedly focused upon sin and suffering; for Kierkegaard, 'being a Christian is neither more nor less, absolutely neither more nor less, than being a martyr. Every Christian – that is, every true Christian – is a martyr' (1848). In contrast, Jung maintains that we are to live our individual lives as responsibly and authentically as Christ lived his; essentially this archetypal Christ is a liberating force driving towards one's self-realisation; I believe this is what Jung means when he writes, 'the real Christ is the God of freedom' (1928–1930: p. 519). During the First World War, Jung embarked upon what he called his 'confrontation of the unconscious'; an extensive self-exploration that occupied him

204 Kierkegaard and Nietzsche: opposites

between the years of 1914 and 1930. Throughout his *Red Book* Jung alludes to the scriptures and there is perhaps scope for viewing this text as a kind of gospel; in it Jung documents the recovery of his soul, attained by allowing the rebirth of a new God-image in his soul. This then is a deeply religious text. Sounding very much like his Christ God of freedom, Jung writes:

> Believe me: It is no teaching and no instruction that I give you. On what basis should I presume to teach you? I give you news of the way of this man, but not of your own way. My path is not your path, therefore I cannot teach you. The way is within us, but not in Gods, nor teachings, nor in laws. Within us is the way, the truth and the life. Woe betide those who live by way of examples! Life is not with them. If you live according to an example, you thus live the life of that example, but who should live your own life if not yourself? So live yourselves. The signposts have fallen, unblazed trails lie before us. Do not be greedy to gobble up the fruits of foreign fields. Do you not know that you yourselves are the fertile acre which bears everything that avails you? Yet who today knows this? Who knows the way to the eternally fruitful climes of the soul? You seek the way through mere appearances, you study books and give ear to all kinds of opinion. What good is all that? There is only one way and that is your way. I will be no savior, no lawgiver, no master teacher unto you. You are no longer little children. Giving laws, wanting improvements, making things easier, has all become wrong and evil. May each one seek out his own way. The way leads to mutual love in community. Men will come to see and feel the similarity and commonality of their ways. Laws and teachings held in common compel people to solitude, so that they may escape the pressure of undesirable contact, but solitude makes people hostile and venomous. Therefore give people dignity and let each of them stand apart, so that each may find his own fellowship and love it.
>
> (2009)

When Christ is made ideal and perfect, as is the case in orthodox Christianity, the 'divine mediator stands outside as an image, while man remains fragmentary and untouched in the deepest part of him' (1944: par.7). According to Jung, Christ can be imitated to the point of stigmatisation without the imitator becoming acquainted with the ideal of its meaning. He notes, 'it is not a question of an imitation that leaves a man unchanged and makes him into a mere artefact, but of realising the ideal on one's own account – *Deo concedente* – in one's own individual life' (ibid.). Ultimately, if we are to assume responsibility for ourselves we must withdraw our projections from the historical Christ. However, even within the boundaries of traditional Christianity the imitation of Christ was important to Jung; addressing Victor White's vocational dilemma he writes,

> Whatever your ultimate decision will be, you ought to realise beforehand that staying in the church makes sense as it is important to make

Kierkegaard and Nietzsche: opposites 205

people understand what the symbol of Christ means, and such understanding is indispensable to any further development. There is no way round it, as little as we can eliminate from our life old age, illness, and death. . . . The vast majority of people are still in such an unconscious state that one should almost protect them from the full shock of the real *imitatio Christi*.

(1951–1961)

Notes

1 Nietzsche's most literary work, *Zarathustra*, promotes a kind of faith, albeit an unconventional one. Jung took absolutely seriously Nietzsche's claim that he felt as though something was writing through him when he wrote *Zarathustra*. Consequently, Jung sought to understand the symbolism that emerges in this work from Nietzsche's unconscious mind, and a psychological interpretation of *Zarathustra* became the aim in the seminar he held at the Zurich Psychological Club from 1934 to 1939. The transcript of these proceedings forms Jung's *Nietzsche's Zarathustra: Notes on the Seminar Given in 1934–1939*, written up into two volumes of over 1200 pages.

2 'Too much of the animal distorts the civilized man, too much civilisation makes sick animals' (1917/1926/1943:par.32).

3 See for example, 'For anyone acquainted with religious phenomenology it is an open secret that although physical and spiritual passion are deadly enemies, they are nevertheless brothers in arms, for which reason it often needs the merest touch to convert one into the other. Both are real, and together they form a pair of opposites, which is one of the most fruitful sources of energy' (1947/1954.par.414).

4 'There can be no doubt that the original Christian conception of the *imago Dei* can be embodied in Christ meant an all-embracing totality that even includes the animal side of man. Nevertheless the Christ symbol lacks wholeness in the modern psychological sense, since it does not include the dark side of things but specifically excludes it in the form of a Luciferian opponent. . . . In the empirical Self, light and shadow form a paradoxical unity. In the Christian concept, on the other hand, the archetype is hopelessly split into two irreconcilable halves, leading ultimately to a metaphysical dualism – the final separation of the kingdom of heaven from the fiery world of the damned' (1951:par.74–6).

5 The pessimistic attitude that the later Kierkegaard adopts is similar to Schopenhauer's. This Schopenharian connection is interesting to us, for Schopenhauer is a figure whom Jung and Kierkegaard both deeply admire. Jung praises the centrality accorded to suffering by Schopenhauer, writing 'every genuine philosophy, every true religion is wrapped in the earthly garment of pessimism as the only accurate mode of reviewing the world befitting man in the awareness of his nothingness'. Jung takes no issue when these life-denying elements appear in the man-hating, poodle-loving figure of Schopenhauer. And if there was ever a philosopher who settled things in his study, then we need look no further than Schopenhauer, the most renown of Pessimists. With this in mind it seems that Jung's rejection of Kierkegaard is indeed of a very personal nature.

Chapter 19

Summary of discussion

Let's take a moment to briefly review what we have discovered thus far. Jung clearly indicates Kierkegaard's inability to individuate; that he rejects the feminine and couldn't tolerate it when his anima appeared in the projected guise of Regine. There is nothing especially unusual here, as Jung himself states 'it is normal for a man to resist his anima, because she represents . . . all those tendencies and contents hitherto excluded from conscious life'(1938/1940: par.129). We have also seen the ways in which the one-sided characteristics of Kierkegaard's and Nietzsche's personalities compliment and contrast one another; Nietzsche's philosophy has the Dionysian emphasis but at the expense of a Christ figure, whilst Kierkegaard's primary focus is on the figure of Christ, but he denigrates those elements that can be considered Dionysian. And finally, we have discerned a very real incompatibility in Jung's and Kierkegaard's understanding of the *Christi imitatio*. An incompatibility that, as I will shortly argue, exemplifies both Kierkegaard's attempt to heal the rift between modern man and Christianity whilst staying within the framework of the conventional Christianity of his father's faith, as well as Jung's stepping outside and beyond the rejected conventional Christianity of his father's faith. I do not believe that any of these factors alone can be regarded as the motivating source of Jung's hostile reception of Kierkegaard. Such hypersensitivity evident in numerous remarks Jung makes of Kierkegaard usually indicates the presence of what Jung calls a 'complex'[1] and whilst Jung possibly does have a Christ complex which he proceeds to unconsciously project upon Kierkegaard, I believe it is Kierkegaard's piousness that is predominantly the source of Jung's anger and which Jung perhaps unconsciously sets himself up to compete with. In fact, there is reason to suspect something resembling a sibling rivalry in Jung's ultimate dismissal of Kierkegaard.

In his PhD on Kierkegaard, Künzli paints a portrait of man who earnestly searches for self-realisation outside of the Church dogma and tradition that he believes all-too lacking in spirit. As we noted earlier, we would have expected the Kierkegaardian emphasis on self-knowledge through God-knowledge to have immediately captured Jung's heart, given his own promotion of such an approach.[2] I suspect Kierkegaard and Jung had much in common and not just theoretically or with regards a shared psychological inheritance, but also – and perhaps most importantly for my argument – with regards their personalities and character traits. Both are individuals who in their youth were particularly aggressive and ambitious. Kierkegaard's character in this respect is well known, but it may surprise the reader to learn that Jung, much like our Danish 'fork' (family nickname for Kierkegaard's sharp tongue), was 'inclined to sharp words' (Antony 1990). In fact, he often showed such a lack of consideration for the feelings or others that contemporaries remarked that he could ride roughshod over people (Brome 1978). As a child, Jung was capable of sudden rages and he never outgrew this emotional variability (Hannah 1991). He could be vibrant and charming one moment and then vociferous and rude the next (Brome 1978). Eugen Bleuler, Jung's boss at the Burghölzli mental hospital, described him as 'cold', whilst the doctors under his supervision complained he was an overbearing bully (Bair 2003).

There is in Kierkegaard's work an underlying tone that evokes uncanny feelings, as if something foreign, something that does not seem to sit well, something sick and un-natural, underpins his words, and I contend this to be residues, symptoms if you like, of his obsession with suffering, an obsession that creates an overwhelming sense of solitude in his writings. His propensity towards self-alienation is evident in Kierkegaard as a child, and it is interesting how the following description of the young Kierkegaard sounds remarkably similar to the description of Jung as a child given by Albert Ori. Frederik Welding comments on Kierkegaard's 'aloofness' and 'self containment':

> S.K. did not reveal his character in the way that boys and young people of school age usually do. He went his own way, almost self-contained, never spoke of his home. To the rest of us, who knew and lived a more genuinely boyish life, S.K was a stranger and an object of pity . . . as far as I can remember, he was not friends with any of the other boys. . . . There was something unusual in his quiet nature, which bore the stamp of the customs of his home and of his own inner self, secrets which were never revealed.
>
> (Kirmmse 1996)

Jung's early memories are devoid of people and reveal a lonely child, somewhat detached, consumed in solitary play; he himself recalls 'playing alone and in my own way. Unfortunately I cannot remember what I played; I recall only that I did not want to be disturbed' (Dunne 2002). Albert Oeri, a lifelong friend, remarked retrospectively that they were brought together by their fathers, themselves old school friends, in the hope that their sons would share a similarly close friendship. However, it became clear that Jung preferred to play alone, 'Carl sat in the middle of the room, occupied himself with a little bowling game, and didn't pay the slightest attention to me. . . . I have never come across such an asocial monster before' (Hannah 1991). Jung's interpersonal relationships seem to have been quite problematic, and he immersed himself in his inner world where he lived a dissociated double life filled with secret rituals of fire-tending, magic stones and a carved manikin to ward off evil that he kept hidden in the attic (it is this secret world that Jung believed 'the essential factor of my boyhood') (1963). He described himself as being two persons; one the son of his parents who had difficulties in school and with relationships, and the other, the old adult, remote from men but close to nature, the night and dreams. His biographer, Bair, records a frightening case of Jung's insensitivity toward his daughter, Gret:

> Unfortunately, Gret was the butt of most of the jokes and 'nasty tricks' Jung liked to play on his children. Once he threw a lighted cracker between Gret's legs that went off and made her deaf in one ear. She [Gret] told her children it was one of the two main reasons she grew up embittered.

I think we might question here Bair's use of the words 'jokes' and 'nasty tricks'; there is no humor in such a deliberately cruel act. It would seem marriage and fatherhood had done nothing to distil either Jung's aloofness or his disinterest in others.

Kierkegaard exhibits many of the perceived behaviours of the narcissistic personality (behaviours that include keeping people at arm's length [being impenetrable], rejecting the interpretations of others, inability to tolerate criticism, having low empathy with others and having a propensity for envy and rage).[3] We can infer from the previous quotes that these are qualities shared by Jung. Indeed, Michael Fordham believes Jung was a narcissistic personality with susceptibility to paranoia that led to dissatisfaction in his feeling towards himself and others. Jung's numerous displays of ego, secrecy, hypersensitivity and aloofness could very well point towards a narcissistic personality. These hidden and unacknowledged aspects of Jung's shadow-self arguably correspond to Kierkegaard's own conscious ego-personality and character. On occasion it has been questioned whether Kierkegaard's philosophy can offer anything to people who have a non-religious outlook.[4] If we were to take away Jung's women, his grounding in the earthly realities and impart a more fervent nature to his religious belief, he might begin to bear an uncanny resemblance to Kierkegaard. Jung contrasts his own experiences of solitude to Nietzsche's self-destructive solitude, maintaining that it was his family and professional work that kept him grounded in reality:

> Nietzsche had lost the ground under his feet because he possessed nothing more than the inner world of his thoughts – which incidentally

possessed him more than he it. He was uprooted and hovered above the earth, and therefore he succumbed to exaggeration and reality. For me, such irreality was the quintessence of horror, for I aimed, after all, at this world and this life. No matter how deeply absorbed or how blown about I was, I always knew that everything I was experiencing was ultimately directed at this real life of mine . . . thus my family and my profession always remained a joyful reality and a guarantee that I also had a normal existence.

(1963)

It is most likely that the tight circle of women that Jung kept around him played the decisive factor in keeping Jung from 'hovering loftily above the earth'. After interviewing many of the women who formed what is often alluded to as Jung's 'Valkyries', Maggy Anthony (1990) concluded that Jung needed these women as much as they needed him. The 'Valkyries' were the group of loyal disciples that Jung collected around himself over the course of his career; like bees to a honey pot, they swarmed over him at conferences, and hung on his words in meetings of the Psychology Club (ibid.). The Club became a hotbed of jealousies as these women had to share Jung with others, and in the midst of all this was Jung, enjoying their attentions, using their energies to further his work, relying on (perhaps even exploiting) their devotion and willingness to put their own resources in his service. Jung does not deny himself the power of Eros. His promiscuous and adulterous behaviour (with his patients, Sabina Spielrein and Toni Wolff, among others)[5] would indicate a narcissist need for admiration and adoration. Unlike Kierkegaard, he is unable to surrender his dependence on women – to reign in his anima so to speak. It is interesting here to note R. D. Laing's intrigue regarding Kierkegaard's inability to sustain a relationship with a woman (a feature of his personality and life that he shared with Nietzsche, whose two marriage proposals to Lou Salome were spurned by her in favor of one from his best friend); both figures remained single throughout life, indicating a deeper problematic relationship with their inner female complexes, namely their ability to integrate the anima. Given this, it lends some credence to my speculative view that Jung's grievances with both Kierkegaard and Nietzsche (the latter of whom, Jung says, 'drips with outraged sexuality') are at least in part, related to issues with his own anima. That is to say, the evident anima issues that affect Kierkegaard and Nietzsche evoke issues within Jung's own psyche, causing his emotional outbursts directed firmly at the two men. Jung certainly emphasises his belief that both Nietzsche and Kierkegaard had problems in their relationships to the feminine.[6]

Jung did not accept Freud's belief that the individual's image of God is formed as a direct consequence of their relationship with their real-life father; he believed instead that the God-image is just one of the many archetypes of the human psyche. And yet, as we considered earlier, it is

210 Summary of discussion

abundantly clear that Jung wholeheartedly believed it was his vocation to restore the instinctual (Dionysian) aspects of life to religious experience and especially to the Christian tradition which, as he saw it, neglected these aspects and repressed them. From the viewpoint of Christianity, such a task made Jung distinctly an outsider to conventional Christian thinking. Aniela Jaffe (1963) reveals that,

> for all his worldwide fame, this verdict was forcibly borne in upon him by the reactions to his writings. This grieved him, and here and there in this book he expresses the disappointment of an investigator who felt that his religious ideas were not properly understood.

Murray Stein (1985) contends that Jung was guided in his writings by an unseen hand, a largely unconscious *spiritus rector*. It was this guiding spirit that Stein believes prompted his mission to heal Christianity, to diagnose the ailments of traditional Christianity and offer it psychotherapeutic help (Stien 1985). At the center of what Stein refers to as Jung's 'Christianity complex', along with his perception of God's dark side, stood Paul Jung, Jung's father. We might then view Jung's becoming a therapist to the Christian tradition as a veiled desire to be his father's therapist. Jung felt that his father had never known the inner, living experience of God, believing his faith and belief to be empty. Is it possible that Jung would have seen his father and his weakened faith in the person and work of Kierkegaard? It is my suspicion that Jung's advice directed towards Kierkegaard is actually more representative of that which he would have liked to have said to his father.

This declaration to Kierkegaard that, 'God is immediately with you and is the voice inside you. You have to have it out with that voice,' certainly has more poignancy and relevance in relation to his clergyman father, to the man who was filled with self-doubt about his calling and faith, than it does to Kierkegaard. Jung saw his lifelong psychic task as overcoming the legacy he had received from his father – to heal his father's psychic woundedness.[7] He was well aware of the legacy of 'wounded fathers'; a wounded man had a wounded father and the father was wounded by his father. Consequently, he was aware too that the same problems run through generations of father-son relationships as part of an emotional inheritance. Whilst chiseling the name of his paternal ancestors on stone tablets, Jung recalls how he became aware of 'fateful links' with his forefathers:

> It has always seemed to me that I had to answer questions which fate had posed to my forefathers, and which had not yet been answered, or as if I had to complete, or perhaps continue, things which previous ages had left unfinished.

(1963)

And yet we should not lose sight of the fact that Jung's efforts to 'heal' Christianity are, arguably, also a very real attempt to recover his own faith as well as that of his father's. Harry Wilmer, a Jungian analyst and professor of Psychiatry, suggests that the wound of the father may have been Jung's salvation, 'just as the wounded wounds himself, so the healer heals himself' (Jung, 1963)[8].

Jung was almost certainly gripped by a negative father complex. It seems clear that he had little respect or admiration for the failure he perceived his father to be. It is hard to imagine that Jung would not have resented his father for his failure not just as a parent but as his mother's partner also, forcing him to grow up long before his years and thereby robbing him of a childhood. On this Jung writes,

> my mother usually assumed I was mentally far beyond my age, and she would talk to me as a grown up. It was plain to see that she was telling me everything she could not say to my father, for she early made me her confident and confided her troubles to me.
>
> (1963)

Mourning her husband's death, Emile Jung spoke to her son in the 'other' voice that had inklings of a world far stranger than the one young Carl knew, declaring, 'he died in time for you'. At the age of three, he was taught by Emile to say the following prayer before sleep each night:

> Spread out thy wings, Lord Jesus mild,
> And take to thee thy chick, thy child,
> If Satan would devour it,
> No harm shall overpower it,
> So let the angels sing (1963).

Jung was confused by the second phrase and thought that Jesus swallowed children reluctantly, like bitter medicine;

> I understood at once that Satan liked chicks and had to be prevented from eating them. So although Lord Jesus did not like the taste he ate them anyway, so that Satan would not get them. As far as that went, my argument was comforting.
>
> (ibid.)

However, this view became supplanted by his observation of funerals and burials:

> But now I was hearing that Lord Jesus 'took' other people to himself as well, and that this 'taking' was the same as putting them in a hole in the

ground. This sinister analogy had unfortunate consequences. I began to distrust Lord Jesus. He lost the aspect of a big, comforting, benevolent bird and became associated with the gloomy black men in frock coats, top hats, and shiny boots who busied themselves with the black box.

(ibid.)

The parallel here to Kierkegaard's own situation is further indicative of a shared religious upbringing; one that combined a childhood (negative) imposition of Christianity with a father's spiritual melancholy and nurtured an environment whereby the father's absence of genuine faith was readily and disconcertingly apparent.[9] Jung observed that children are educated by what the grown-up is and not by his talk, an observation perhaps partially informed through the experience of his relationship to Paul Jung; 'what he said sounded stale and hollow, like a tale told by someone who knows it only by hearsay and cannot quite believe it'. Both Kierkegaard and Jung were old beyond their years, a consequence of them both having been robbed of childhood by their fathers. Nearing the end of his life, reflective and serene, Kierkegaard wrote that his father's fault 'consisted not in a lack of love but in mistaking a child for an old man' (1848/1859). In a similar vein, Jung told Van der Post that the failure of his father as a parent forced him to grow up long before it was normal. Kierkegaard would surely argue that much damage was done by the mother's insistence of a nightly recital of this religious poem. Children have no use of Christianity, in their innocence they can only misunderstand, he asserts, 'the danger is that the child in that situation is almost provoked to draw a conclusion about God, that God is not infinite love' (JP: 1850). Early in this work I explained that it is not unreasonable to suggest that both Kierkegaard's and Jung's works were modelled by their respective unconscious relationships to their father. I am now in a position to go further here and put forth the possibility that Jung's comments regarding Kierkegaard touch upon his own unconscious issues with father. Jung sought to downplay the influence of his father, perhaps motivated by his need to reject Freud's reductive interpretation of his own religious ideas. Jung writes,

Naturally [Freud] assumed that my more positive ideas about religion and its importance for our psychological life were nothing but an out-crop of my unrealized resistances against my clergyman father, whereas in reality my problem and my personal prejudice were never centred in my father but most emphatically in my mother.

(1951–1961)

In his attempt to heal the ailing religious tradition, Jung steps outside Christianity, rejecting outright both his father's religion and any influence his father may have had upon his 'more positive ideas about religion'. Jung's understanding of the *imitatio Christi* carries with it the implication that traditional Christianity has misunderstood both Christ and the Incarnation. The incarnation continues in and through the individual, who must understand that his relation to the infinite is to realise the incarnation as an ongoing and continuing process.[10] According to Jung, to exist as an authentic individual requires that we break away from and go beyond conventional Christianity in pursuit of a higher religion.[11] In contrast, Kierkegaard emulates his experiences of his father; his faith is entwined with the close relationship he has with his father, and from whom he 'gained a conception of divine fatherly love' (JP: 1840). As I discussed in Part Three: 'To Marry or to Martyr', Kierkegaard rejects the possibility of married life with Regine, arguably, owing to his father's confession of a sexual indiscretion. Consequently, it is this carnal nature demonstrated to him in his disappointment with the father, and his lifelong brooding about it that causes Kierkegaard to distance himself from sexuality. With his broken engagement to Regine, Kierkegaard severs his ties to sexuality, so as to become a better man than his father before him. He not only emulates the father (with regards his theological outlook), but also seeks to surpass him. I contend therefore that Kierkegaard's imitation of Christ is an imitation of the kind of father he sought to idealise and embody for himself. Whilst for Jung, by contrast, Christ is an example of how one can live and not necessarily to imitate; rather, for Jung, – the individual must ultimately find his or her own way through to a relationship with a more complete God within. In contrast to Kierkegaard, Jung extols a very different relationship between Christianity and sexuality, one that essentially sexualises the Godhead (perhaps most strikingly portrayed in a dream that was to preoccupy him for life whereby he found himself confronted with the underground phallus, the man-eater so associated with Lord Jesus, sitting upon a golden throne). It is not surprising then that Jung accuses Kierkegaard of having 'took to his heels' when 'God appeared to him in the shape of Regina' (1951–1961). Naturally God would appear in a sexual form for Jung.

Both Jung and Kierkegaard sought to transform perceptions and understandings of Christianity through their own personal experiences of the God within. We might consider their common aim as a struggle for the inward deepening of Christianity to emphasise the personal relationship with God within us as individuals. Kierkegaard's central task as an author is to encourage his reader to make the truth his or her own; 'my whole life', wrote Kierkegaard, 'is an epigram calculated to make people aware' (JP: 1848). 'I have worked for a restlessness orientated toward inward deepening . . . to keep people awake, in order that religion may not again become an indolent habit' (1851). Individual truth ('the idea for which I can live and die') and Christianity are essential concerns of Kierkegaard's life and works, he writes:

> through my writings I hope to achieve the following: to leave behind me so accurate a characterization of Christianity and its relationships in the world that an enthusiastic, noble-minded young person will be able to find in it a map of relationships as accurate as any topographical map from the most famous institutes.
>
> (JP: 1848)

Such a map would lead one from the degenerated Christianity of Danish Lutheranism to Kierkegaard's conception of the authentically existing Christian. In contrast, to this Kierkegaardian re-introduction of Christianity into Christendom, we have in Jung the re-introduction of the symbolic content of Christianity to Christendom; as a consequence he presents us with something equivalent to an archetypal map of the soul. Human interiority is the focus of both Kierkegaard and Jung's reinterpretation/development in Christianity. Self-awareness is one's path to knowledge of the effects of, and relationship with God, and to this extent the instinctive religious factor is discovered in the depths of one's psyche. And yet both Kierkegaard and Jung are unable to live up to their own expectations and fulfill these ideal states, in this respect, as we have noted previously, Kierkegaard acknowledges his deficiencies as a Christian and his failure to reach his *Knight of Faith* ideal; indeed, he reveals in his journal 'it becomes more and more clear to me that I am so) constituted that I just never manage to realise my ideals' (JP: 1846).

Both Kierkegaard and Jung attempt to heal the rift between traditional Christianity and the inner spiritual faith of modern man. Kierkegaard maintains his inherited faith whilst remaining within the framework of traditional Christianity, which we can perhaps interpret as a staying true to his father. The analogy of a perceived sibling rivalry between Jung and Kierkegaard may very well be an apt one; the sincerity of Kierkegaard's faith is readily apparent. Unlike his father whose cursing of God upon a Jutland heath is well known, Kierkegaard never takes God's name in vain, not even in his most despairing moments. Kierkegaard never lifted his hands to heaven and cursed God for his suffering; rather he believed his suffering and his melancholy evidence that he stood as a witness for truth. Consequently, he does not lament the thorn in his flesh but accepts it and embraces it, allowing it to be a source of his own empowerment and creativity.[12] In essence, Kierkegaard knew what it was that he was to do and he had found that which he could live or die for. Kierkegaard's leap to faith allows him to accept that God forgives our sins; it describes the transformative effect that

Kierkegaard's own discovery of faith had wrought in his own life. Kierkegaard wrote,

> what marvellous boldness of faith is involved in believing that the sin is entirely forgotten, so that the memory of it has nothing alarming about it, thus truly believing oneself into being a new man, so that one can scarcely recognize oneself again.
>
> (Lowrie 2013)

In short, we can argue that he had resolved those issues of religious doubt and sin that had afflicted his father. In contrast, Jung's famous declaration regarding his personal religious convictions – notably, his proclamation that 'I do not believe [God exists], I know' (Hull 1980) – seems to possess all the dogma that Jung believed had entrapped his father's theological thinking, cutting him off from faith altogether. In the same interview in which Jung made this claim, he remarks that, 'the word "belief" is a difficult thing for me. I don't believe. I must have a reason for a certain hypothesis. Either I know a thing, and then I know it – I don't need to believe it'. Not only does such a statement seem completely out of kilter for an author who delights in esoteric knowledge and paradox, it also contradicts his assertion that doubt is an inevitable part of the journey toward a complete life.[13] One can argue that all spiritual truths are paradoxes, but strangely not in the case of Jung's conception of his own faith. In response to Jung's claim 'to know', Kierkegaard would no doubt reassert his belief that in order to have faith in God, one cannot *know* that there *is* a God. Although Jung believes himself to have discovered God alive and active within the unconscious, I do not think he managed to recapture his lost faith in God (a point similarly made by Stein, among others). It would certainly seem that his attempt to heal the split with his father and his father's religion was ultimately unsuccessful.

In his twilight years Jung became increasingly subject to depression. Writing to Laurens Van der Post (1988), he confesses, 'I am an increasingly lonely old man, writing for other lonely men'. Michael Fordham who visited Jung just a few days before Jung's death found him in low spirits, feeling that 'he had failed in his mission' and was 'misunderstood and unappreciated' (Urban 2015). Furthermore, in the last paragraph of his 'autobiography', he writes, 'it seems to me that the alienation which has so long separated me from the world has become transferred to my own inner world, and had revealed to me an unexpected unfamiliarity with myself' (1963). These examples, which point towards Jung's feelings and experiences of alienation and loneliness, are of interest to our argument, for alienation is often understood by Jungians to be symptomatic of an inner psychological disunity. As we have already seen, according to Jung, material in the unconscious is often experienced in waking life through our projection of it onto others in the outside world.[14] The material that is cut off from our conscious awareness is more often than not projected onto the outside world, manifesting itself in conscious feelings of alienation from our surroundings. Given this, we might then share in Kaufmann's (1992) belief that Jung's account of his own individuation process does not reflect the journey of a man who had successfully 'faced up to his own shadow and attained a degree of self knowledge'. I find such a statement unduly harsh; perhaps Jung remained a solitary individual, ultimately disconnected from others and disconsolate at his life's work but does this not point toward just how difficult a task facing existence as an integrated whole is? Fordham experienced Jung's air of disconsolation approaching his death as a severe blow to any residual fantasy that he was a sort of Mahatma who could determine his death. On the contrary, he died like an ordinary man' (Urban 2015). This need to immortalize and worship Jung as a God does a great disservice to Jung, the very ordinary flesh and blood man, who struggled in earnest and with immense courage, a man who had many shortcomings but whose attempt at a self-cure leaves us with an extraordinary corpus of work.

Notes

1 According to Jung, a complex (e.g., a mother or father complex) is an unconscious constellation of cognitions, memories, images, impulsions, opinions, beliefs, associations and other content emanating from a core of repressed or dissociated emotion, drive or instinct. Complexes can behave like relatively autonomous 'splinter personalities', powerfully influencing consciousness, cognition, affect and behaviour. Jung wrote, 'we all have complexes; it is a highly banal and uninteresting fact . . . it is only interesting to know what people do with their complexes; that is the practical question which matters' (1935:par.175).
2 For example, commenting on the older mystical religious tradition Jung writes, 'they were very pious people who maintained that self-knowledge paves the way to knowledge of God' (1952:par.661).
3 The DSM-IV definition of narcissistic personality disorders lists grandiosity, lack of empathy and the expectation that others will accommodate to the individual's desires as criteria for the disorder.
4 An issue raised by Stephen Evans (2006), *Kierkegaard on Faith and the Self: Collected Essays* (Baylor University Press) and Claire Carlisle (2006), *Kierkegaard: A Guide for the Perplexed* (Continuum).
5 In a letter to Freud dated January 30, 1910, Jung wrote: 'the prerequisite for a good marriage, it seems to me, is the license to be unfaithful'. Little doubt exists that Jung had several extramarital affairs. Frank McLynn (1996) has alleged that Jung was a notorious womaniser who frequently had affairs with his patients and former patients. It is his claim that Jung's 'mother complex' caused him to harbor animosity toward his wife while destining him to a life of promiscuity. F. McLynn, (1996), *Carl Gustav Jung*. New York: St Martin's Press. See also, J. Kerr, (1993), *A Most Dangerous Method: The Story of Jung, Freud, and Sabina Spielrein*. New York: Knopf. And, A.C. Elms, (1994), *Uncovering Lives: The*

Uneasy Alliance of Biography and Psychology. New York: Oxford University Press.

6 We have previously discussed Jung's prejudice that Kierkegaard did not have much of a relation to the feminine; in the following passage we discover that this prejudice also extends to the figure of Nietzsche: 'it all comes from the fact that we have no anima in Zarathustra. Only very near the end anima figures appear in the erotic poem "Unter Tochtern der Wuste." . . . It takes the whole development of Zarathustra to call Nietzsche's attention to the fact that there is an anima' (1934–1939:p.533).

7 In this respect, Jung is fulfilling Freud's model, by seeking to overcome the father and trying to negotiate the guilty feelings of wanting to surpass the father's authority. It is this surely, that keeps Jung's feelings about his father somewhat repressed and available for projecting onto Kierkegaard.

8 See Smith, Robert. The Wounded Jung: Effects of Jung's Relationships on His Life and Work. Northwestern University Press: Illinois, 1997.

9 'It is a dubious thing to bring up a child in Christianity. . . . The child has no actual consciousness of sin. What then? Take an analogy. Describe the family physician to a child as a very rare and lovable man. What happens? The child thinks it is very possible that there is such a rare man. I would gladly believe it, but I would also rather stay clear of him. The fact that I might became the object of his special love means that I am sick, and to be sick is no fun. Therefore, I am far from being happy at the thought that he has been called.

. . . When one is actually sick and the sickness is serious, then one is very happy that there is a physician, but when one is not sick, has no idea at all of what it is to be sick, then "the physician" is really a disagreeable thought. In the relation of Christianity to the child, either what is really Christian must be left out, and then what does upbringing in Christianity mean then! – or it must be said, and then the child is prompted more to be afraid of Christianity than to be happy for it' (JP:1850).

10 'The future indwelling of the Holy Ghost in man amounts to a continuing incarnation of God. Christ, as the begotten son of God and pre-existing mediator, is a first-born and a divine paradigm which will be followed by further incarnations of the Holy Ghost in the empirical man' (1952a:par.693).

11 In 1949, Max Zeller shared the following dream with Jung: 'A temple of vast dimensions was in the process of being built. As far as I could see – ahead, behind, right and left – there were incredible numbers of people building on gigantic pillars. I too was building on a pillar. The whole building process was in its very first beginning, but the foundation was already there'. Jung's response to Zeller's dream was to say, 'that is the temple we all build on. We don't know the people because, believe me, they build in India and China, and in Russia, and all over the world. That is the new religion'. Jung told Zeller that it would take six hundred years before the temple would be built. When Zeller asked him how he knew this, Jung replied, 'From dreams. From other people's dreams and my own. This new religion will come together as far as we can see'. – Max Zeller, quoted in Kammen and Gold, *Call to Connection: Bringing Sacred Tribal Values into Modern Life*, 1998).

12 'O my God, how clearly it now all stands out before me, how endlessly much has already been done for me. It is not difference that I must pray myself out of, that is not the task, but alas, I shall never know security, which consists in being like others. No, I remain different. I have suffered so very much in the past year and had to consider everything so seriously that doubtless I am a good deal changed . . .

I feel peaceful and happy, perhaps more definitely so and with a more tranquil confidence than that in 1848' (JP:1852).

13 A proposition he puts to his long-time correspondent, Father Victor White: 'There is no place where those striving after consciousness could find absolute safety. Doubt and insecurity are indispensable components of a complete life. Only those who can lose this life really, can gain it. A "complete" life does not consist in a theoretical completeness, but in the fact that one accepts, without reservation, the particular fatal tissue in which one finds oneself embedded, and that one tries to make sense of it or to create a cosmos from the chaotic mess into which one is born' (1951–1961).

14 For instance, Jung notes, 'the psychological rule says that when an inner situation is not made conscious it happens outside, as fate' (1951:par.126).

Chapter 20

Conclusion

Jung sought the therapeutic remedy for those suffering souls caught in the net of a one-sided, strangulating Christian tradition – the same net that Stein reminds us had crippled his father's spirit and yet as I see it Jung's cure is similarly one-sided. Jung's passionate assertion that whilst God is present everywhere He is most accessible to us within our own souls is one that Kierkegaard would agree with heartedly; however, he would not be too accepting of Jung's elevation of experience over and above faith rather than through faith. Jung's formulation simply leaves no room for faith. I find it especially striking that until the publication of 'The Significance of the Father in the Destiny of the Individual' (1909) there is very little discussion of religion to be found in Jung's work. Here he endorses Freud's claim that all divine figures have their roots in the father-imago. This delights Freud who believes that Jung has correctly understood that the Oedipus complex is at the root of religious feeling (see Palmer 1997). This is interesting to note as, I do believe, for reasons I will explain, that Jung's Oedipus complex may well be at the root of his religious feeling. Tellingly, Jung's thinking around religion only begins to diverge from Freud's own around the time that their collaboration comes to an end. Jung's understanding of Christianity is entrenched not only in his own self-understanding but also in this oedipal battle. In fact I suspect that his genuine desire to heal his spiritually defeated father and act as physician to an ailing religious tradition were in conflict with his need to separate himself from and essentially surpass his father. The father's dismissal of his son's curiosity with the exhortation that first he had to believe and trust, only then could he know and understand must have been a crushing disappointment to the young boy. Jung recalls his father's habit of saying:

> 'you always want to think. One ought not to think, but believe.' I would think, 'No, one must experience and know,' but I would say, 'Give me this belief,' whereupon he would shrug and turn resignedly away.
>
> (1963)

220 Conclusion

It would seem that Jung is still living out this angry, stubborn battle with his father, and if this indeed the case, which I believe it is, this points towards Jung's never having fully mourned his father's passing. This is certainly something which might possibly further link Kierkegaard with Jung; that both men defend against the pain of these losses in order to maintain their position of narcissistic omnipotence. When dealing with inner traumatic experiences there can be a tendency towards defending ourselves by either fusing with an inner image of an 'other' or separating entirely. Could it be that Jung dissociates from his father and to a certain extent becomes his own father whilst Kierkegaard, whose God-image is fused with the memory of his father, stays the eternal son?

There are those, such as Richard Noll, who taking quite literally statements such as 'I must become a Christ, I am made into Christ, I must suffer it' (2009) conclude that Jung had become victim to inflation, identified with Christ and had founded a new religion. I cannot follow such a line of thought; indeed Jung was prone to inflation and he does repeatedly stress the importance of undergoing the original religious experience (that which underlies the age-old symbols of Christian faith) but this has more to do with correcting the devitalised religion of his father than it does with any sort of Christ complex. There are times when Jung does lapse into grandiose, narcissistic inflation but we must balance this with Jung's hard won self-awareness that allowed him to recognise such inflation. Serrano quotes Jung shortly before his death in 1961 as saying 'what I have tried to do is to show the Christian what the redeemer really is, and what the resurrection is. Nobody today seems to know, or to remember, but the idea still exists in dreams' (Stein 1985). This is a reformulation – perhaps more accurately, a revitalisation – by Jung the prophet for there is something radically new in his reformulation of religion. This does beg the question, is Jung's reimagining of Christianity an evolution or does he (perhaps unconsciously) seek to substitute it with analytical psychology? Whether there is any genuine concern for Christianity or Christians in Jung's writings is quite an issue. Whilst some are inclined to view his work as essentially narcissistic and primarily concerned with his own personal struggle for self-coherence (Homans), others such as Stein are of the view that Jung was indeed genuinely concerned with Christianity (even if this interest was deeply intertwined with his own personal psychology). Could it be that both Stein and Homans are correct that there is a genuine concern for Christianity but this desire to be the dutiful son and heal his father's religious wound is in conflict with Jung's need to exceed the father, reject faith and go his own way? Jung puts Christianity onto his therapist's couch and recommends that it acknowledges and integrates that which has been excluded by its one-sidedness. However, the therapist is never outside of the relationship, being very much an active participant in the therapeutic alliance whom changes as a result of his engagement with the patient. Jung is always on the outside of Christianity. This diagnosing of his father and his father's religion is an oedipal victory in itself and not some sort of atonement for the guilt and remorse he felt over his astonishing oedipal victory that Stein point towards. As I will expand upon shortly, Jung does not allow for doubt or uncertainty into the religious experience and in this respect he defends his own faith (or lack of) with all the rigid dogmatism of his father. Consequently, with this absence of doubt combined with the distanced stance he takes towards Christianity there can be no conflict and therefore no synthesis; essentially, a new element is never allowed into consciousness. The therapist who himself is not open to change will not affect a change in the patient either.

In psychotherapists or the clergy, Jung writes that 'it is indeed high time for the clergyman and the psychotherapist to join forces to meet this great spiritual task' (1932a). The spiritual task that he speaks of here is the restoration of a living religion, a religion of vibrancy and vitality, capable of healing. However, I am not convinced that Jung allows for both clergy and psychotherapists in this role of healer. The problem as Jung saw it was the conflict between faith and knowledge; between religious and scientific truth, this resulting from the historical split of the European mind:

> Had it not been for the – psychologically speaking – unnatural compulsion to believe, and an equally unnatural belief in science, this conflict would have no reason to exist. *One can easily imagine a state of mind in which one simply knows and in addition believes a thing which seems probable to one for such and such reasons. There are no grounds whatsoever for any conflict between these two things. Both are necessary, for knowledge alone, like faith alone, is always insufficient.*

Whilst the church preaches blind faith, the universities inculcate an intellectual rationalism and so faith and reason are continually at war with one another. 'Tired of this warfare of opinions', writes Jung,

> the modern man wishes to find out for himself how things are. And through this desire opens the door to the most dangerous possibilities, we cannot help seeing it as a courageous enterprise and giving it some measure of sympathy. It is no reckless adventure, but an effort inspired by deep spiritual distress to bring meaning once more into life on the basis of fresh and unprejudiced experience.
>
> (1932a: par.529)

Jung undertakes this dangerous possibility and experiences the 'intensely personal, reciprocal relationship between man and an extra mundane authority' that provides the foundations of man's freedom and autonomy. Unfortunately, whilst intellectually Jung understands the necessity of faith and knowledge, emotionally he is unable to hold these two elements in tension

222 Conclusion

which leads to the reduction of the religious into the psychological. This subject of religious belief, faith and knowledge is one that is far too emotionally charged for him still. When it comes to healing within the sphere of the psychotherapeutic, Jung talks with ease about belief: 'His (the Physicians) belief is what does the trick. If he really believes, then he will do his utmost for the sufferer with seriousness and perseverance, and this freely given effort and devotion will have a curative effect' (1935b: par.4). The contrast when he speaks of belief within the context of religion is stark indeed: 'I think belief should be replaced by understanding; then we would keep the beauty of the symbol, but still remain free from the depressing results of submission to belief. This would be the psychoanalytic cure for belief and disbelief' (1917/1926/1943). It is difficult to understand this as anything other than the assertion of his religious attitude that places psychological experience as the primary dimension and belief as a secondary. I do not mean to imply that Jung held analytical psychology as somehow superior to religion but that it does perhaps point towards never having reconciled this problem of faith and the father. In Jung's understanding it is 'incontrovertible' experience that liberates and not 'ethical principles, however lofty, or creeds, however orthodox' (1957: par.509). Given the centrality of undergoing the powerful and disturbing original religious experience the negativity that surrounds his feelings concerning creeds is understandable but this negativity around belief is not so easily understood. Jung's clear desire to eliminate belief from faith is readily apparent in the following statement:

> All that I have learned has led me step by step to an unshakable conviction of the existence of God. I only believe in what I know. And that eliminates believing. Therefore I do not take his existence on belief –
> I know that he exists.
>
> (Sands 1955)

With his statement 'I do not believe, I know,' Jung is standing, patronisingly so, outside of his father's religion. Such statements seethe with unconscious doubt and indicate a clear need to quieten uncertainty by dogmatically defending religious experience. Faith and knowledge through personal experience exist so uncomfortably in Jung's thinking that to my mind this really does limit the degree to which we can view Jung as a sensitive and sympathetic spiritual pilgrim. Jung perhaps viewed his knowledge of God as superior to some arbitrary deciding to believe in something; regardless this dichotomy between faith and reason remains. When it comes to his own belief in God Jung simply cannot maintain the tension between belief and knowledge and consequently his personal God-self-image is reduced to a process of self-determination.

Freedom, in terms of being authentic, has practically become synonymous with self-knowledge; there is the common perception that until we can understand why we do what we do, we are not truly free. Freedom then is seen as resting in lessening the degree to which we are controlled by the things around us (our ever-shifting external world) and strengthening our self-determination. The beginnings of engagement in true selfhood for Jung and Kierkegaard lies in the strengthening of self-determination through God. This makes God, or at least the Self-ego axis the truest relationship. Jung strongly fought against a purely intellectual belief divorced from any actual experience of God; 'it is of the highest importance that the educated and "enlightened" should know religious truth as a thing living in the human soul, and not as an abstruse and unreasonable relic of the past' (1951–1961) and I wonder whether he may have fallen into so strongly defending the original experience of God that he severs it from belief and faith altogether. How can we have a fuller realisation of Christian faith where faith, that which is Kierkegaard's anchor has been cast aside and left behind on the seabed? Jung erodes and undervalues belief. This is religious experience viewed through a monocle. A mature faith requires both belief and knowledge, faith and reason. All belief is a leap of faith – but not all leaps of faith are created equal. Ultimately, Kierkegaard and Jung each lack something crucial required for the other's conception of authentic religious feeling; in Kierkegaard's case he lacks the dark weight of the world symbolised in the form of a Lutheran opponent whilst Jung is lacking in that which was so fundamental to Kierkegaard, a devoted faith.

There can be little doubt that Kierkegaard's solitude does indeed catalyze his personal growth, that his fundamental aloneness and sacrifice of Regine are understood to be his destiny: 'there are men whose destiny it is to be sacrificed in one way or another for others in order to bring the idea out – and I with my peculiar cross was one of them' (JP: 1853).[1] Loneliness does not result from having no people around but from being unable to communicate things that seem so very important to us and which we often hold so very closely to our hearts. Loneliness is apathetic, lacking as it often does the care and concern that is part and parcel of interpersonal relationships. Intimacy makes us vulnerable; it demands trust and therefore carries an inescapable risk. And yet, if we cannot allow ourselves fully into relationship, if we cannot marry our internal world with the outer world then we condemn ourselves to psychological aloneness and desolation. Love and intimacy require that we are open, honest and able to give ourselves freely, despite uncertainty and the very real possibility of grief, sorrow and heartache. In fact desire, passion, eroticism and love all demand such uncertainty. With amazingly acute insightfulness on his 'own thorn in the flesh' Kierkegaard writes; 'He who cannot reveal himself cannot love and he who cannot love is the most unhappy man of all' (1843a).[2] It does seem to be the case that Kierkegaard never manages to return from loneliness; he spends his entire life conceiving of his self through his authorship and yet these pseudonyms remain a unified chorus of voices. Rather than return to himself and marry

224 Conclusion

his inner world to that which goes on around him, Kierkegaard confines himself in this painful imaginary world.

Only when we are thrown back on our resources through solitude and isolation do we discover 'the helpful powers of our own natures'. Writing of the healing experience that is driven by one's egoism and linking this egoism to God's will, Jung concedes that:

> If I wish to effect a cure for my patients I am forced to acknowledge the deep significance of their egoism. I should be blind, indeed, if I did not recognise it as a true will of God. I must even help the patient to prevail in his egoism; if he succeeds in this, he estranges himself from other people. He drives them away, and they come to themselves – as they should, for they were seeking to rob him of his 'sacred' egoism. This must be left to him, for it is his strongest and healthiest power; it is, as I have said, a true will of God, which sometimes drives him into complete isolation. However wretched this state may be, it also stands him in good stead, for in this way alone can he get to know himself and learn what an invaluable treasure is the love of his fellow beings. It is, moreover, only in the state of complete abandonment and loneliness that we experience the helpful powers of our own natures.
>
> (1932a: par.525)

In searching out the pain of existential loneliness there is a precarious balance to be struck for there is both reward and risk involved in such estrangement from others. This deepening of one's self-understanding and the love found for one's fellow beings that Jung speaks of do not necessarily follow from one's retreat into oneself. As I suspect to be the case with Kierkegaard, not everyone safely returns from loneliness and yet we should take care not to ascribe those who do not successfully reemerge into society as failing to have attained a sufficient understanding of themselves or of others. I have previously drawn a distinction between Jung's call to submit to the Self and Kierkegaard's more familiar fulfillment of God's will. But what we see in the above quotation is a sacred egoism that is one and the same time the true will of God. Jung is bringing to the forefront here something that I feel is vitally important, that as individuals we are driven not only by intense intrapsychic connection but interpersonal connection also. Writing on the kinship libido Jung explains that

> it wants the human connection. That is the core of the whole transference phenomenon, and it is impossible to argue it away, because relationship to the self is at once relationship to our fellow man, and no one can be related to the latter until he is related to himself.
>
> (1946: par.445)

It is hard not to see Kierkegaard's religiosity as a highly defensive retreat before the overwhelming presence of 'other'; that which threatens something fundamental to his sense of identity. This withdrawal from society could then be understood as an attempt to preserve individuality, or perhaps more accurately that which allows for the retaining of a fragile core. Participation involves risk – it is not unreasonable to put forward the suggestion that Kierkegaard feared losing that part of himself that had allowed for the development of faith within his heart. This spark of hope that has arisen through his relationship to God enlivens him:

> My reserve and self-isolation are broken. . . . My whole being is changed. God's love overwhelms me. What he has done for me is indescribable. My father's death has really pulled me up. I dared not believe that the fundamental misfortune of my being could be resolved. But now a hope has awakened in my soul that God may desire to resolve the fundamental misery of my being.
>
> (JP: 1848)

It is this relationship to God that he cannot risk losing and so, understandably, he shrinks from life as a country pastor and as a husband to his beloved. After all, despair, writes Kierkegaard, is not 'the loss of the beloved – that is unhappiness, pain, suffering – but despair is the lack of the eternal' (1847b). Could it be that Regine and taking up the position of country pastor undermine the self-world relationship that Kierkegaard had built? It might be very tempting to pause here and declare that living in such a narrowed and constrictive world can only block growth and development. It is my feeling that such a statement is terribly belittling; it also undervalues the real contribution Kierkegaard gives to the world through his Christian authorship. Can we really say that Kierkegaard turns against himself, that he fails to actualise a deeper sense of self – does he deceive and deny his true authentic self? Kierkegaard faces his potentialities and the conflicts that he perceived to be set into motion; he is a passionate, relentless and an incredibly intense self. Does he ever cease to be the person he was to be? Only Kierkegaard himself could answer such a question. It intrigues me though that three years after his broken engagement Kierkegaard writes:

> It is now my intention to qualify as a pastor. For several months I have been praying to God to keep on helping me, for it has been clear to me for some time now that I ought not be a writer any longer, something I can be only totally or not at all. This is the reason I have not started anything new along with proof-correcting except for the little review of *The Two Ages*, which, I repeat, is final.
>
> (JP: 1844)

226 Conclusion

Whilst he has taken to his heels and fled from romantic intimacy with Regine, here we see that he is still trying to participate in life or to put it in Kierkegaard's own language he is still venturing into the realm of social commitment. Whilst Kierkegaard engages with his self on a very deep level, he can only attempt to venture into the outer world through this intention to become a pastor. He desires to bring the spiritual and the social together but cannot. Writing in his journal (1847a) Kierkegaard speaks of his intention to cease with the intellectual work that protects him from his melancholy:

> (I shall) not begin on a new book, but try to understand myself, and really think out the idea of my melancholy together with God here and now. This is how I must get rid of my melancholy and bring Christianity closer to me. Hitherto I have defended myself against my melancholy with intellectual work which keeps it away.

He succeeds in bringing Christianity closer to him but melancholy is never metamorphosed to a more gentle forgiveness or acceptance. I strongly suspect that Kierkegaard's overwhelming sense of guilt would not allow this to happen. Unable to escape a grief ridden and traumatic past he can make no commitments to the future. Perhaps Kierkegaard really could not have preserved his sense of identity in the midst of a romantic relationship but it is saddening indeed to sense that he deeply desired to take his place in society with his fellow human beings, that he was so constituted that he could not come back from his solitary endeavors.

The conviction of Jung's entire authorship is that it is the ego-self relationship that guides the individuation process leading to a deeper and more authentic sense of selfhood. And if the development of personhood to its absolute fullness laid solely in the movement that centers life in a union with God then we would have no problem in seeing Kierkegaard's path as a creative and individuating one. However, I suspect very few Jungians would be happy, and rightly so, to accept that individuation is possible when participation with other selves is omitted. There is no doubt that we are more than our social interactions, and yet without them our experience of self is, I believe, severely limited. Jung emphasised that 'individuation does not shut out from the world, but gathers the world to oneself'. Kierkegaard's spiritual development does not 'gather the world to himself' nor does it foster a 'love for his fellow beings'; in fact Kierkegaard's spiritual sustenance always conflicted with his social existence. The spiritual and the social, for Kierkegaard, were certainly not two sides of the same coin. A common phrase in Jungian literature is 'it is the relationship that heals', therapy creates the safe space in which individuals can begin to unravel their past and find hope for the future, however, it is the relationship between analyst and analysand that is genuinely restorative. By this I mean that there is seemingly something quite powerful in the understanding and acceptance provided by

Conclusion   227

another who holds the patient in both mind and heart. Both Kierkegaard and Jung tell us to look within, to find that which we always possessed – to reacquaint the patient with their inner potential is absolutely at the heart of the therapeutic task. Importantly, the therapist is not the agent of treatment but a fellow participant in a process of individual development who has the unenviable task of becoming the personal embodiment of his patient's interpersonal world. When individuation is embarked upon through analysis, this interpersonal element is readily apparent and difficult to avoid; however, people may individuate without analysis: poets through their poetry, artists through their art, philosophers through their philosophy. This reaching out to another, to give of ourselves and receive into ourselves is less obvious when the vehicle for one's individuation is through artistic endeavor. The creative experience of loneliness can often make us better observers of the social world – many of our greatest artists, writers and philosophers were outsiders and this is no coincidence. There is something of a painful irony here for Kierkegaard, through his vocation as a religious author he discovers his meaning but it is this authorship that drives him into isolation, bringing him closer to Christianity but further separated from his fellow man. I simply cannot accept that Kierkegaard was disconnected from his inner life, it is with a sense of great urgency that he hears the call to be a self and arrives at a profound understanding of who he was and who he could (and could not) be. If we are to take seriously Nietzsche's advice 'follow you, not me', then we are forced to concede there can be no simple, universally applicable understanding of what human development looks like; however, it has to include meaningful relationships. And this is where I feel Jungian individuation distinguishes itself from other philosophical processes of self-realisation, for individuation demands participation in one's social world. That we care about others and allow ourselves to be cared for, that we accept others and are in turn able to accept acceptance – it is these interpersonal relationships which put one in harmony with one's self and world. Essentially, individuation is a being and becoming in intercourse with the world.

Notes

1 See also: 'I cannot quite say that my work as an author is a sacrifice. It is true I have been unspeakably unhappy ever since I was a child, but I nevertheless acknowledge that the solution God found of letting me become an author has been a rich, rich pleasure to me. I may be sacrificed, but my authorship is not a sacrifice; it is, in fact, what I unconditionally prefer to keep on being' (JP:1849).
2 On never having been able to reveal himself, Kierkegaard writes: 'it may well be my duty to God. To have to talk about how I spend my time in prayer, how I literally live in relationship to God as a child to a father (mother) etc . . . never in my life have I spoken to one single person the way two people ordinarily speak together – I have always kept my interior life to myself (JP:1849).

Epilogue
Jung and Kierkegaard: a legacy considered

If indeed Jung did read Künzli's thesis on Kierkegaard, it is likely that the image he discerned was of a man who sought to heal the rift between Christianity and humankind, and who ultimately came nearer to closing this rift than Jung himself. Furthermore, his reading may well have evoked interconnected unconscious issues for Jung pertaining to his difficult relationship with his own father, for it is likely that he became aware of Kierkegaard's capacity to resolve his own, as well as his father's, deeply felt religious angst, in the process of writing and developing his religious ideas. The authenticity of Kierkegaard's spiritual experiences would have been readily apparent to Jung, and it is the genuine piety of Kierkegaard's religious belief that comes across in his writings, and undoubtedly in Künzli's work about him, which is, I contend, at the heart of Jung's rejection and misinterpretation of Kierkegaard.

With their unique visions for Christendom, both Kierkegaard and Jung isolated themselves from their contemporaries. And yet, even if time and space had placed the two thinkers in closer proximity, it is highly unlikely that a serious dialogue or engagement between them could have occurred, for such attempts would have been seriously hampered by Jung's shadow issues that are evoked by Kierkegaard's personality and experiences. Laurens Van der Post (1976) remarked of Jung, 'as great as he was, he must also have had a great shadow'. As far as we can determine the extent to which Kierkegaard became a shadow figure for Jung, we can indeed concur with Van der Post that Jung's shadow was indeed great. It is improbable that Kierkegaard would have recognised Jung's therapeutic method as a valid one, for the deepening of one's self-knowledge must always be, for Kierkegaard, dependent upon God, and not the therapist's ability to construct a conducive environment for the exploration of the psyche and its apparently divine depths. However, I do believe Kierkegaard would have recognised in Jung individuation, the potential for profound healing; although he perhaps would have taken issue, as many theologians have, with Jung's attribution of this healing power to the psyche. And yet, psychological maturity and authentic religious experience go hand in hand for both Kierkegaard and

Jung; constituting the kind of 'holy healing' that we explored at the very beginning of this book. Both Jung and Kierkegaard grasp and articulate the movement, the continual becoming and spiritual momentum that characterise human existence. In Jung we have a 'therapist-pastor', and in Kierkegaard we see the 'pastor-therapist'. Both men sought to respond to what they perceived to be the urgent need of contemporary humanity, a more authentic relationship with God from within, the true moorings of the essential authentic self. The finger of accusation being pointed in the same direction, at the passive acceptance of traditional, institutional Christianity. Both are concerned with emphasising the unconscious forces that pull the personality towards wholeness – Jung from a therapeutic background and Kierkegaard from that of existential philosophy. Furthermore, life's meaning is intrinsically involved in self-realisation for Jung and Kierkegaard; each advocate finding personal principles that are worth living for. In becoming there is a sense of overcoming – the overcoming of the lies we tell ourselves and the imaginative ways in which we deceive ourselves, so often found to be at the very heart of our greatest sufferings. Kierkegaard and Jung provide us with more than a compelling analysis of the human condition – their work is an overture of illumination, a powerful analysis of the despair that arises when we turn away from our potentialities, a transgression against one's self that can only result in estrangement from our own selves and others.

As human beings we are born into this very unique condition where we need to find out who we are, what we care about, what kind of person are we going to be. We look around ourselves and conform all too readily, we avoid those difficult conversations with ourselves and neglect the personal truth of our individuality. This looking outside of ourselves for answers that can only be found by looking within really is a kind of suicide. Knowing oneself is profoundly difficult; there is always going to be the inevitable elements of distortion in our beliefs and acts. But if we are able to find the courage and resolve to dare to know, to dare to be wise then we will find and awaken passion. Jung and Kierkegaard dare to follow the dictates of their own individual internal truth and they each discover personal principles worth living for. Henry David Thoreau once said that government 'has not the vitality or the force of a single living man'; government and institutions cannot be the moral arbiter of our existence, this comes from the individual who is at the very center of moral progress. And this is why to my mind Kierkegaard and Jung are delightfully relevant to us today, for theirs is a powerful reminder that responsibility for change and growth lays within the individual. Communities are built from the inside out, not through politicised 'big society' projects and the like – they are built and driven by us and through us. Individuation is an incredible endeavor, one that demands an ethical obligation, for 'acceptance of oneself is the essence of the moral problem and the acid test of one's whole outlook on life'. Jung is clear that individuation strengthens our relationship with others, and there is then a sense in which we could state that we have a moral responsibility to carry our personal development out and into the world. Perhaps to not take one's abilities into the community and contribute to the whole is an act of transgression that results in despair similar to that which Kierkegaard describes as arising when one refuses to accept his true vocation, a betrayal of the individual's innate potential and creativity. We might then seek to marry the ethical obligation of individuation with the Kierkegaardian call to action, for it is not enough for an individual to have attained a degree of self-knowledge; personal truth only exists insofar as the individual himself produces it in action. Writing of his own age Jung suggested that 'if ever there was a time when self-reflection was the absolutely necessary and only right thing, it is now, in our present catastrophic epoch' (1917/1926/1943: preface). Perhaps in our own age we have a plentiful amount of self-reflection, perhaps what we so desperately need in our increasingly alienated and divided age is passion and social generosity. Nevertheless, the proclamation that an individual has an ethical obligation to be a citizen of the world is one that takes me into territory that I feel deeply uncomfortable in.

I do not mean to suggest that one's interpersonal relationships are the *sine qua non* of mental or emotional health – they are not. I do not believe that one does find life's meaning – his or her personal truth – in interpersonal relationships themselves; there is little doubt that for Jung and Kierkegaard the meaning of life is to be found primarily in the personal realm. Despite the central importance of the relationship between analyst and analysand it does remain that individuation is a personal journey conducted though a great deal of solitude, but not complete isolation; the analyst whilst actively encouraging the independence of his patients' personal development is at the same time always available to guide and intervene when necessary. Similarly, Kierkegaard's relationship with God provides a constant orientation towards the impersonal through which he experiences a sense of unity and a change of attitude towards life. Our inner world and that of our outer world are in a constant relation; the personal and the impersonal, self and society, solitude and solidarity interact with one another pulling us in one direction and then the other. For some individuals there is very little conflict between such opposing forces but there are those among us who in order to be our true creative selves need to be free of interpersonal relationships and social commitments. That out of loneliness is born the possibility of love is one of Jung's most charming insights; his hypothesis that the reduction of psychic disharmony within the psyche brings to birth a new orientation towards life and a better relation to one's outer world is a delightful insight. But I do feel that we must exercise great caution if we are to judge an individual's personal development by his social connectedness, for we each differ significantly in regards to the kind of intimacy and depth of relationships we require from others. This is particularly so given our cultural bias towards viewing marriage, children and career as indicators of one's health and happiness. Ann Casement's restrained description of the ethical stance as living in a reciprocal relationship with one's surroundings so that one will usually enter into marriage, have a job or useful occupation and conduct one's civic duties in a responsible manner is incredibly wise. The key here is 'usually', not necessarily – commitment to one's fellow human beings can manifest in many different forms, it need not follow such a prescriptive course. Whether we gravitate and orientate ourselves more towards others or to solitude is of no special importance, what is important is that we do not idealise or denigrate either state for both are necessary. The individual must be receptive and strive towards a state of harmony between one's inner and outer world. Where this balance lays is a profoundly personal matter. Of course such a state of equilibrium is inevitably unattainable; a new unity arises and a new hypothesis which reconciles previously incompatible ideas is created but such a state necessarily cannot last for 'adaptation is never achieved once and for all . . . in the last resort it is highly improbable that there could ever be a therapy that got rid of all difficulties; they are necessary for health' (1916/1957: par.143).

Jung's empathising of responsibility, freedom, commitment, decision making, suffering, self-acceptance and self-becoming combined with his understanding of inner conflicts, loss of self and the significance of self-awareness certainly places him firmly within the world of existentialism. Anxiety, uncertainty and doubt challenge our self-world relationship: we have to embrace and live with such anxieties in order to be transformed by it – running from anxiety only serves to maintain a status quo in the most personally stifling way. The key is not to drown out such dis-ease with the noise of everyday existence or to bury it with one's dogmatic or fanatical beliefs but to embrace it. Confronting uncertainty and its attendant anxiety plays a key role in an individual's transformation. 'Doubt is an unpleasant condition, but certainty is absurd', wrote Voltaire. The uncomfortable truth is that we don't know anything for certain. We might think we do, but we don't. We might have a strong belief, which is backed up by strong evidence and perhaps even constantly reinforced by experience but we still do not know that thing for certain. Belief shapes our very world and what we believe has absolutely nothing to do with how true they may be – and this is especially so in regards to the beliefs we hold about ourselves. The transformation of our own self-beliefs is crucial in overcoming suffering. With a wonderful clarity Jung writes 'it is not that something different is seen, but that one sees differently. It is as though the spatial act of seeing were changed by a new dimension' (1939d: par.891). It is the discovery of this new dimension that allows us to bring to birth something new within ourselves and this is directly related to our capacity to act on our insights. By this I mean to say that how we perceive things seems integrally related to our intentionality. Therefore should we be incapable at that present moment to act, essentially if volition is lacking, then this process of re-perceiving is not possible.

Whether we are striving to become a Kierkegaardian self or seeking to proceed along the path of Jung's individuation, anxiety needs to be courted and doubt demands to be embraced – it is fine to be half sure, so long as one is wholly committed. Kierkegaard and Jung teach us this not only with their philosophies but in how they chose to live their own lives, that they never reached their ideals does not invalidate their work, quite the contrary, for they show us the courage and resolve that is required to engage in the perpetual uphill battle that is knowing thyself.

Bibliography

Allen, E. L. *Kierkegaard, His Life and Thought* (London: Stanley, 1935).
Anthony, M. *Jung's Circle of Women: The Valkyries* (Nicolas-Hays: U.S, 1999).
—— *The Valkyries: The Women Around Jung* (Element Books: England, 1990).
American Psychiatric Association. *Diagnostic and Statistical Manual of Mental Disorders*. Text Revision (4th Edition) (DSM-IV-TR) (Washington, DC: American Psychiatric Association, 2004).
Argyle, M. Psychology and Religion: An Introduction (London: Routledge, 2000).
Aquilina, Mike. *A Year with the Church Fathers: Patristic Wisdom for Daily Living* (Saint Benedict Press: North Carolina, 2010). Bair, D. *Jung: A Biography* (Boston: Little, Brown and Co, 2003).
Beebe, J. and Falzeder, E. (Editors) *The Question of Psychological Types: The Correspondence of C. G. Jung and Hans Schmid-Guisan, 1915–1916*, translated by Ernst Falzeder (Princeton University Press: New Jersey, 2012).
Benner, D. *Care of Souls: Revisioning Christian Nurture and Counsel* (Baker Books: Michigan, 1998).
Bishop, P. *The Dionysian Self: C.G. Jung's Reception of Friedrich Nietzsche* (Walter de Gruyter: Berlin, 1995).
Blanch, S.Y. *Living by Faith* (W.B. Eerdmans Publishing: Michigan, 1984).
Bly, R. *A Little Book on the Human Shadow* (Harper Collins: New York, 2009).
Bockus, F.M. The Archetypal Self: Theological Values in Jung's Psychology in Moore, R. (Editor) *Jung and Christianity in Dialogue* (Paulist Press: New Jersey, 1990).Brome, V. *Jung* (London: Palgrave Macmillan, 1978).
Brooke, R. (Editor) *Pathways into the Jungian World: Phenomenology and Analytical Psychology* (London: Routledge, 2004).
Buber, J (Editor). *Martin Buber's on Psychology and Psychotherapy: Essays, Letters, and Dialogue* (Syracuse University Press: New York, 1999).
Carlisle, C. *Kierkegaard: A Guide for the Perplexed* (Continuum: London, 2006).
Casement, A. (Editor) *Post-Jungians Today: Key Papers in Contemporary Analytical Psychology* (Routledge: London & New York, 1998).
—— *Who Owns Jung?* (Karnac Books: London, 2007).
Chessick, R. *What Constitutes the Patient in Psychotherapy: Alternative Approaches to Understanding Humans* (Jason Aronson Incorporated: Maryland, 1992).
Cole, P. *The Problematic Self in Kierkegaard and Freud* (Yale University Press: Connecticut, 1971). Cooper, M., N. Thulstrup and M. M. Thulstrup (Editors) *Kierkegaard's Classical Inspiration* (Reitzel: Copenhagen, 1985).

234 Bibliography

Daniels, M. *Shadow, Self, Spirit: Essays in Transpersonal Psychology* (Imprint Academic: England, 2005).

Davenport, J. and Rudd, A. (Editors) *Kierkegaard After Macintyre: Essays on Freedom, Narrative and Virtue* (Open Court Publishing: Chicago, 2001).

Dourley, J.P. *Paul Tillich, Carl Jung, and the Recovery of* Religion (London and New York: Routledge, 2008).

——— *On Behalf of the Mystical Fool: Jung on the Religious Situation* (Routledge: London: 2009).

Dourly, J. The Jung, Buber, white exchanges: exercises in futility. *Studies in Religion/ Sciences Religieuses,* Volume: 20 issue: 3, page(s): 299–309.

Dourley, J.P. Jung, Tillich, and aspects of Western Christian development in Moore, R. (Editor) *Jung and Christianity in Dialogue* (Paulist Press: New Jersey, 1990).

Dunne, C. Carl Jung: Wounded Healer of the Soul: An Illustrated Biography (Continuum: London, 2002).

Edinger, E. *The New God-image: A Study of Jung's Key Letters Concerning the Evolution of the Western God-Image* (Chiron Publications: Illinois, 1996).

Ellenberger, H. F. Discovery of the Unconscious: The History and Evolution of Dynamic Psychiatry (Basic Books: New York, 2008).

Eller, V. *Kierkegaard and Radical Discipleship: A New Perspective* (Princeton University Press: Princeton, 1968).

Evans, S. *Søren Kierkegaard's Christian Psychology: Insight for Counseling and Pastoral Care* (Regent College Publishing: Vancouver, 2005).

——— *Kierkegaard: On Faith and the Self, Collected Essays* (Baylor University Press: Texas, 2006).

Fenger, H. *Kierkegaard: The Myths and Their Origins,* translated from Danish by George C. Schoolfield (New Haven, CT: Yale University Press, 1980).

Ferguson, H. *Melancholy and the Critique of Modernity: Søren Kierkegaard's Religious Psychology* (Routledge: London & New York, 2005).

Fratoli, E. Me and my anima: through the dark glass of the Jungian/Freudian interface in Young-Eisendrath, Terence Dawson (Editors), *The Cambridge Companion to Jung* (Cambridge University Press: Cambridge, 2008).

Friedmann, R. *Kierkegaard: The Analysis of the Psychological* Persona (Peter Nevill Ltd: London, 1949).

Furtak, R.A. *Kierkegaard's 'Concluding Unscientific Postscript': A Critical Guide* (Cambridge University Press: Cambridge, 2010).

Furtak, R.A. *Wisdom in Love: Kierkegaard and the Ancient Quest for Emotional Integrity* (University of Notre Dame Press: Indiana, 2005.

Freeman, J. "The 'Face to Face' Interview," 1959, in *C.G. Jung Speaking: Interviews and Encounters,* edited by McGuire & Hull (Princeton University Press: Princeton, 1987).

Gardiner, P. *Kierkegaard* (Oxford University Press: Oxford, 1988). Garff, J. *Søren Kierkegaard: A Biography* (Princeton University Press: Princeton, 2005).

Glover, E. *Freud or Jung* (Northwestern University Press: Illinois, 1950), p. 163.

Goldenberg, N. *Changing of the Gods* (Beacon: Boston, 1979).

Gordon, R. 'Reflections on Curing and Healing', *Journal of Analytical Psychology* 24.3 (1979): pp. 207–217.

Gouwens, D. *Kierkegaard as Religious Thinker* (Cambridge University Press: Cambridge, 1996).

Bibliography   235

Greenhalgh, K. On Reading Narcissistic Texts: An Object Relation's Theory View of the Life and Works of Søren Kierkegaard (Ph.D. Thesis, University of Stirling, 2008).

Hayman, R. *A Life of Jung* (Bloomsbury Publishing: London, 2002).

Hanna, C. B. *The Face of the Deep: The Religious Ideas of C.G. Jung* (The Westminster Press: London, 1967).

Hannah, B. *Jung: His Life and Work. A Biographical Memoir* (Chiron Publications: North Carolina, 1976).

Hannay, A. *Kierkegaard* (Routledge: London, 1982).

—— *Kierkegaard: A Biography* (Cambridge: Cambridge University Press, 2001).

—— Kierkegaard and Philosophy: Selected Essays (Routledge: London, 2013).

Helweg, H. *Søren Kierkegaard. En psykiatrisk-psykologisk studie,* (H. Hagerup: Copenhagen, 1933). Hillman, J. *Healing Fiction* (Station Hill Press: New York, 1983).

—— *Insearch: Psychology and Religion* (Spring Publications: Zurich, 1994).

Hoggart, R.*The Tyranny of Relativism: Culture and Politics in Contemporary English Society* (Chatto & Windus, London, 1995).

Homans, P. *Jung in Context* (University of Chicago: Chicago, 1979).

Howland, J. *Kierkegaard and Socrates: A Study in Philosophy and Faith* (Cambridge University Press: Cambridge, 2006).

Hunt, S. 'The Anthropology of Carl Jung: Implications for Pastoral Care' in Moore, R. (Editor) *Jung and Christianity in Dialogue* (Paulist Press: New Jersey, 1990). Huskinson, L. *Nietzsche and Jung: The Whole Self in the Union of* Opposites (Routledge: London, 2004).

Jacobi, J. *Psychology of C.G Jung* (Routledge: London, 1999).

Jaspers, K. *General Psychopathology*, translated by J. Hoenig and Marian W. Hamilton (Baltimore and London: John Hopkins University Press: Maryland, 1997).

Jegstrup, E. *The New Kierkegaard* (Indiana University Press: Indiana, 2004).

Judd, Antony. Carl Gustav Jung: A Missed Connection. In *Kierkegaard's Influence on the Social Sciences,* edited by Jon Stewart (Routledge: New York, 2011).

Jung, C. G. *Collected Works of C. G. Jung,* edited by H. Read, M. Fordham, G. Adler, translated by F. F. C. Hull (Routledge: London & New York).

1912 – New Paths in Psychology (Vol. 7)

1912/1952 – Symbols of Transformation (Vol. 5)

1916 – The Structure of the Unconscious (Vol. 7)

1916/1957 – The Transcendent Function (Vol. 8)

1917/1926/1943 – The Psychology of the Unconscious (Vol. 7)

1921 – Psychological Types (Vol. 6)

1925 – Marriage as a Psychological Relationship (Vol. 17)

1925 – *Introduction to Jungian Psychology: Notes of the Seminar on Analytical Psychology Given in 1925*, edited by William McGuire, revised and introduced by Sonu Shamdasani (Princeton, NJ: Princeton University Press, 2011).

1927 – *Women in Europe* (Vol. 10)

1928a – Psychoanalysis and the Cure of Souls (Vol. 11)

1928b – On Psychic Energy (Vol. 8)

1928–1930 – Dream Analysis 1: Notes on a Seminar Given in 1928–1930 (Vol. 10)

1928/1931 – The Spiritual Problem of Modern Man (Vol. 10)

1929a – The Relations Between Ego and the Unconscious (Vol. 7)

236 Bibliography

1929b – Freud and Jung: Contrasts (Vol. 4)

1929c – Commentary on 'The Secret of the Golden Flower' (Vol. 13)

1930/1931 – *The Stages of Life* (Vol. 8)

1931a – Basic Postulates of Analytical Psychology (Vol. 8)

1931b – The Aims of Psychotherapy (Vol. 16)

1932a – Psychotherapists or the Clergy (Vol. 11)

1932b – *The Psychology of Kundalini Yoga: Notes of the Seminar Given in 1932*, edited by Sonu Shamdasani (Princeton University Press: Princeton, 2012).

1934 – The State of Psychotherapy Today (Vol. 10)

1934–1939 – *Nietzsche's Zarathustra: Notes of the Seminar Given in 1934–1939*, edited by James Jarrett, Vol. 2 (Routledge: London & New York, 1989).

1934/1954 – Archetypes of the Collective Unconscious (Vol. 9: Part 1)

1935a – The Tavistock Lectures (Vol. 18)

1935b – Principles of Practical Psychotherapy (Vol. 16)

1936/1954 – Concerning the Archetypes and the Anima Concept (Vol. 9: Part 1)

1938/1940 – Psychology and Religion: The Terry Lectures (Vol. 11)

1939a – *The Symbolic Life* (Vol. 18)

1939b – Psychological Commentary on the Tibetan Book of the Great Liberation (Vol. 11)

1939c – Sigmund Freud: An Obituary (Vol. 15)

1939d – Introduction to Zen Buddhism (Vol. 11)

1940/1950 – *Concerning Rebirth* (Vol. 9: Part 1)

1942/1948 – A Psychological Approach to Dogma of the Trinity (Vol. 11)

1942/1954 – Transformation Symbolism in the Mass (Vol. 11)

1943 – Psychotherapy and a Philosophy of Life (Vol. 16)

1944 – Psychology and Alchemy (Vol. 12)

1945 – Medicine and Psychotherapy (Vol. 16)

1906–1950 – *Letters*, Vol. I: 1906–1950, Selected and edited by Gerhard Afler in collaboration with Aniela Jaffe with translation by F. F. C. Hull (Routledge: London & New York, 1973).

1946 – Psychology of the Transference (Vol. 16)

1947/1954 – On the Nature of the Psyche (Vol. 8)

1951 – *Aion* (Vol. 9: Part 2)

1951–1961 – *Letters*, Vol. 2: 1951–1961, Selected and edited by Gerhard Afler in collaboration with Aniela Jaffe with translation by F.F.C Hull (Routledge: London & New York, 1976).

1952a – Synchronicity: An Acausal Connecting Principle (Vol. 8)

1952b – *Answer to Job* (Vol. 11)

1955 – Mysterium Coniunctions (Vol. 14)

1956–1957 – Jung and Religious Belief (Vol. 11)

1957 – The Undiscovered Self (Vol. 10)

1958 – A Psychological View of Conscience (Vol. 10)

1959 – Good and Evil in Analytical Psychology (Vol. 10)

1961 – Symbols and the Interpretation of Dreams (Vol. 18)

1963 – *Memories, Dreams, Reflections*, Recorded and edited by Aniela Jaffé, translated from the German by Richard and Clara Winston (Fotana Press: Illinois, 1995).

Bibliography   237

2009 – *The Red Book: Liber Novus*, edited by Shamdasani (W.W Norton: New York, 2009).

Kangas, D. *Kierkegaard's Instant: On Beginnings* (Indiana University Press: Indiana, 2007).

Kast, V. Anima/animus in Renos K. Papadopoulos (Editor) *The Handbook of Jungian Psychology: Theory, Practice and Applications* (Routledge: London & New York, 2006).

Kaufmann, W. A. From Shakespeare to Existentialism: An Original Study: Essays on Shakespeare and Goethe, Hegel and Kierkegaard, Nietzsche, Rilke, and Freud, Jaspers, Heidegger, and Toynbee (Princeton University Press: Princeton, 1980).

———— *Nietzsche, Heidegger, and Buber* (Transaction Publishers: New Jersey, 1980).

Kierkegaard, S. *Søren Kierkegaard's Journals and Papers*, edited by Howard Vincent Hong, Edna Hatlestad Hong (Indiana University Press: Princeton, 1978).

1843a – *Either/Or*, edited and translated by Howard V. Hong and Edna H. Hong (Princeton University Press: Princeton, 2013).

1843b – *Fear and Trembling/Repetition*, edited and translated by Howard V. Hong and Edna H. Hong (Princeton University Press: Princeton, 2013).

1844a – *Philosophical Fragments*, edited and translated by Howard V. Hong an: Pd Edna H. Hong (Princeton University Press: Princeton, 1985).

1844b – *The Concept of Anxiety*, edited and translated by Howard V. Hong and Edna H. Hong (Princeton University Press: Princeton, 2013).

1845 – Stages on life's way: Studies by various persons, edited and translated by Howard V. Hong and Edna H. Hong (Princeton University Press: Princeton, 1988).

1846a – *Concluding Unscientific Postscript*, edited and translated by Howard V. Hong and Edna H. Hong (Princeton University Press: Princeton, 2013).

1846b – *Two Ages: The Age of Revolution and the Present Age, a Literary Review*, edited and translated by Howard V. Hong and Edna H. Hong (Princeton University Press: Princeton, 1978).

1847a – *Eighteen Upbuilding Discourses*, edited and translated by Howard V. Hong and Edna H. Hong (Princeton University Press: Princeton, 1990).

1847b – *Works of Love*, edited and translated by Howard V. Hong and Edna H. Hong (Princeton University Press: Princeton, 2013).

1847c – *Upbuilding Discourses in Various Spirits*, edited and translated by Howard V. Hong and Edna H. Hong (Princeton University Press: Princeton, 2009).

1848 – *Christian Discourses*, translated by Walter Lowrie (Princeton University Press: Princeton, 1971).

1848/1859 – *The Point of View for My Work as an Author*, edited and translated by Howard V. Hong and Edna H. Hong (Princeton University Press: Princeton, 1998).

1849 – *The Sickness Unto Death*, edited and translated by Howard V. Hong and Edna H. Hong (Princeton University Press: Princeton, 2013).

1850 – *Practice in Christianity*, 1849a – *The Sickness Unto Death*, edited and translated by Howard V. Hong and Edna H. Hong (Princeton University Press: Princeton, 1991).

1851 – *For Self Examination: Judge for Yourself*, edited and translated by Howard V. Hong and Edna H. Hong (Princeton University Press: Princeton, 1990).

1854 – *Attack Upon "Christendom"*, edited by Walter Lowrie (Princeton University Press: Princeton, 1968).

238 Bibliography

The Diary of Søren Kierkegaard, edited by Peter Preisier Rohnde (Philosophical Library: New York, 1960).

The Essential Kierkegaard, edited by Howard Vincent Hong and Edna Hatlestad Hong (Princeton University Press: Princeton, 2000).

Parables of Kierkegaard, edited by Thomas C. Oden (Princeton University Press: Princeton, 1989).

The Prayers of Kierkegaard (University of Chicago Press: Chicago, 1956).

Provocations: Spiritual Writings, edited by Charles E. Moore (Plough Publishing House: New York, 1999).

The Soul of Kierkegaard: Selections from His Journal, edited by Alexander Dru (Courier Dover Publications: New York, 1959).

Kirmmse, B. (Editor) *Encounters With Kierkegaard: A Life as Seen by His Contemporaries* (Princeton University Press: Princeton, 1996).Lachman, G. Jung the Mystic: The Esoteric Dimensions of Carl Jung's Life and Teachings (Penguin Group: London, 2010).

Lake, F. *Clinical Theology: A Theological and Psychological Basis to Clinical Pastoral Care* (Darton, Longman and Todd: London, 1986).

Lacan, J. *The Four Fundamental Concepts of Psycho-analysis* (W.W. Norton: New York, 1998).Lawson, T. *Carl Jung, Darwin of the Mind* (Karnac Books: London, 2008).

León, C. *The Neither, Nor of the Second Sex: Kierkegaard on Women, Sexual Difference and Sexual Relations* (Mercer University Press: Georgia, 2008).

León, C. and Walsh, S. (Editors) *Feminist Interpretations of Søren Kierkegaard* (Penn State Press: Pennsylvania, 1997).

Lorentzen, J. *Kierkegaard's Metaphors* (Mercer University Press: Georgia, 2001).

Lowrie, W. *A Short Life of Kierkegaard* (Princeton University Press: Princeton, 2013).

Lubcke, P. 'Kierkegaard and Indirect Communication', *History of European Ideas* 12.1 (1990): pp. 31–40.

Malantschuk, G. *The Controversial Kierkegaard* (Wilfred Laurier University Press: Ontario, 1980).

Manheimer, R. *Kierkegaard as Educator* (University of California Press: California, 1977).

Martin, H. V. *Kierkegaard: The Melancholy Dane* (Epworth Press: London, 1950).

McCuire, W. (Editor) *The Freud/Jung Letters: The Correspondence Between Sigmund Freud and C. G. Jung*, translated by Ralph Manheim and R. F. C. Hull (The Hogarth Press and Routledge & Kegan Paul: London, 1977).

Mcguire, W. and R. F. C. Hull (Editors) *Jung Speaking, Interviews and Encounters* (Pan Books: London, 1980).

McLynn, F. *Carl Gustav Jung: A Biography* (St. Martin's Press: New York, 1998).

Meckel, D. and R. Moore (Editors) Jung and Christianity in Dialogue: Faith, Feminism, and Hermeneutics (Paulist Press: New Jersey, 1990).

Nordentoft, K. *Kierkegaard's Psychology*, translated by Bruce H. Kirmmse (Duquesne University Press: Pittsburg, 1978).

Ostenfeld, I. *Søren Kierkegaard's Psychology*, translated by Alistair McKinnon (Wilfred Laurier University Press: Ontario, 1978).

Otto, R. *The Idea of the Holy*, translated by John W. Harvey (Penguin Books: london, 1959).

Palmer, M. *Freud and Jung on Religion* (Routledge: London, 1997).

Papadopoulos, R. (Editor) *Carl Gustav Jung: Critical Assessments* (Routledge: London, 1992).

—— *The Handbook of Jungian Psychology: Theory, Practice and Applications* (Routledge: London & New York, 2006).

Pattison, G. *Kierkegaard: The Aesthetic and the Religious* (Palgrave Macmillan: London, 1992).

Perkins, R. (Editor) *The Moment and Late Writings* (Mercer University Press: Georgia, 2009).

Plekon, M. 'Anthropological Contemplation': *Kierkegaard and Modern Social Theory', Thought* 55 (1980): pp. 346–369.

—— 'Kierkegaard', *Anglican Theological Review* 64.3 (1982): pp. 327–352.

Podmore, S. 'Kierkegaard as Physician of the Soul: On Self-Forgiveness and Despair', *Journal of Psychology and Theology* 37.3 (2009).

Podmore, S. Kierkegaard and the Self before God: Anatomy of the Abyss (Indiana University Press: Indiana, 2011)Poole, R. *Kierkegaard: The Indirect Communication* (University of Virginia Press: Virginia, 1993).

Poole, R. and Stangerup, H. (Editors) *A Kierkegaard Reader: Texts and Narratives* (Fourth Estate,: London, 1989).

Rae, M. *Kierkegaard and Theology* (Continuum: London, 2010).

C: \Users\Tara Grover Smith\AppData\Local\Temp\Temp2_32-0533 Cook to CE.zip\15032-0533-Ref Mismatch Report.docx - LStERROR_54—— *Kierkegaard's Vision of the Incarnation: By Faith Transformed* (Oxford University Press: Oxford, 2004).

Ryce-Menuhin, J. (Editor) Jung and the Monotheisms: Judiasm, Christianity, and Islam (Routledge: London, 1994).

Saarni, C. *The Development of Emotional Competence* (Guilford Press: New York, 1999).

Sagi, A. Kierkegaard, Religion, and Existence: The Voyage of the Self (Rodopi: Amsterdam, 2000).

Samuels, A. The Plural Psyche: Personality, Morality, and the Father (Routledge: London, 1989).

Sanford, J. *Dreams, God's Forgotten Language* (Lippincott: Philadelphia:, 1968).

Sartre, J. P. *Jean Paul Sartre: Basic Writings*, edited by Stephen Priest (Routledge: London, 2002).

Sartre, J.P. *Existentialism and Human Emotions* (Philosophical Library: New York, 1957). Schaer, H. Religion and the Cure of Souls in Jung's Psychology (Routledge: London & New York, 1957).

Segal, R. A. Explaining and Interpreting Religion: Essays on the Issue (Peter Lang: New York, 1992).

Segal, R. Is Analytical Psychology a Religion? Rationalist and Romantic approaches to Religion and Modernity. *Journal of Analytical Psychology*, Volume 44, Issue 4 October 1999, pp. 547-560.

Shamdasani, S. Is Analytical Psychology a Religion? In Statu nascendi. *Journal of Analytical Psychology*, Volume 44, Issue 4 October 1999, pp. 539–545.

Shamdasani, S. *Jung and the Making of Modern Psychology: The Dream of Science* (Cambridge University Press: Cambridge, 2003).

—— Jung Stripped Bare by His Biographers, Even (Karnac Books: London, 2005).

240 Bibliography

—— C. G. Jung: A Biography in Books (W.W. Norton: New York, 2012).

Sharf, R. S. Theories of Counseling and Psychotherapy: Concepts and Cases (Cengage Learning: Boston, 2010).

Shelburne, W. A. 'Existential Perspective in the Thought of Carl Jung', *Journal of Religion and Health* 22.1 (Spring 1983): pp. 58–73.

Shestov, L. *Kierkegaard and the Existential Philosophy* (Ohio University Press, 1969).

Simms, E.M. 'In Destitute Times: Archetype and existence in Rilke's *Duino Elegies'* in Brooke, R.*Pathways Into the Jungian World: Phenomenology and Analytical Psychology* (Routledge: London, 2003).Singer, J. *Boundaries of the Soul: The Practice of Jung's Psychology* (Doubleday: New York, 1972).

Sobosan, J. G. 'Kierkegaard and Jung on the Self', *Journal of Psychology and Theology* 3 (1975): pp. 31–35.

Smith, R. The Wounded Jung: Effects of Jung's Relationships on His Life and Work (Northwestern University Press: Illinois, 1997).Stein, M. *Jung's Treatment of Christianity: The Psychotherapy of a Religious Tradition* (Chiron: North Carolina, 1985).

—— *Jungian Psychoanalysis: Working in the Spirit of Carl Jung* (Opeb Court: Chicago, 2010).

Stewart, J. (Editor) *Kierkegaard's Influence on the Social Sciences* (Ashgate: Surrey, England, 2011).

Stewart, J. and N. J. Cappelørn (Editors) *Kierkegaard Revisited* (Walter De Gruyter: New York, 2007).

Stewart, J. *Kierkegaard's Relations to Hegel Reconsidered* (Cambridge University Press: Cambridge, 2003). Stiener, R. *Freud, Jung, and Spiritual Psychology* (Anthroposophic Press: Massachusetts, 2001).

Stokes, J. G. and A. Bube (Editors) *Kierkegaard and Death* (Indiana University Press: Indiana, 2011).

Storr, A. *Nietzsche and Jung: J.R. Jones Lecture.* Delivered at the University on 20 November 1996 (University of Wales: Swansea, 1996).

Storr, A. Is analytical psychology a religion? Jung's search for a substitute for lost faith. *Journal of Analytical Psychology*, Volume 44, Issue 4 October 1999, pp. 531–537.

Swenson, D. *Something About Kierkegaard* (Mercer University Press: Georgia, 2000).

Tacey, D. J. Remarking Men: Jung, Spirituality and Social Change (Routledge: London, 1997).

Taylor, M.L. The Hermit Emerges Victorious. Contempt for Woman in Kierkegaard's Attack upon the (Male) Ecclesiastical Establishment. *The Moment and Late Writings* edited by Robert L. Perkins (Mercer University Press: Georgia, 2009). Thompson, J. (Editor) *Kierkegaard: A Collection of Critical Essays* (Anchor Books: New York, 1972).

Thompson, J. *Kierkegaard* (Victor Gollancz: London, 1974). Tinder, G. "Can We Be Good Without God?' *Atlantic Monthly*, December 1989, pp. 69–85.

Tisdell, E.J. *Exploring Spirituality and Culture in Adult and Higher Education* (Jossey-Bass: New Jersey, 2003).Ulanov, A. *Spirit in Jung* (Daimon: Switzerland, 2005).

Bibliography 241

Ulanov, A. and B. Ulanov. *Religion and the Unconscious* (Westminster Press: Philadelphia, 1975).

Urban, E. 'Michael Fordham and the *Journal of Analytical Psychology*: The View from Hangman's Hill', *The Journal of Analytical Psychology* 60.4 (September 2015).

Van Der Post, L. *Jung and the Story of Our Time* (Random House: New York, 1976).

―――― *A Walk With a White Bushman* (Random House: New York, 2010).

Walsh, S. Living Christianly: Kierkegaard's Dialectic of Christian Existence (Penn State Press: Pennsylvania, 2008).

―――― *Kierkegaard: Thinking Christianly in an Existential Mode* (Oxford University Press: Oxford, 2009).

Washburn, M. Transpersonal Psychology in Psychoanalytic Perspective (Suny Press: New York, 1994).

Watkin, J. *Kierkegaard* (Continuum: London, 2001).

Watkin, J. The Logic of Søren Kierkegaard's Misogyny, 1854–1855 in Léon and Walsh (Editors) *Feminist Interpretations of Søren Kierkegaard* (Penn State Press: Pennsylvania, 2010). Wehr, D. S. *Jung and Feminism* (Beacon: Boston, 1987).

Weigert, E. 'Søren Kierkegaard's Mood Swings', *International Journal of Pyscho-Analysis* 41 (1960): pp. 521–525.

Welch, J. Spiritual Pilgrims: Carl Jung and Teresa of Avila (Paulist Press: New Jersey, 1982).

Wilson, C. *C.G. Jung: Lord of the Underworld* (Maurice Bassett: Florida, 1988).

Winnicott, D. W. *Psychoanalytic Explorations*, edited by C. Winnicott, R. Shepherd, M. Davis (Karnac: London, 1989).

Winnicott, D. 'Review of *Memories. Dreams. Reflections* by C.G. Jung,' *International Journal of Psychoanalysis*, 45, 2–3, 1964. Wulff, D. *The Psychology of Religion* (Wiley: New York, 1991).

Young-Eisendrath (Editor) *The Cambridge Companion to Jung*, edited by Young-Eisendrath and Dawson (Cambridge University Press: Cambridge, 2008).

Index

Adler, Gerhald 66
aesthetic life 28–30, 112
Aion 95, 102
"Ancient Tragical Motif as Reflected in
  the Modern, The" 148
Andersen, Hans Christian 168, 172n2
angst 24, 101
anima 138, 139–40, 154–5, 169, 206
Answer to Job 64
Anthony, Maggy 209
Antigone 148–9, 172
anxiety 187–90
archetypal compensation 167–72
archetype, God 68–9
authenticity 24, 50, 85–6, 182–3;
  conflict and 107; deepening and
  broadening of self for 109–10;
  despair and 116–17; existentialism
  and 123–4; neurosis and 115–16;
  passion and 119–20; pure
  contemplation and 122–3; in
  reconciliation of immanence and
  transcendence 117–18; redemption
  and 120–1; self-acceptance and
  110; self-consciousness in 118;
  self-knowledge and 118–22;
  self-reflection and 121–2; shadow
  self and 108–9; sin and 110–11;
  through surrender to God 112–13;
  see also self

Binswanger, Ludwig 23
Bishop, Paul 191, 194
Bleuler, Eugen 207
Bly, Robert 108
Bockus, Frank 114–15
Boesen, Emil 134, 160
Boisen, Eline Heramb 135–6
Boss, Medard 23

Brandes, Georg 3, 156
Bremi, Willi 187
Brøcner, Hans 136
Buber, Martin 62, 67

Camus, Albert 23, 24
Carlisle, Claire 147
Cartesian philosophy 62
Casement, Ann 5, 43–4, 101,
  139, 178
castration anxiety 144, 164–5
Catholicism 75n1; patriarchal nature of
  73; reception of Jung's work 78–9
"C.G. Jung: A missed connection" 5
Christ: freedom through 203–4;
  imitation of 202, 204–5; Jung on
  withdrawal of projections of 200–1;
  as one-sidedly perfect and *image dei*
  198–200; as savior 183–4; suffering
  and 95–6, 104–5, 201–2
Christendom 59–61
Collected Works 47, 71, 178
communication, indirect 79–81
community as goal of selfhood 91–2
compassion 91
compensatory self 38
*Concept of Anxiety: A Simple
  Psychologically-Oriented Reflection
  on the Dogmatic Problem of Original
  Sin, The* 16, 24, 26, 171, 188
Concept of Irony 130
Concluding Unscientific Postscript
  31, 142
consciousness: moral vs ethical forms of
  87; painful states of 96–7; of sin 97,
  103, 110, 112; suffering as intricate
  facilitator of 96–7; three-stage theory
  of 27–30; and unconscious coming
  together 18, 37–40

Index   243

contemplation, pure 122–3
Corsair, The 23, 163, 168, 173n5
cure versus healing 8

Dehing, Jef 70
despair 14, 15–16, 19n2, 20n6, 24,
  54–5; authenticity and 116–17;
  proper 97–8; Søren Kierkegaard's
  spiritual castration and 145–7;
  spiritlessness as 14–15, 97–8
Die Angst Als Abendlandische
  Krankheit: Darges-Tellt Am
  Leben Und Denk en Soeren
  Kiergaards 190
Dionysian 197–8, 206
division of labour 14
Douglas, Clare 36
Dourley, John 5, 180, 184, 192

Edler, M. D. 88
ego 11n2, 37, 100, 224
Either/Or 23, 26, 29, 30, 85, 129, 169,
  187; on authenticity 110–11, 120;
  Kierkegaard's spiritual castration and
  148, 151; Regine Olsen immortalized
  in 154
Eller, Vernard 168
Epicurean life 31
Erickson, Erik 23
Eros 138, 154, 164, 209
ethics 112; compassion and 91;
  individuation and 87–8, 90; and
  morality from within 88, 92–3n3;
  mysticism and 80; passions and
  85–6; personal meaning creation and
  85; responsibility 87–8; stage of life
  30–1
evil 183
existentialism 24, 123–4
Existentialism and Human Emotions 24

faith 27; as being oneself before God
  113; ethics requiring passion of 85–6;
  finding joy in sorrow through 105–6;
  Jung and therapeutic value of 76–9;
  Kierkegaard and therapeutic value of
  79–83; transformation experienced
  by groups and 78; *see also* God;
  religion
faithlessness 103
father(s): abandonment of conventional
  religious self because of 59; Jung
  relationship with 44–8, 59, 210–12,

219–20; Kierkegaard's relationship
  with 48–55, 59, 213–14
Fear and Trembling 23, 61, 90
Fenger, Henning 131, 158, 168
first immediacy 28
Fordham, Michael 208, 215
For Self Examination 141, 170
freedom: versus security 14; through
  Christ 203–4
Freud, Sigmund 7, 27, 48, 64, 77, 200,
  212, 219; Oedipus Complex 143–4,
  148; on one's conception of God the
  father 150, 209–10; on religion as
  obsessional neurosis 196
Freud and Jung on Religion 196
Fromm, Erich 23
Furtak, R. A. 25–6

Gabriel, Merigala 81
Gardiner, Patrick 138
Glover, Edward 19
God: archetypal 66–9; authenticity
  through 112–13, 121; awareness
  of 19; belief and knowledge of
  68–9; denied by Nietzsche 193–4;
  faith as being oneself before 113;
  human beings anchored in 12, 180;
  individuation as relation with God
  8, 10–11, 20n6, 72–3, 229–30;
  Jung on dependence on 179; Jung on
  Kierkegaardian neurosis and 180–91;
  Jung on making peace with 9; Jung
  on raison d'être as 8, 10; Jung's
  personal relation to 63–4, 114–15;
  Kierkegaard on removal of 59–60;
  meaning in life related to 90–1;
  oedipal roots of one's conception
  of 150, 209–10, 219; psychological
  nature of Christian doctrine of 64–6;
  rebellion against 110–11; relating
  to, as self 13–14; residing within us
  179–80, 229; rest(ing) transparently
  in 12, 15, 114; spirit and 13–15,
  40–1; unconsciousness identified with
  72, 192; *see also* faith; religion
Goethe, Johan Wolfgang von 122, 168,
  172n4
Gordon, Rosemary 8
Greenhalgh, Kenneth 136–7

Hanna, Charles 19
Hannah, Barbara 63
Hannay, Alistair 50, 79–80

244 Index

healing: versus cure 8; individuation and 10–11; psychological, in terms of the religious 9; through dialectical relationship with the unconscious 9–10
hedonism 31
Hegel, Georg W. F. 81, 168, 172n4
Heiberg, Peter Andreas 132
Heidegger, Martin 24
Helweg, Hjalmer 131
Hillman, James 114, 122
Homans, P. 220
Hostie, Raymond 78–9
Hunt, Swanee 73
Huskinson, Lucy 191, 194

immediacy, first 28
indirect communication 79–81
individuation 8, 10–11, 20n6, 37, 39, 72–3, 202–3, 216, 227; ethics and 87–8, 90; midlife and 100–1; process and stages 74; two principal aspects of 92n1
inflation 220
introspection 16–17

Jaffe, Aniela 27, 210
Jaspers, Karl 23, 192
Jung, Carl: abandonment of conventional religious self by 59, 220–3; on absence of religion as neurosis 196; analysis of overlap between Kierkegaard and 3–6, 206–16; on anima 154–5; on the anima concept 140–1; on anxiety 187–90; attitude toward women 35–6; on authenticity 107–8, 114–24; childhood of 207–8; on the Christian trinity 73–4; on clash between traditional symbols and psychological experience 74–5; on collision between actual and ideal self 85; on the conscious and unconscious 37–8; contrasted with Freud 7–8; dialogues with his minister father 44–5; on Eros 154–5; on ethical responsibility 87–8; on finding spiritual home outside traditional religion 114; on Freud 48; on funerals and burials 211–12; on God as within 179–80; God-image of 66–8; on healing through dialectical

relationship with the unconscious 9–10; on his own psychology 43, 129–30; hostile reception of Kierkegaard 178; on imitation of Christ 202, 204–5; on individuation 8, 10–11, 20n6, 37, 39, 72–3, 74, 202–3; inflation and 220; on Kant 70; on Kierkegaardian neurosis 180–91, 200; on kinship libido 224; on losing religion as a child 44; on meaning in life related to relationship with God 90–1; on mistaking genuine psychological rebirth for transformation in group experiences 78; on moral vs ethical form of consciousness 87; on neurosis 102–3, 115–16; on Nietzsche 193–205; Oedipus Complex recognized by 143; optimistic tone of 7; parents and wife of 34–6, 44–7, 207–8; on personality 36–7, 39; personal relation to God 63–4, 114–15; on psyche as *naturaliter religiosa* 66; on psychological nature of Christian doctrine of God 64–6; on psychology of religion 13, 20n4, 63, 68, 70–2, 221–2; on the *Red Book* 8; on redemption 120–1; rejection of Freud 209–10, 212; relationship with his father 44–8, 59, 210–12, 219–20; on the self as entity of potentiality 40; sense of divinely bestowed destiny 55–6; on the shadow self 108–9, 163–4; similarities to Kierkegaard in views on religious experience 10–11, 177–8, 228–9; as solitary figure 34–5, 215–16; split personality in 36; on staying touch with reality 170–1; struggle to understand himself 43; on subjective nature of religious experience 48; on suffering 95, 99; *Terry Lectures* 8–9; on therapeutic value of faith 79–83; tight circle of women around 209; on the unconscious and conscious 37–40, 203–4; unconscious as comparable to spirit 15; warning against exalting intellect above all faculties 62
Jung, Emma 34, 211
Jung, Paul Achilles 35, 44–6, 55, 210, 212

Kafka, Franz 22–3
Kant, Immanuel 70
Kaufmann, Walter 16, 98
Keener, Helene 65–6
Kierkegaard, Ane 135–42, 147–8
Kierkegaard, Michael 21, 44, 48–51,
  55; Søren Kierkegaard's spiritual
  castration and 143–53
Kierkegaard, Peter 50
Kierkegaard, Søren 69; abandonment
  of conventional religious self by
  59; analysis of overlap between
  Jung and 3–6, 206–16; anima
  concept and 138, 139–40, 154;
  archetypal compensation 167–72;
  on authenticity 24, 50, 107–14,
  182–3; on battle between sensuous
  aesthetic immediacy and endless
  ethical reflections 26–7; bitter attacks
  by 168–9; commentaries on 23–4,
  33n2; conception of God 150; on
  crises in stages to adult development
  100–2; on despair 14, 15–16, 19n2,
  54–5, 97–8, 116–17; diagnosed as
  manic depressive 131; diagnosed as
  paranoid 21; Edifying Discourses
  81; on faith 27; on feminine silence
  141–2; final years of 167–72; finding
  himself through his work 52; on first
  immediacy 28; on freedom versus
  security 14; on goal of selfhood
  91–2; identification with Antigone
  148–9; immersion in religious life
  and religious ideal 170–2, 214–15,
  225; on indirect communication
  79–81; on intellectual types within
  Christianity 61–2; Jung on neurosis
  of 180–91, 200; later negative views
  of marriage 169–70; loneliness
  and 99–100, 223–4; melancholic
  description of himself 25, 55,
  131–2, 161, 226; mental health of
  21–2, 207; on need of psychology
  in re-education of Christians 24–5;
  on not marrying Regine 165–6;
  Oedipus complex in 152; parents
  and wife of 21–3, 33n2; on passion
  and authenticity 119–20; on
  passion and ethics 85–6; physical
  weaknesses of 130; pseudonyms
  used by 82–3, 123, 132–4;
  psychological analysis of 130–1;

psychological value of work of 24;
  on psychological wholeness 156–7;
  public recognition of 23–4; on
  radical individualism 89; on relating
  to God in self 13–14; relationship
  with his father 48–55, 59, 144–53,
  213–14; relationship with his
  mother not mentioned by 135–42,
  144; religious ideal as life-denying
  161–2; on removal of God from
  Christendom 59–60; repression
  of sexuality 155–60, 167–8; on
  rest(ing) transparently in God 12,
  15, 114; on the rotation method 29;
  on sacrifice 152; sadism in 158; on
  salvation through decisiveness of
  spirit 14–15; secretiveness of 129;
  sense of divinely bestowed destiny
  56; sense of religious purposefulness
  53–4; on shadow elements within
  ourselves 108–9; shame and
  136–8, 147; similarities to Jung
  in views on religious experience
  10–11, 177–8, 228–9; spiritual
  castration of 143–53; on starting
  with understanding the self 16–17;
  struggle to understanding himself 43;
  on suffering as essence of religious
  life 94–5; therapeutic aspects of
  79–83; on therapeutic value of
  faith 79–83; three-stage theory of
  consciousness 27–30; on two types of
  religious life 31–2; on urge to write
  and silence 81–2; see also Olsen,
  Regine
Kierkegaard: The Melancholy
  Dane 20n3
"Kierkegaard and Jung on the Self" 18
Kierkegaard's Influence on the Social
  Sciences 5
"Kierkegaard's Mood Swings" 49
Kinney, William 90
Kirmmse, B. 169
Künzli, Arnold 5, 133, 190, 206–7, 228

Laing, R. D. 23
language and direct communication
  79–80
Literary Review 14
Logos 138
loneliness 99–100, 223–5
Lowrie, Walter 50, 138

246 Index

Lowtzky, Fanny 132, 152, 165
Lubcke, Poul 81
Lukács, Georg 89
Lund, Henriette 135, 141

Martensen, Hans L. 136
Martin, H. V. 20n3
May, Rollo 23
Memories, Dreams, Reflections 34,
41n4, 44, 48, 55, 63, 194
Meyer, Raphael 153
Moller, Paul 168, 172n5
Mynster, Jacob 168, 173n6–7
Mysterium Coniunctionis 66

National Liberal Party 168
naturaliter religiosa, psyche as 66
neurosis 102–3, 115–16; anxiety
and 187–90; Freud on religion
as obsessional 196; Jung on
absence of religion as 196;
Jung on Kierkegaardian
180–91, 200
"New Paths in Psychology" 14
Nietzsche, Friedrich 24, 133, 170,
191, 206; claim of God's death
193–4; Jung on insanity of 193;
self-destructive solitude of 208–9
Noll, Richard 220
numinous encounters 10, 107

Oedipus complex 132, 143, 148, 152,
209–10, 219
Oeri, Albert 63
Olsen, Regine 22–3, 34, 51–2, 82,
160, 161, 187, 206; as "angel of
salvation" 157–8; as anima 138–41,
154; Kierkegaard on not marrying
165–6; Kierkegaard's sacrifice of
161–3; Kierkegaard's spiritual
castration and 144, 152–3
*On Reading Narcissistic Texts: An
Object Relations Theory View of the
Life and Works of Søren Kierkegaard*
136–7
Ori, Albert 207
Ostenfeld, I. 131
Otto, Rudolf 10

Palmer, Michael 48, 66, 67–8, 196; on
self-images 88–9
Pannwitz, Rudolf 4, 185
Pascal, Blaise 24

passion: authenticity and 119–20;
ethics and 85–6
Pedersen, Michael 147–52, 153, 159
persona 37, 116
personality 36–7, 39
personhood 117
Podmore, S. 21
*Point of View for My Work as an
Author, The* 51, 79, 82
Poole, R. 149
Postscript 26
Practice of Psychotherapy, The 72
Preiswerk, Emilie 35
pseudonyms of Kierkegaard 82–3
psyche: as *naturaliter religiosa* 66;
psychological wholeness and 156–7;
self-regulating 38–9; spiritual
dimension of 73
psychic energy 37
psychic wholeness 96–7
Psychological View of Conscience, A 87
psychology: analytical, as religion 75;
Kierkegaard on need for, in Christian
re-education 24–5; in nature of
Christian doctrine of 64–6; of
religion, Jung on 13, 20n4, 63, 68,
70–2, 221–2; religion reduced to
70–2; traditional view of religion 64
Psychology and Religion 20n4, 64, 67
Psychology Club 209
Psychology of the Unconscious 77
Psychotherapists or the Clergy 76, 100
pure contemplation 122–3

radical individualism 89
Red Book 8, 123
redemption 120–1
religion: Christian trinity 73–4; cultural
forces and spiritlessness in 14; faith
and 27; finding spiritual home
outside 114; individuation through
8, 10–11, 20n6; intellectual types
and poisoning of 61–2; Jung and
Kierkegaard rebellion against 60;
Jung on losing his own 44; Jung
on psychology of 13, 20n4, 63, 68,
70–2, 221–2; Kierkegaard on his
sense of religious purposefulness
and 53–4; Kierkegaard on need of
psychology in 24–5; Kierkegaard
on removal of God from 59;
Kierkegaard's spiritual castration
from 143–53; numinous encounters

10; power to produce psychological health and well-being 77; reduced to psychology by Jung 70–1; salvation and 14–15, 17, 32; suffering and 104–5; *Terry Lectures* on 8–9; traditional psychologists' views of 64; and two types of religious life 31–2; *see also* faith; God

Religion and the Psychology of Jung 78

Repetition: A Venture in Experimenting Psychology 23, 24, 65

revelation 73

rotation method 29

Rudd, Anthony 5

sacrifice 152, 161–3

sadism 158

Salome, Lou 209

salvation 14–15, 17, 32

Samuels, Andrew 88

Sartre, Jean Paul 23, 24

Schopenhauer, Arthur 24, 94, 205n5

Seducers Diary, The 140

Segal, R. A. 68–9, 75

self 5; collision between actual and ideal 85; compensatory 38; versus ego 11n2; as entity of potentiality 40; equivalency between Christ and 95–6; goal of selfhood and 91–2; individuation of 8, 10–11, 11n1, 37, 39, 72–3, 74; journey to, as religious 10–11; Nietzsche on 194–5; personal meaning creation and 85; shadow 108–9, 163–4; starting with understanding of 16–17; as synthesis of immanence and transcendence 117–18; true 12–13, 17–18, 19n1; unity and 110; *see also* authenticity

self-acceptance 110

self-actualisation 18

self-archetypes 66

self-centeredness 16

self-consciousness 118

self-images 89

self-knowledge 118–22, 206–7

self-realisation 88

self-recovery 100

self-reflection 121–2

self-regulating psyche 38–9

sexuality: Jung on inseparability of spirituality and 197; Kierkegaard's repression of 155–60, 167–8

shadow self 108–9, 163–4

Shamdasani, Sonu 34, 75

shame 136–8, 147

Shelburne, W. A. 123

Sickness Unto Death: A Christian Psychological Exposition for Edification and Awakening, The 13–14, 16, 24, 26, 110, 170, 171

"Significance of the Father in the Destiny of the Individuals, The" 219

silence: feminine 141–2; solitude and 81–2

Simms, Eva Maria 122

sin: authenticity and 110–11; consciousness of 97, 103, 112

Sobosan, Jeffrey 18

"Solomon's Dream: When Despair Intensified, How May It Affect the Whole of One's Existence?" 147

Spielrein, Sabina 209

spirit: as capacity for and urge towards conscious relationship to God 40–1; equal balance of flesh and 40, 196–7; as freedom 20n5; spiritlessness 14–15, 97–8

Stages on Life's Way 85, 145–6

stagnation of spirit 14

Stein, Murray 44, 210, 219, 220

Stewart, Jon 3, 79

Storr, Anthony 44

suffering: alleviation of 104; Christ as symbolic of 95–6, 104–5, 201–2; consciousness of sin and 97; despair 14, 15–16, 19n2, 20n6, 54–5, 97–8; as essence of religious life 94–5; faith and finding joy in 105–6; as intricate facilitator of consciousness 96–7; Kierkegaard's consolation in 164–5; loneliness as 99–100; at midlife 100–1; neurosis and 102–3, 115; psychic 99; in stages of adult development 100–2

symbolism 74–5, 79, 121–2, 203

Symbols of Transformation 143

systematic blindness 179

Taylor, Mark Lloyd 168

Terry Lectures, The 8–9

three-stage theory of consciousness 27–30

Thus Spoke Zarathustra 194

Tisdell, E. J. 124

Training in Christianity 170

transcendentalism 179, 192

248 Index

Transformation Symbolism in Mass, The 70
trinity, Christian 73–4
Troels-Lund, Troels Frederick 136, 141, 142
Two Essays on Analytical Psychology 88

Ubermensch 195
Ulanov, Ann Belford 154–5
unconscious, the: coming together with the conscious 18, 37–40; despair and 16; healing through dialectical relationship with 9–10; identified with God 72, 192; Jung's confrontation of 203–4; religion providing vehicle for encountering 68; revelation and 73; spirit as comparable to 15
Undiscovered Self, The 12
urbanisation 14

Van Der Post, Laurens 212, 215
vismedicatrix nature 15

Washburn, M. 100
Watkin, Julia 168
Weigert, E. 33, 49
Welding, Frederik 207
"What Meaning and What Joy There Are in the Thought of Following Christ" 202
White, Victor 67, 204–5
Wilmer, Harry 211
Wilson, Colin 122
Winnicott, D. W. 36
Wisdom in Love 25
Wittgenstein 80
Wolff, Toni 209
Works of Love 30, 104, 136